THATCHERISM AT WORK

THATCHERISM AT WORK

Industrial Relations and Economic Change

by John MacInnes

Open University Press

Milton Keynes • Philadelphia

Open University Press
12 Cofferidge Close
Stony Stratford
Milton Keynes MK11 1BY
England

and

1900 Frost Road, Suite 101
Bristol, PA 19007, USA

First Published 1987
Reprinted 1989
Copyright © 1987 John MacInnes

British Library Cataloguing in Publication Data

MacInnes, J. (John)
    Thatcherism at work: industrial relations
    and economic change.
    1. Industrial relations — Great Britain
    2. Great Britain — Economic conditions
    — 1945-
    I. Title
    331'.0941   HD8391

    ISBN 0-335-15517-0
    ISBN 0-335-15516-2 Pbk

Library of Congress Cataloging in Publication Data

MacInnes, John
    Thatcherism at work.
    Bibliography: p.
    Includes index.
    1. Industrial relations — Great Britain. 2. Great
Britain — Economic policy — 1945-. 3. Great Britain—
Economic conditions — 1945-. I. Title. II. Series.
HD8391.M26 1987   338.941   87–24722
ISBN 0-335-15517-0
ISBN 0-335-15516-2 (pbk.)

Typeset by Burns & Smith, Derby
Printed in Great Britain by
St Edmundsbury Press, Bury St Edmunds

Contents

List of Tables

To my mother and the memory of my father.

If you in this conference defeat composite 1A you will not stop trouble: it will make trouble ten times more for years to come. You give the prize for what has been done not to the working people of Britain but you hand it over to, yes, Thatcher, Joseph and Heseltine and all of that ilk of privilege. The benefits of North Sea oil are on the horizon. The benefits of a stronger balance of payments are also on the horizon. And they are going to the party of privilege. Instead of being free you will put the mighty in the seat and kick the people of low degree in the teeth. That is the danger.

Jack Jones, TGWU Conference, 6 July 1977,
supporting the Social Contract and opposing
(unsuccessfully) the call for a return to free
collective bargaining.

Preface

This book is about Thatcherism at work. It explores the effects of the first two Thatcher governments on industrial relations in the broadest sense of how people work together and the conditions of work they experience, as well as the wider effects these have – on earnings or productivity for example – and the system of relationships between government, employers and trade unions within which this all takes place. In doing so this book looks closely at the relationship between the economy and industrial relations because it has been important in two complementary ways. First Thatcherism argued that poor industrial relations were a major cause of Britain's poor economic performance after the Second World War and of rising unemployment in the 1970s. Second Thatcherism's main weapon for changing industrial relations was the way it handled the economy: it argued that governments could not be held responsible for the level of unemployment and let it rise to very high levels in order to 'discipline' the trade unions.

Work has always had a central role in Thatcherite ideology. The 1979 general election was fought under the slogan 'Labour isn't working': a comment aimed at the increase in unemployment under Labour, the economic difficulties Britain had faced and the breakdown of the Social Contract: Labour's attempt to develop a consensus between government, employers and unions about the running of the economy which disintegrated in the 'Winter of Discontent'. Similarly a fundamental theme of the 1987 general election was that Thatcherism had made the British economy 'great' again. While this book was completed before the 1987 election took place, the campaign and its result are both relevant to the following chapters. It is worth spelling out here some of the ways the analysis presented in this book contribute to understanding the mechanics of the 'success' of Thatcherism and what lessons for this book's analysis were contained in the election result.

In the general election the Labour campaign was reckoned to be superior to that of the other parties and marred by none of the disasters typical of 1983, yet the Conservative Party won virtually the same percentage share of the vote while Labour took 3 per cent from the Alliance. Labour increased its share of the unskilled and semi-unskilled workers' vote and that of women, particularly young women, but its share of trade union members' votes only rose from 39 to 42 per cent, in line with the overall improvement in the Labour vote (*Sunday Times* 14 June 1987).

The Conservative campaign focused on its claim to have achieved a substantial economic revival (the phrase 'back to work' was studiously avoided for obvious reasons). Amid many references to the Winter of Discontent and Labour's recourse to an International Monetary Fund (IMF) loan in 1976, Mrs Thatcher claimed that Britain under Labour had been 'a strife-torn, strike-ridden, divided society'. By contrast her policies had 'cut down over-mighty trade union bosses, reduced inflation and transformed the economy into Europe's success story' (Financial Times, 10 June 1987). Norman Tebbit argued that the public had 'six key choices' in the election which, apart from defence, all concerned the economy. These were between high and low taxes, between economic collapse and success, between 'inflation through the roof' and lower inflation, between a state controlled society and a property owning democracy and between industrial anarchy and good industrial relations (Financial Times 5 June 1987). Mrs Thatcher argued that Labour would bring back secondary picketing and that this would lead to the return of violence and intimidation: 'Don't let Labour ruin our new found prosperity .... The unions would be back in the driving seat ... Under Labour production lines would grind to a halt, orders would be lost and investment plans cancelled. Foreigners would no longer be able to rely on the prompt delivery of British goods and the country would cease to pay its way in the world' (*Financial Times* 3 June 1987). These arguments were given a media backdrop by what one correspondent described as a 'relentless trudge' by the Prime Minister round various industrial sites for 'photo opportunities' associating her with images of a vibrant and dynamic industrial scene.

In fact, Chapter 5 below presents evidence which suggests that the performance of Britain as a national economy has been very poor indeed since 1979 and the rest of this book presents evidence that the underlying problems of inflationary pressures and disorganised industrial relations remain unsolved. By dint of careful selection of the base years and countries against which comparisons were made, the Conservative Party produced statistics which purported to show that the economy was in fine shape. There were three main reasons why this was possible. The first was paradoxically the very depth of the recession which Conservative economic policies had provoked between 1979 and 1982. This made rates of economic progress measured from the start of recovery from the slump look quite good even though aggregate performance from 1979 was awful. Second because the recession hit other European countries later than Britain, partly because of the international repercussions of Britain's severely deflationary stance, it was possible to draw flattering comparisons between British performance during the upswing in the business cycle with European performance across both a downward and upward phase. Finally the international environment for the first two Thatcher governments was more favourable in two ways. Commodity and raw material prices fell steeply throughout almost the entire period. This removed a powerful source of inflation and effectively represented a transfer of wealth from the third world to the developed industrial countries like Britain. British wage earners could maintain their standard of living without large increases in their money wages because the prices of many imports were falling. By contrast the 1970s had seen dramatic rises in raw material prices and the unprecedented hike in oil prices at the start of the decade. The Conservatives also had the considerable benefit of North Sea oil. This not only generated jobs, but also made a major contribution to growth of output, boosted tax revenues and increased exports, thus easing balance of payments difficulties.

There is nothing unusual about parties making exaggerated or misleading claims about the success of their policies at election time. But it is difficult for a party to make ridiculous assertions without its opponents or other interested groups successfully challenging them. Yet the opposition concentrated its fire on the government's record on social services rather than challenging its economic record head-on. This was despite the fact that the promises of both Labour and the Alliance to reduce unemployment by one million or more were credible. The director of the National Institute for Economic and Social Research estimated that it would be possible to reduce unemployment by up to 1.5 million without inflation reaching double figures (*Financial Times* 3 June 1987). Nor was there much protest voiced by industry itself which appeared to endorse the Conservatives' policies as strongly as in pre-Thatcherite days. Meanwhile the unions were largely silent in the course of the campaign: the Labour Party viewed them as an electoral liability rather than an asset. Does this all mean that the Conservatives' claims about the economy and industrial relations in fact have substance? This book suggests not and it also points towards some of the factors underlying the Conservatives' electoral success.

How is it then that after two terms the government was able to secure endorsement for economic policies which had produced results so far at variance with the claims made for them? The key to the answer lies in appreciating the difference between the aggregate performance of the whole economy and the fortunes of individuals and individual enterprises within it. According to Thatcherite ideology this is a distinction which does not or should not exist. If everyone pursued their own economic interests and left it to the market to sort out their competing or contradictory claims, then all would be for the best. By contrast attempts by governments to improve on the market and address the interests of society as a whole simply stop the market mechanism working properly and cause inflation. Hence the Conservatives cheeky adoption of the slogan 'Power to the People'. It was intended to encapsulate their conviction that the state should not be able to regulate people's economic lives in the name of the general interest, instead people should be free to get what they can from their endeavours on the market. According to this view the private world of markets is almost inevitably positive while the public world of regulations and institutions is negative: the most fruitful relationships between people are those dependent on money. Chapter 2 examines just how powerful and historically deep rooted such ideas are in Britain.

Yet the evidence of the book suggests that the key to understanding the problem of the economy and industrial relations in Britain today lies in the contradiction between individual or sectional interests and the collective or national interest and that the problems of the 1970s perhaps stemmed from too little rather than too much collectivism in the British industrial order and its workplace industrial relations. This contradiction also explains how within a generally poor economic performance, substantial groups within the economy have done very well during the first two Thatcher governments. While unemployment and cutbacks in public spending on benefits has increased poverty dramatically, it has enabled those with more secure jobs to use free collective bargaining to increase their real earnings at an unprecedented rate since 1982. The distribution of economic cheer and gloom has been very skewed. Those plants and companies which survived the crash of 1980–81 have enjoyed increased profits and rising productivity. This lies behind the degree of electoral support for Thatcherism: it has brought increased personal prosperity for a substantial minority of the population. But such individual prosperity does not mean that the claims made about economic revival are well founded for it has resulted not *despite* but rather *because* of the poverty of Britain's overall performance. It has been possible to let market forces reign not in spite of high unemployment but because of high unemployment. By contrast many of the troubles governments faced in the 1970s stemmed from their attempts to maintain full employment as a priority. In abandoning this goal Thatcherism has had its greatest impact on the British industrial relations system; not by undermining union bargaining power (the main assumption of most analyses) but by taking the unemployed out of the reckoning and letting employers and workers pursue policies which maximised their own returns regardless of the consequences for the aggregate level of employment.

While commentators have focused on the North–South divide revealed in the election results, it is important to recognise that this divide has increasingly become an economic divide too. Chapter 5 shows how the geography of recovery from the recession precipitated by the government between 1979 and 1982 has been very uneven. In the 'hands off' environment of Thatcherism it has been the South which has seen the main benefits of the upturn in the economy. Unemployment — the major 'cost' of the government's policies — has been unevenly spread, so too has economic prosperity. This is the essence of the North–South split. Thus if we arrange the parliamentary constituencies in order of their unemployment rates as measured by the Unemployment Unit we find some staggering results. Of the 84 constituencies in Britain with unemployment rates of over 20.0 per cent only 9 returned Conservative MPs. Apart from Nottingham East and Wolverhampton North East there were no Conservatives returned in the 50 constituencies with the highest unemployment rates. In the prosperous areas the results were even more dramatic. With the exception of Paddy Ashdown's Yeovil constituency (139th lowest, 8.3 per cent unemployment) the 181 constituencies with the lowest unemployment returned Conservative MPs. Of the 204 constituencies with rates below 10.0 per cent on the Unemployment Unit's count, there were only one Labour (Oxford East) and three Liberal members returned. The election result therefore confirms not the economic success of Thatcherism but rather its sharpening of divisions between those who have enjoyed the fruits of market based prosperity and those at whose expense such prosperity has been enjoyed.

Class is a concept which social scientists have always found hard to pin down. In the British case, as we discuss below in Chapter 3, this confusion has been compounded by the paradox of the strength of class identity in the sense of the adversarial nature of shopfloor industrial relations and the weakness of class organisation in the sense of class based challenges to the established social, economic or political order. Class is a theme running throughout this book. Perhaps what stands out most clearly in the aftermath of the election result is the weakness of class in Britain in the sense of a political identity rooted in a consciousness of collective economic position in contrast to its strength in terms of pursuit of sectional interest. Many workers, including manual workers in the prosperous South, could vote Conservative in the knowledge that Thatcherism promised to look after their economic interests. So long as they could avoid unemployment and particularly if they held well paid or well organised jobs, free collective bargaining and tax cuts meant living standards increasing faster than ever before except for the 'costs' of deteriorating social services. This counted for more than their potential collective interest in a government which sought to reduce unemployment (thereby spreading employment chances more evenly) but at the cost of curbs on wages growth or higher taxes. But it would be premature to conclude on the basis of such political behaviour and on the claims made about strikes and changes in industrial relations that class attitudes and structures in Britain have undergone a fundamental change. As Chapters 3 and 7 discuss there is a sense in which the British working class has always been prone to 'middle class' and individualist ways of thinking and acting and far from conflicting with the tradition of adversarial industrial relations — a tradition which Chapter 6 argues is still very much intact — it is a basic part of that tradition. Nor does it mean that the traditional relationship between the Labour Party and the trade unions is about to fall apart, or that Labour's traditional sources of electoral support have been newly undermined by economic change. But it does mean that the pressures on the relationship between the political and industrial arms of the labour movement discussed in Chapter 7 remain acute.

The general election showed that there were still sufficient numbers of people doing well enough out of the Thatcherite industrial order to deliver a third victory at the polls in the context of a divided opposition. But as this book argues it would be premature to take this as evidence of the creation of a new industrial and economic order in Britain. It showed that people were more strongly influenced by the evidence from their pockets than the credibility of the opposition's promises of higher employment. Thatcherism has made greed respectable. Whether it has achieved anything else, as this book explores, is open to doubt.

Many people helped me in the course of writing this book and pursuing the research which lay behind it by giving me technical or secretarial assistance, providing data, discussing through the issues or being supportive: Phillip Bassett, John Brady, Sabine Citron, Pauline Connelly, Peter Cressey, John Eldridge, Nigel

Haworth, Tim Holmes, Jeff Hyman, Morag Lamont, Alan McGregor, Archie Onslow, Tim Pickles, Harvie Ramsay, Maureen Robb, Mary Ryan, Gordon Smart, Sheila Stallard, Anne Stewart and Simon Watkins. Officials in the Department of Employment, Department of Trade and Industry, Industry Department for Scotland, Scottish Development Agency and the Treasury answered many queries about published data and supplied valuable unpublished material. I have also to thank the staff of Glasgow University Library and the Adam Smith Library. Part of the research on which the book is based was made possible by a Fellowship from the Royal Society of Edinburgh and by a grant from the Scottish Economic Society. I am grateful to both these bodies for their financial support, but neither body should be held responsible for the views expressed here. Lesley Baddon, Geraldine Hackett, Paul Marginson, Bert Moorhouse and Alan Sproull read earlier drafts of the manuscript and provided me with many useful comments. I am particularly grateful to Janette Steele who produced two drafts of the entire book in a very tight schedule indeed. Finally Juliet Webster gave me loads of much needed support and encouragement.

Without the help of all these people this book would have been poorer; for the errors and omissions which remain I am, of course, solely responsible.

John MacInnes
University of Glasgow
1 July 1987

CHAPTER 1

Introduction: Some Myths About Thatcherism

Most people have a picture of the recent development of the economic system and industrial relations in Britain that goes something like this. From the Second World War onwards both Conservative and Labour governments followed a social democratic consensus (which is referred to hereafter as the Post-War Settlement) in their policies towards the economy and worked closely with employers and the trade unions to carry it out. Through public expenditure, taxation and more direct intervention in the private economy the government took responsibility for ensuring virtually full employment and also provided the 'social wage' of the welfare state: housing, education and health services. Within a world economy which grew faster in the 1950s and 1960s than ever before, this system worked fairly well. But there were also nagging problems which meant that when the world economy faltered after the steep rise in oil and other raw material prices in the early 1970s, the social democratic consensus on which the British economy was based fell apart.

During the boom period full employment increased the bargaining power of unions and shifted the balance of power within them from the leadership towards the rank-and-file members and their spokespeople, the shop stewards, in the factories. This encouraged rising wage claims and frustrated improvements in productivity. Relatively poor economic performance, combined with competing demands for wages and better public services (a higher social wage) caused inflation and produced regular balance of payments crises. The problems facing governments in trying to reconcile competing claims to national resources with poor economic growth and international economic competition came to a head in the mid-1970s. Unemployment passed the symbolic 1 million mark. Inflation reached 25 per cent. A loan from the IMF was needed because of the acute balance of payments problems. In the 'Winter of Discontent' of the early months of 1979 the incomes policy of the Labour government fell apart as low-paid public sector workers and others struck. Meanwhile Conservative shadow ministers argued that the social democratic consensus was leading to a collectivist stranglehold on the private sector of the economy. The state regulated a wide range of markets including prices, incomes and currency exchange and through taxation and public borrowing was coming to control half the economic activity in the country. In turn the state, they argued, was becoming a captive of union power: it was forced to concede rises in wages and improvements in the social wage which could only be financed by printing money and thus increasing inflation.

May 1979 brought to power a Conservative government set firm against the social democratic consensus. This was not just a product of electoral disillusionment with Labour. There were longer-term changes in social structure and attitudes which paved the way. The decline of manufacturing employment, particularly in old staple industries like coal, steel, shipbuilding, heavy engineering and textiles, and the destruction of old urban working-class communities by urban housing renewal programmes, eroded the material basis of both the industrial and political arms of the labour movement. Economic restructuring was working powerfully against unionism. Manual jobs were being replaced by white-collar, full-time by part-time, jobs for men by jobs for women. Tony Lane (1982) argued that 'trade unionism in most of the larger towns and cities was dominated by manual workers concentrated in perhaps a handful of industries'.

These centres of unionisation were the focus for its spread throughout urban areas. However, new manufacturing plants were opening up in smaller centres of population, often on greenfield sites employing labour less familiar with union traditions, and more scattered geographically. Fothergill and Gudgin (1982) showed how in the 1960s and 1970s manufacturing employment fell in the conurbations, and rose in smaller towns and rural areas. Lever (1984) suggested that one explanation for these moves was the possibility of greater control over labour forces in labour markets dominated by a single large employer. Lane (1982, p. 9) pointed out that the organisational structure of large firms, with larger numbers of establishments of various sizes ultimately owned by single corporations, made them less reliant on any one particular workforce and encouraged a more sectional form of plant based unionism. Mulhearn (1984, p. 11) quoted a GLC study of manufacturing relocation from London which found that firms found labour elsewhere more quiescent and more productive: 'It's a question of attitude. It's better here, it's a different type of labour. It's not a question of wages — they're about the same. It's about being able to manage. People are more mature here. They've got mortgages and kids.'

Workers in new industries living in new areas were developing new lifestyles and allegiances (see, for example Beaumont 1987). The Labour vote declined steadily after 1951. Higher wages and shorter working hours brought changes in leisure and lifestyle, opening up new consumer markets (including home ownership) to working people and providing practical experience of the contrast between market choice and bureaucratic public provision (see, for example, Hobsbawm 1981).

Thatcherism in Britain, like Reaganism in America and monetarist-inspired economic philosophies elsewhere, seemed to be an idea which had found its time. Breaking decisively with past Conservative policy, the new government proceeded to 'roll back the frontiers of the state' by abandoning the commitment to full employment (arguing that government attempts to raise employment simply caused inflation), abolishing controls on exchange, incomes and prices, cutting public expenditure and taxation, raising interest rates and cutting the money supply with the aim of reducing inflation: the symbol of 'collectivism' in the system. It introduced legislation designed to curb union power and ended the principle of the government acting as a 'fair employer' setting model conditions for the private sector. It set about introducing market forces to the public sector through cash limits on expenditure and introducing competitive tendering or privatisation.

These policies hit the labour movement in four main ways. Legislation limited the ways unions could act and they were no longer consulted by government nor their agreement or cooperation on economic policy sought. The harshness of the new economic regime slashed revenues in manufacturing leading to a collapse of profits, record bankruptcies and a fall of about one-third in employment in established firms. This produced a very hostile climate for unions in the workplace. In the public sector, unions also faced job losses and a hostile government and usually a new hostile management too, such as Michael Edwardes at British Leyland, and, more spectacularly, Ian MacGregor at steel and then coal. Finally unemployment, which rose by more than two million, weakened unions directly by reducing their membership and income and indirectly by threatening their workplace bargaining power. The unions suffered a series of severe defeats: particularly that of the miners, barely ten years after they could claim to have brought down a Conservative government. The unions were powerless to resist the government's challenge, much of which was popular with their own members. Unions expressed fears about the activity of union-busting consultancies of the kind used in the United States, where union membership had fallen steadily to less than one-fifth of the workforce. The TUC was racked by divisions and threatened splits, particularly over how it should respond to the government's employment legislation, while the Labour Party actually did break apart with the formation of the Social Democratic Party in 1981.

Traditional labour-movement solidarity tended to give way to 'enterprise consciousness'. Workforces were more likely to be interested in the fortunes and fate of their own firm than in the struggles of fellow members elsewhere (Brown 1986). Managements could take advantage of the mood of 'new realism' encouraged by high unemployment to marginalise or sack militants, and establish new forms of communication and involvement with their workforces to educate them in 'the realities of business'. While the number of strikes plummeted, profit-sharing and share-ownership schemes spread: a further potent aspect of employer–employee collaboration. Many new firms found no need to recognise unions, while in 'high-tech' areas like electronics unions such as the Amalgamated Engineering Union (AEU) and the Electric, Electronics, Telecommunications and Plumbing Union (EETPU) began to offer single-union deals and no-strike agreements.

On the basis of this account or something quite like it, government ministers claim that in six or seven years they have wrought a thoroughgoing revolution in industrial relations and with it the social and economic structure of the country as a whole. They have created an 'enterprise culture' out of a collectivist one. Opponents, including opposition and union spokespeople and theorists further to the left, also tend to agree that a revolution has been achieved, but argue that the changes have only produced widespread unemployment, greater inequality and poverty, poorer working conditions and more authoritarianism in the workplace, all for no lasting benefit in terms of Britain's long-term economic performance. Not everyone would accept every last detail of that account, in particular some industrial relations academics have been more cautious in their evaluation of the extent of change (see Nichols 1986, p.190). But the consensus about the general direction of economic change and social relations in industry and the causes and effects of change is quite surprising. Most disagreement is not so much about what has happened or why, but rather about whether it is good or bad and what the meaning of these changes for the future will be.

The trouble with this account, convincing as it at first sight appears to be, is that there are important pieces of the picture that just do not fit, and others that are seriously distorted or inconsistent. The contrast between the periods before and after 1979 is easily overdrawn. The extent of the fall in industrial action and the degree of improvement in labour productivity and economic growth both depend heavily on which dates are chosen for comparison. On yardsticks such as reduction in the proportion of national income taken by taxation or devoted to government expenditure the record of the previous Labour government was better. The change in public attitudes is also far from clear-cut. Mrs Thatcher and the Conservative Party may be popular, but many of the policies and attitudes which they advocate are not. It is easily forgotten that Michael Edwardes was the appointee of a Labour government and that Ian MacGregor's appointment to British Steel was organised by Jim Prior — a prominent 'wet' and critic of Thatcherism. Macho management, and the other side of the coin, 'participative management', often catch the headlines, but are not necessarily representative of what is happening in most factories, shops and offices. There are more shop stewards today than in 1979 and workplace trade unionism and bargaining remain intact. The actual number of workers covered by single-union and no-strike deals is tiny and is unlikely to have increased much. Unions have indeed lost members, but most of the loss is to be explained by the massive rise in unemployment, and some by the shift in employment towards services, where unions have never been strong.

The decline of older industries is not a product of Thatcherism. Employment in manufacturing in Britain has been falling now for over 20 years. As far back as 1960 the service sector employed more than manufacturing. It was the 1950s and 1960s that saw the dismantling of old working-class communities and the growth of manufacturing employment in new areas away from the metropolitan strongholds of unionism. Indeed the initial result of Thatcherism, as chapter 5 below suggests, was to *slow down* these trends in restructuring! Nor was poor economic performance in terms of low growth or declining share of world trade a problem of the 1960s. Just these problems were dogging the British economy in the 1870s. Indeed, compared to the first half of the twentieth century when Britain's balance of payments depended crucially on rentier payments from abroad, Britain's growth performance since 1945 has been rather good. Prior to 1979 one of the major obstacles to higher growth was held to be that wages rose too fast. Wage inflation caused problems both for competitiveness and the balance of payments. But one thing which has evidently not changed since 1979 is wage inflation. Indeed, since 1979 it has become significantly higher in real terms. By 1986 settlements were averaging above 7 per cent — over twice the rate of inflation — while labour productivity growth had flattened out.

These facts sit ill with a picture of union evisceration. Meanwhile, in October 1986 the government, or rather the Governor of the Bank of England, announced as quietly and as obscurely as possible, the dropping of sterling M3 money supply targets as an object of economic policy. In the same month a balance of payments crisis forced a rise in interest rates to historically unprecedented levels in real terms. There seemed to be Thatcherism without monetarism and with many of the economic ills of the period of social democratic consensus.

This book tries to make sense of these conundrums by looking carefully at the links between economic change and social relations in industry over the period from 1979 to 1986. As well as putting the empirical record straight, it aims to illuminate the relationship between industrial relations in the workplace and poor British economic performance. By doing so it can examine whether the actual changes taking place during the two Thatcher administrations of May 1979 to June 1987 have provided an environment for better economic performance in the future or not, and also evaluate the accuracy of the claims of Thatcherites and others that bad industrial relations were the root cause of the problems of the 1960s and 70s. Looking at a period which is so close is made hazardous by the historical foreshortening of perspective involved. A space of ten or 20 years affords the social scientist the considerable benefit of hindsight. However, that hindsight is itself partly composed of the consensus that develops about the relative importance and meaning of events and changes. As this introduction has made clear, the current consensus about Thatcherism and industry seems muddled and misleading. It also tries to shed light on the relationship between economic change and industrial relations. Again both the Thatcherites and their opponents have seen industrial relations issues as central to Britain's comparatively poor economic performance. Thatcherism has blamed over-powerful unions and a collectivist restrictive spirit. Labour critics have argued about management inadequacies and the failure to promote industrial democracy. In contrast to this, the period after 1979 gives us a chance to view the impact on industrial relations of tremendous economic changes. A slump in manufacturing output of one-sixth, a fall in gross domestic product (GDP: the output of the whole economy) of nearly one-twentieth and a rise in unemployment of two million constituted a deep shock to the system. How did industrial relations react to this economic 'experiment', as J.K. Galbraith called it? (Keegan 1984).

In order to fully understand the significance of what is happening now, Chapters 2 and 3 review the origins and development of the British economy and industrial relations. It is important to do this, although it might seem odd in a work which is concerned with the present, because many of the explanations of what is happening now are to be found there. In eschewing 'pragmatism', blaming the Post-War Settlement and trade unions for Britain's economic ills and espousing 'Victorian values', Thatcherism has a strong historical component to its analysis. This makes it desirable to measure its claims against the historical evidence. This is important not just to set the record straight but also to identify the social and economic forces which lie behind Thatcherism and to understand both the logic of its policies and why they have had the effects which this book describes. One of the fundamental themes explored throughout the following chapters is that in contrast to its claims to represent a 'new' social and economic order capable of reversing the country's economic decline, Thatcherism in fact represents the recrudescence of fundamental forces in British economy and society which date back at least to the eighteenth century and whose impact was hardly lessened in the Second World War and its aftermath. To the extent that this is the case Thatcherism may not be the 'cure' for the 'British disease' but rather the latest manifestation of the disease itself.

In doing so, this book takes material from a number of academic disciplines — sociology, economics, history and politics — but tries to present them in a way which is rigorous enough to avoid being simplistic, but plain enough to be understood by someone who is not an expert in any or all of these. Only the reader can decide if this has been successful. It is therefore also a work of social science. Given the political passions and controversies aroused by Thatcherism and the changing fortunes and circumstances it has brought to different people, it is worth recalling what a work of social science can do. To prove whether Thatcherism is right or wrong, or good or bad is beyond the scope of this work. What is within its scope is to examine the adequacy of those theories about how the economy and industrial relations work that are central to Thatcherism and analyse what the actual as opposed to expected results of policies based on these theories have been in practice. The results of this exercise can also throw light on how the system as a whole works and what the effect of other policies might be. Such ideas will always be inconclusive to an extent. A perfect social science would imply that history and society take a very determinist shape, leaving little role for human creativity. It will also become clear that the author himself profoundly disagrees with the sentiment and purpose of Thatcherism. However, it is hoped that the material and analysis in the book stand independently of such a judgement.

CHAPTER 2

The British Economy and
Industrial Relations System

The origins of British industrial relations

Each nation's system of industrial relations and pattern of economic development is to some extent distinctive; this is especially true of Britain because it was the first capitalist industrial nation. It would be wrong to attribute everything including the country's present predicament to this starting point, but it would be just as mistaken to ignore it. It had decisive consequences for the nature of industry. Many of the central features of British industrial relations which were forged in the genesis of industry itself endured right through to the 1970s. In order to understand what is happening now it is important to see how the system worked before and why it fell apart when it did.

The history of decline is relevant to Thatcherism, since it claims that many aspects of nineteenth century economic policy were correct and that Britain's economic problems were caused by too indulgent an attitude to trade unions from the 1870s onwards and too much state intervention in the economy after 1945. In contrast to these claims this chapter suggests that economic decline was endemic from the 1870s and more likely to be rooted in the way the British economy emerged from the industrial revolution itself. The distinct form of relations between classes in industry, the way these classes were organised and came to define their interests in relation to one another, the relationship between different branches of capital and the state: in short the social relations of production constituted a system which not only retarded economic development but was also highly resistant to reform and frustrated the pursuit of economic modernisation. Industrial relations, particularly at workplace level, were a central part of this system. If the arguments presented in this chapter are accepted then Thatcherism can be seen in a new light: not as an attempt to create a new social and economic order but, on the contrary, an attempt to preserve an older one riddled by economic weakness from attempts to reform and modernise it.

Perhaps the most fundamental aspect of the development of the social relations in British Industry was the commitment to *laissez-faire*, to the market and to individual liberty (in terms of freedom to do with private property as one liked, and freedom from state control or interference). This climate, as Thompson (1965, p. 43) points out, was originally fostered not by industrialists but by the rural gentry 'a superbly successful and self-confident capitalist class.' The industrial bourgeoisie did not have to create a 'new' social order. *Laissez-faire* was built in part by the use of the law against the powers of the state, and in particular common law rights of property and freedom to trade which judges 'found' in custom, rather than being enacted by Parliament. 'Freedom', a fundamental concept of the emerging capitalist order, came to have

> a largely negative connotation in English political argument. What was debated was always freedom against some dominating force — crown, aristocracy, bishops, feudal monopoly or courtiers privilege ... even for substantial sections of the higher classes liberty was defined in terms of wariness towards the central state apparatus (Fox 1985, p.18).

One result was that patriotism and national consciousness came to be 'defined in terms of aversion to and protections against, any threat of the absolutist state' (Fox 1985, p.17). The weakness of national consciousness (except when defined in relation to other nations, when it could turn to jingoistic imperialism and xenophobia) meant that identity and solidarity were often more local in character: to a region, a class, a trade, for example.

The weak position of the state in nineteenth century Britain had other causes and consequences too which have been discussed by Anderson (1986), Leys (1983) and Ingham (1984). As the first industrial nation Britain originally faced only weak international competition. Unlike the United States or Germany there was no felt need for the state or private enterprise itself to organise production consciously to catch up and compete with Britain. There were few links between domestic industry and the state. But fears of absolutism at home did not prevent imperial conquest abroad. As well as fuelling the industrial revolution this made Britain the world's foremost military as well as economic power which turned the city of London into the commercial and financial capital of the world. Ingham (1984) argues that what was becoming a global trading system required a world currency and international commercial clearing house and that the City and sterling adopted this role. The City's links with the state, particularly the Treasury which from early on stood for *laissez-faire* and minimum public expenditure and borrowing, ensured that when the interests of the City and domestic industry conflicted, as they increasingly did from the late nineteenth century onwards, it was the City which regularly won out. Domestic industry was too fragmented and disorganised to challenge the City's role. In addition as it developed an increasingly imperial and multinational character it came to share some of the City's interests.

Laissez-faire was therefore more than a belief in the benevolence of markets. It described the material absence in Britain of any institutions powerful enough to direct the course of economic development at a local, industrial or national level. Individual employers guarded their autonomy and saw little need to recognise interests or forces which markets did not represent. Indeed this avoidance of any conscious regulation of production often extended to the factory itself. Rather than setting out to control the management and organisation of work employers simply relied on subcontractors (Hobsbawm 1968).

Laissez-faire also precluded any effective paternalist rule of the working class. The emphasis on the rights of private property, sovereignty of the market and the perils of state interference with market forces meant that neither the state nor individual employers pursued any active social policy towards the emerging proletariat. In Britain, as in all other industrialising countries, the proletariat was seen as a new and potentially dangerous political factor. Elsewhere both state and employers tended to pursue a mixture of paternalist social policies providing minimum living and welfare standards, and fierce repression of independent working-class economic or political activity. But in Britain both these measures were precluded by the strength of the ideology of economic individualism and weakness of the state. Employers felt few obligations to or responsibility for their workforce. Fox (1985, p. 50) quotes Mantoux: 'He owed his employees wages, and once these were paid, the men had no further claim on him: put shortly, this was the attitude of the employer as to his rights and duties.' Therefore the emerging British working class was left to fend for itself but crucially it was also left with significant resources and political space to do so. In a complementary manner to *laissez-faire*, the 'rule of law' came to be an important tool not only for guarding against state absolutism but also for securing the consent of the mass of the population both to government and to the vast economic changes of the industrial revolution. The rule of law, as Thompson (1977) and Hay *et al.* (1975) have argued, was a potent and at times savage instrument but it had a crucial ambiguity in that its effectiveness depended on its ability to legitimate authority and command consent: it had to be seen to be just, fair, and on occasion, merciful in order to work. It therefore afforded considerable space for the rising proletariat to organise and struggle for economic and political rights both within the political state and economically against their employer. Thus direct state repression of trade unions on behalf of the employers was conceivable only if the whole social order was to be abandoned. This option at times became a real one in the aftermath of the French Revolution. Measures like the Combination Acts which attempted to outlaw unionism and events like the Peterloo Massacre or the transportation of the Tolpuddle Martyrs bear this out. But as Fox (1985) points out, what is more significant was the general pattern of eschewing repression of unionism in favour of weakening, taming and integrating it. Combinations and later national unions were allowed to carve out a widening and steadily less vulnerable avenue for struggle over economic conditions and political rights, provided, however, such struggle stayed within the bounds of a liberal economic order.

There were in any case other forces encouraging it to adopt these forms. The complement to the instrumental attitude of employers towards labour as a commodity was that of labour as a commodity to its prospective owner. Its 'enterprising' strategy was to affirm the conflict of interest in the market for the purchase and sale of labour power and to organise to extract the highest possible price from the employers. The political space open to the emerging unions was paradoxically a function of the *laissez-faire* social order. Both employers and the state were keen to see trade unions and workers' combinations put down, but in order not to injure the authority of the law (or rely upon means of repression that were simply not available) it was important that this was done legally, through the courts. The state complained about the 'want of spirit' in employers in prosecuting combinations because they were in restraint of trade. It wanted employers to take the lead because such battles had to be seen as economic rather than political in character, with the law arbitrating between competing claims about property rights. For their part, employers showed only sporadic enthusiasm: their business was to make money, not to pursue social order. Too aggressive an attitude to combinations when trade was slack might rebound on an employer when labour was scarce. They complained about the 'want of spirit' in the state. In more buoyant economic times, when the workforce enjoyed more bargaining leverage, employers could be forced to heed the union's claims, even if they preferred officially not to admit its existence. Till the late nineteenth century unions therefore existed in legal limbo. In themselves they were not illegal (though the law on conspiracy was always a potential threat) but virtually any action they took to further their demands was liable to be so. However, at times it would be in the immediate interests of either government or employer to avoid invoking the law.

This particular set of social and economic relations and attitudes produced a particular structure and strategy of trade union organisation in Britain as they developed in the nineteenth century. The focus of organisation was local employers, its objectives were overwhelmingly economic in character and its methods sectional. The 'bottom-up' growth of British trade unions and traditions of direct democracy they inherited worked strongly against any centralisation of power, either nationally or by industry. Relations between employers and workers at local level were likely to be volatile, determined by the state of trade, characterised by mutual distrust and dependent on the ability of the union to control the supply of labour. Unions did this by enforcing traditions of craft skill and 'custom and practice' of the trade to exert control over how work was done and, through apprenticeships, who was to do it. At any point the employers might decide that the costs of attacking union organisation were less than co-operating with it. However, such mutual antagonism was primarily economic rather than political. It was more about the terms of operation of market forces than whether they should operate. It was a form of organisation open principally to those already in a stronger market position who often desired to maximise the distance between themselves and the unorganised poor, and draw closer to the employers themselves.

It was also a form open mainly to men, who sought to exclude access to women, sometimes under the barrier of protective legislation, as in the mines. To this day, 'skilled' work remains work done by men, regardless of the actual technical complexity or manual dexterity in the job. Indeed 'craft' work has been an important source of modern masculinity itself (Cockburn 1983a). Allied to this was the union strategy of bargaining for 'family wages'. It was argued that if married women did not or could not work, then men should be paid wages sufficient to cover family rather than personal subsistence. Struggles were as much between worker and worker (between craftsman and unskilled, or between men and women) as between worker and employer. The deep antagonism between employer and worker generated in the course of such struggles did not necessarily imply any wider conflict between labour and capital as such.

Just as the radical rhetoric of union rule books and the socialist leanings of individual union activists were submerged in practice by the liberal, economistic and constitutionalist focus of day-to-day union and worker behaviour, so too were the anti-union fulminations of exasperated employers and creative refinement of common law doctrine against combinations and conspiracies outweighed by the recognition that in practice it was preferable to treat with the unions rather than to attempt to destroy them. But this relationship of 'practical' people on both sides did not extend to any great mutual trust or legitimacy. Rather the other party was to be endured as a regrettable but for the most part unavoidable fact of life. Indeed to develop such trust would be to risk losing substantial bargaining power by relying on the other side not to take advantage of their new position. Were unions to accord management the right to organise production without any union restrictions, or management to invite trade unions to decide jointly on the running of the business each might find that they had lost their power.

The nature of their relationship also had relevance for the power of the two parties. The concept of power in industrial relations is a notoriously difficult and elusive one but it is also central to the theme of this book. The power relationship between employer and union (or indeed unionised workforce) was not simply zero-sum, in the sense of what one gained the other lost. There were costs as well as benefits in either side trying to push a potential advantage too far. Given that unions had few visions of any alternative economic order or realistic ideas about how it might be achieved, they had an immediate interest in the survival of an employer or an industry. They sought 'fair' wages, not abolition of the wages system. Too strident demands, or too militant a posture, might threaten their respectability or public sympathy and could ultimately provoke a more intransigent or hostile stance from Parliament or the courts. Conversely, employers had an interest in the way unions could regulate the labour market and in ensuring that they kept within the liberal constitutionalist order, rather than turning to more radical ideas.

The power of each side over the other tended also to be of a negative rather than positive character: each could resist and prevent the full aspirations of the other but neither had the ability (or the desire perhaps) to initiate or impose a substantial change of attitude or behaviour. Employers could attempt to forestall restrictive practices or sack recalcitrant or militant workers, but they could not summon forth an active commitment to their aims, from union or non-union workforce. Trade unions could enforce trade practices or bargain up wages, but they were allowed no positive role in running the workplace.

What joint regulation there was centered on wages. A *laissez-faire* attitude to the rights of employers to direct labour as they wished (the idea of absolute employer authority was enshrined in the Master and Servant Laws) was still consistent with bargaining over the price of labour with trade unions which simply helped the labour market work in a more orderly fashion. But in essence much of labour's bargaining power (whether formally organised into a combination or not) depended on the ability unilaterally to restrict what the employer could get from the workforce: whether by means of a go slow or by the enforcement of custom and practice. In a very real sense the ability formally or informally to bargain the terms of cooperation with the employer were a form of working-class property rights. However, they could not, except in exceptional times, be admitted to exist by employers, who had at least to profess to believe in their prerogatives and 'right to manage'.

Respectability held out real advantages for unions. From enabling them to avoid state repression, it brought them the attention of politicians keen to secure the support of the better off workers for their party through the extension of the franchise and legal reform which could curb the interference of the courts. The most important measure here was Disraeli's Conspiracy and Protection of Property Act in 1875. It placed union action beyond the reach of the conspiracy laws, and permitted peaceful picketing. Another reform rendered breaches of contract by workers (for example, by going on strike) a civil rather than legal matter. Further measures in later years obliged the state to ensure that contractors it engaged paid the 'going rate' to employees, what became the 'Fair Wages Resolution', and the state began, in a piecemeal fashion, to intervene to sustain minimum rates of pay in 'sweated' trades, what was to be the origins of the Wages Council system. The Victorian Age was therefore one in which a stable political democracy was founded upon extensive state concern for the economic interests of the working class, but as far as possible left it up to employers and unions to regulate matters themselves. Thus arose a major unique feature of the British system. Rather than acquiring positive rights in law (to organise or strike, for example) unions achieved immunities from prosecution under common law for interfering with trade. Beyond this both unions and employers preferred to keep the law out of their affairs. Unions preferred to rely on their own efforts rather than legislation to secure improvements. As Lord Wedderburn (1986, p. 1) summarised it, 'Most workers want nothing more of the law than it should leave them alone'.

Thus, we come to two further fundamental aspects of the British system: the separation of economics and politics, and the idea that the state 'held the ring' between capital and labour. Both are summed up by the term 'voluntarism'. As long as both employers and unions preferred to deal directly with each other and accepted the context of a free market environment without state interference, then politics could remain largely aloof from economic affairs. Rather the role of the state was to maintain the conditions under which a liberal economic order might flourish: protection of the laws of property, on the one hand, but a watchful eye on the over-zealous interpretation of the law by the courts, on the other. Within the rules of the game set by the state, employers and unions proceeded autonomously and voluntarily. State regulation was kept to a minimum.

There were, however, ambiguities in this arrangement. It was not clear and could not be clear at what point permissible 'economic' unionism became a political challenge, either to the rights of individual employers or to the liberal economic system. According to the Master and Servant Laws governing labour contracts, the servant was obliged to obey his or her employer. But the whole foundation of unionism was based in practice on limiting and challenging that obligation. In practice unionism was tolerated by government and the courts so long as its bargaining power allowed it to advance only such claims as employers individually and the state collectively found it practicable and expedient to meet. One feature of this was the seemingly infinite ability of the courts to discover new legal impediments in common law to union activity. Another feature was the development and reinforcement of a complex of attitudes on the shop floor amongst unionists and non-unionists alike, about the relationship between the employer as manager and the worker. These relationships were cemented in the context of a booming British economy from 1850 to 1880, with protected empire markets and all the benefits of world economic leadership. The lack of product market pressure on British employers allowed them not to define too narrowly what was 'practicable and expedient'. They no more were forced to deal radically with unionism than they were to think innovatively or constructively about how to train, organise or motivate labour. For their part workers and their unions could pursue their economic interests through the leverage they could exert at the workplace over the organisation of work and supply of labour. They could extract material concessions from the employer without having to address potentially divisive political questions about the fairness of a *laissez-faire* economic order or about capitalist exploitation. Just as they saw little need to concern themselves with the economic system, so too there was little need to be concerned about how the individual enterprise ought to be managed or labour deployed. Beyond the tactical challenge to managerial prerogative involved in workplace collective bargaining lay the strategic acceptance that it was the employers' business to direct labour and run the enterprise.

The reactions to the deliberations and report of the Whitley Committee just after the First World War illustrate many of these features of industrial relations. The Committee, composed of academics and representatives of employers, unions and the state, had been charged with reviewing the state of industrial relations and the problems caused by disputes. It recommended that joint industrial committees be established at national, regional and workshop level between unions and employers. These would not just bargain over wages but would aim to develop greater cooperation between employers and workers through discussing all aspects of the business. In private industry the impact of the Whitley recommendations was marginal and short-lived. Employers had little interest in developing any personnel policy towards their workforces or attempting to refashion their relationship so as to incorporate employees into the process of management. They maintained their *laissez-faire* attitude and continued to bargain over what unions were able to force them to concede. The state for its part saw no need to attempt to regulate how employers approached industrial relations, there was no question of joint councils becoming a statutory requirement, for example. But Whitley did create a distinct approach to industrial relations in the public sector. Here the Whitley model was adopted for the civil service and later for local government employees, teachers and health service workers. The extensive system of consultation in the nationalised coal industry after 1945 was also based on the Whitley model. The adoption of Whitleyism by the state was facilitated by some of the distinct features of public sector employment. The public sector did not face market forces directly and its 'products' were more diffuse, often constituting a public service. This meant that managers' objectives were distinct — to uphold the standard of service rather than maximise profits, for example — and so correspondingly was their approach to labour. It was more likely to be organised bureaucratically with training opportunities and the potential for promotion through a career structure. Negotiations were conducted nationally rather than locally. There was more opportunity for both management and employee to identify and share common objectives and interests — and to reward mutual loyalty. Unionism was more firmly established and tolerated. This did not mean that public sector industrial relations were perfect. There were problems of inefficiency, traditionalism and low pay. In the 1960s and 1970s pressures to increase efficiency and reorganise management, along with the political problems caused when the ultimate employer in the public sector — the government — introduced incomes policies, combined to make public sector industrial relations more explosive.

Trade unions and the Labour Party

The final piece in the British system arrived with the creation of the Labour Party by the unions. At first sight this appears to contradict the pattern of development outlined so far which has stressed the apolitical, sectional and divided character of British unionism. But once we examine this process closely, it actually confirms it. The spur to the formation of the Labour Party came from a particularly harmful court decision, the 'Taff Vale' judgement, which threatened to render most union action unlawful once again. As always, the unions looked to Parliament to 'hold the ring' fairly and redress the balance. But in order to formalise this protection role, it was decided to support 'Labour' candidates who would guard the unions' interests in the legislature. The result was very successful. Indeed its very success raised considerable problems.

If Labour MPs were to form a party in the House of Commons, this implied having policies on a whole range of issues besides the legal position of trade unions. But it was not clear how these policies were to be formulated given the absence of any mass popular base for the new party, its dependence on union finance and the explicitly non-political stance of most unions. Nor could the unions be tied too closely to an opposition party when they had to get on with whichever party formed the government of the day. The solution adopted was that while the constitution of the party gave control of its conference to the unions, real power lay with the Parliamentary Party. In turn, the unions formed what Robert McKenzie called a 'Praetorian Guard' for the parliamentary leadership against more radical elements from the constituencies at conference: in Crouch's (1982, p. 181) words,

> the union leadership would support the parliamentary leadership, while the latter would ensure that a Labour Government would respect the union's secured preserve of free collective bargaining ... each group of leaders would respect and protect the autonomy of the other.

This position was made clear by the first leader, Keir Hardie (McKenzie 1982, p. 192), and was very consciously upheld by the unions who explicitly recognised that regardless of the letter of the constitution, this was the fundamental spirit (Flanders 1961b).

The implications of the looseness of this special relationship were not lost on acute observers like Winston Churchill, who argued against assuming that it bound the working class to Labour, or that working-class Conservatives or Liberals would see the link as illegitimate.

> They do not mind, in practice and as a general rule in the great majority of cases, paying for their union politics, which they regard as advancing the interests of their class, then voting for a different political party which they regard as advancing political affairs upon another road at the same time. (Quoted in Coates and Topham 1985, p. 119).

From 1913 onwards unions were obliged to finance their support for Labour and other political activities from political funds to which their members paid the 'political levy'. Churchill's comments also point towards the particular conditions which made this relationship possible: the separation of economics and politics. As long as the state could leave industrial relations to voluntarism, and as long as the trade unions' economic interests did not lead to a particular political outlook towards state policy (beyond the demand that it should 'hold the ring') then such a loose and informal relationship was possible.

This relationship between the industrial and political aims of the labour movement, known as Labourism, became immensely politically successful, eclipsing the Liberal Party and from the Second World War onwards becoming a major party of government. But there was a very important thing which this relationship was not. It was not, from the outset, a socialist movement, despite the importance of socialist ideas alongside Liberal and radical ones. In this it contrasted starkly with the path of development in many European countries where the industrial arm of the movement — the trade unions — were created by the political arm, a socialist party. *Laissez-faire* and liberalism in Britain choked off the development of a mass socialist movement for the same reasons that it fostered and allowed to flourish a mass trade union movement. Nor was the allegiance of the mass of workers to the Labour Party necessarily a decisively *political* one. In some ways, as Hobsbawm (1981, pp. 7–8) has argued, it was a question of culture and identity. 'A common style of proletarian life' emerged in the 1880s and 1890s:

> I am thinking not only of the rise of the socialist movement and the Labour Party as the mass party of British workers, the changes in trade unionism, the enormous and unbroken increase in the number of co-op members from half a million in 1880 to three million in 1914, but of non-political aspects of working-class life; of the rise of football as a mass proletarian sport, of Blackpool as we still know it today, of the fish-and-chip shop.

This common style of life underpinned a crucial political relationship: 'class = support for the Workers' party = being against capitalism = for socialism' (Hobsbawm 1984, p. 11). However it was a loose relationship: not the expression of an active political movement.

British industrial relations were therefore a direct product and central feature of the *laissez-faire* economic order. It was precisely the acceptance of both sides in industry of the separation of economics and politics and the legitimacy of conflict within the boundaries of the market system that produced both the absence of any substantial challenge to the system as a whole and the inability of either side to break out of the mutual distrust and conflict which characterised their approach to each other (Fox 1985).

While *laissez-faire* ushered in the industrial revolution, it failed to compete with more dirigiste systems once the boom of the 1850s and 1860s faded. From then on growth and productivity faltered and dropped behind that of the United States and Germany. As the international economy and the technology it used became more complex, simply reliance on market forces became less efficient than the 'visible hand' of the modern integrated corporation in tandem with the state or finance institutions. At first the profits of Empire and the substantial earnings of the City cushioned decline. Investment abroad provided rentier incomes and prevented a trade deficit. Much debate has taken place on the causes of decline. Many of the factors are difficult to separate out, such as poor training, poor management organisation and union job control strategies. Kilpatrick and Lawson (1980) have emphasised the strength of workplace trade unionism, Nichols (1986) has argued that management organisation was more important. Ingham (1984) has stressed the increasing conflict between the needs of industry and the City. Others have explored the role of low investment, slow innovation, short term horizons and insufficient long term planning. But what was perhaps the most significant common factor in all these issues was the inability of the state or capital or labour to mount any programme to reorganise and modernise industry. Instead what stood out was the way in which each found it easier to guard their own mutual autonomy which reform would inevitably have threatened.

The Second World War and the Post-War Settlement

However, the Second World War presented a major challenge to *laissez-faire*. The separation between economics and politics became impossible to sustain because production was vital for the war effort. This meant greater state regulation not only of industry, but of industrial relations and wider aspects of the social order too, in order to secure the commitment of labour. Together with the military need for greater state intervention in the market economy went the ideas of economic theorists such as Keynes that the state could and should intervene to secure full employment which markets could not sustain if left to themselves. Alongside such an economic policy stood the concept of the welfare state, of standard rights to subsistence, health care and education that every citizen should enjoy, paid for by progressive income taxation. These ideas were not the sole prerogative of socialists. Keynes and Beveridge, two of the major architects of the post-war social and economic order, were Liberals. They were supported by Conservatives like Macmillan and Butler. The spirit of the age was caught in a *Times* leader of July 1940 (quoted in Calder 1971, p. 158):

> If we speak of democracy, we do not mean a democracy which maintains the right to vote but forgets the right to work and the right to live. If we speak of freedom, we do not mean a rugged individualism which excludes social organization and economic planning. If we speak of equality, we do not mean a political equality nullified by social and economic privilege. If we speak of economic reconstruction, we think less of maximum production (though this too will be required) than of equitable distribution. The European house cannot be put in order unless we put our own house in order first. The new order cannot be based on the preservation of privilege, whether the privilege be that of a country, of a class, or of an individual.

Lord Halifax in the same month was aware of the connection between the aims of the war and the social order that would emerge from it.

> We were all conscious as the talk proceeded of the contrast between the readiness of the Nation, and particularly the Treasury, to spend £9,000,000 a day in war to protect a certain way of life and the unwillingness of the administrative authorities in peace to put up, shall we say, £10,000,000 to assist in the reconditioning of Durham unless they could see the project earning a reasonable percentage (quoted in Carlton 1986).

Churchill appointed Ernest Bevin, the leading trade unionist of the day, to be Minister of Labour: probably the most important post in the government. Bevin only accepted on condition that his ministry helped organise production too (Morgan 1985, p. 28). He used state direction of labour supplies to promote trade unionism, collective bargaining and workplace rights. Regulations such as Essential Works Orders and Order 1305 (which banned strikes) were used to persuade employers to improve conditions and recognise unions. Minimum wage legislation grew to cover up to 4.5 million workers by 1950. Trade union membership, halved in the inter-war depression, grew by one-third from 1938 to 1943, despite the fact that almost 5 million people were drawn into the armed forces in the period. Over the same five years women's civilian employment grew by 47 per cent. Unemployment effectively disappeared. In 1943 60,000 were classified as unemployed, equivalent to $\frac{1}{4}$ per cent of the workforce. As well as directing the supply of labour to difficult industries, government directed war industry to depressed regions.

From 1941 a heavily progressive income tax structure was introduced, while rationing restricted the advantage of higher incomes. In December 1942 the immense public reaction to the Beveridge Report on Social Insurance forced Churchill's government to prepare for the post-war Welfare State. 1944 saw White Papers on Full Employment, on Social Insurance and on a National Health Service, and the passing of Butler's Education Act.

It is important not to overstate wartime changes, great as they were. As a whole wage earners, particularly manual workers, improved their standard of living absolutely and relatively, while full employment gave them a new economic security. But they did so by working long and arduous hours, and forces pay was low. Women's employment increased but state provision for child care remained poor, and their share of domestic labour did not decrease. An amendment to the Education Bill to give equal pay to women teachers was heavily defeated. The share of wealth enjoyed by the top 1 per cent of the population declined from 14 per cent in 1938 to 11 per cent in 1947, but the economy was still a private one: despite the Excess Profits Tax there were fortunes to be made in the war. Nor did these changes usher in overnight a period of industrial harmony and efficiency. Working days lost in strikes (formally banned) reached nearly 3.7 million by 1944. Nor was labour productivity or managerial efficiency revolutionised. Barnett (1986) cites many examples of the maintenance of mutual distrust between labour and management in the wartime factories.

It was therefore in the course of the war that the main elements of what came to be known as the Post-War Settlement were laid. Its aims could be summed up as government intervention in the economy to promote full employment, a Welfare State of equal rights to health care, education, a job or subsistence. Its means were to be the fuller involvement of labour in its achievement both industrially and politically. The 1945 Labour government which laid the foundations of the Settlement was one of continuity rather than innovation, despite its landslide victory: in Pimlott's (1985) words,

> Instead of dismantling wartime controls, as happened after 1918, the Attlee Government kept them. Instead of removing wartime direction of industry, Labour nationalised. Instead of giving back the rentiers and high salary earners their pre-war incomes, Labour retained the steeply progressive wartime system of taxation.

The Conservative opposition, traumatised by Churchill's defeat at the polls, did not even oppose Labour's early measures, while, apart from the nationalisation of steel, Conservative governments after 1951 accepted the main direction of policy. It could be argued that this new consensus represented the forced acquiescence of the Conservatives in the new order in order to ensure their political survival. Alternatively, Barnett (1984) and others, such as Nairn and Anderson (1965), have argued that this demonstrated the failure of Labour to produce real change in the post-war period, and to set post-war British society on a true course of 'modernisation'. But the birth of the Post-War Settlement occurred in a context of extremely hard economic circumstances which are seldom appreciated today. In the course of the war, Britain lost the equivalent of a quarter of its national wealth. Its overseas assets had been sold off to pay for the war. In 1914 they had equalled total domestic wealth. Income from these assets had enabled Britain to run a large deficit on the balance of trade. The wartime sale of overseas assets ended all that. By 1945 net overseas assets were negative. Britain's export industry had been converted to wartime production so that there were virtually no sources of foreign exchange with which to pay for the imports of food and raw materials that Britain required. The post-war export drive reduced (but did not eliminate) the deficit on trade sufficiently to allow growth to proceed without balance of payments crises forcing the government to deflate the economy, dampen growth and drive up unemployment in order to curb imports. Only the negotiation of a £4 billion loan from the United States (on terms much harder than the government originally hoped) avoided what would almost certainly have been economic collapse (Morgan 1985, pp. 144ff; Pimlott 1985; Feinstein 1983, pp. 6–7). An early indicator of the Government's commitment to full employment was its reaction to the first post-war currency crisis: rather than deflate the economy — a measure which would cut imports and reduce the need for foreign exchange but also raise unemployment — Attlee devalued sterling by nearly one-third from $4.03 to $2.80. The Distribution of Industries Act was used to direct industry to areas of high unemployment.

In the event, a seemingly virtuous circle of economic growth, full employment, public provision and personal prosperity ensued for nearly 30 years. Indeed, in comparison to Britain's economic performance from the 1870s onwards, the post-war period was one of 'outstanding betterment' (Phelps Brown 1983, p. 208).

This Post-War Settlement ran against the grain of *laissez-faire* and the voluntarist system of industrial relations at its heart. State responsibility for full employment implied a closer link between economics and politics and less autonomy for both labour and capital if the measures necessary to ensure full employment were to be taken. One of the economists whose thinking lay behind the Settlement, Kalecki (1943, p. 331) argued that 'full employment capitalism' would need 'new social and political institutions which will reflect the increased power of the working class'.

The problem was that in the context of not only full employment but a government guarantee to maintain full employment, bargaining power in the labour market would lie overwhelmingly with employees and their trade unions: they would be able to bid up wages to inflationary levels. But others such as Beveridge emphasised that greater economic security could promote less defensiveness on the part of trades unions and encourage more positive cooperation with employers. Unemployment was in his view an ineffective way of securing labour discipline. In practice, however, few new institutions or radically different economic policies emerged, or were seen to be necessary. In the context of fast-expanding world trade full employment was achieved without massive government interference with the market or extensive government controls over companies' decision-making. Where the government did intervene, for example in the Distribution of Industries Act which directed employment away from the overcrowded South East to the depressed areas, its activities were accepted by both unions and employers as in the general interest. Nationalisation was not used to introduce industrial democracy into the new public corporations, although union recognition was encouraged. The extent of public ownership was largely confined to public monopolies where it allowed more efficient co-ordination of supply (power, transport) and to the coal industry, where the neglect and myopia of the owners made public control inevitable.

An explicit polity of tripartism was developed, whereby government sought a consensus with leaders of industry (who only formed a unified pressure group in 1965 after much coaxing from government itself) and the TUC. This position was formalised further by the creation of the National Economic Development Council (NEDC) and its associated Office (NEDO) in 1962. But this tripartism did not constitute a corporatist system whereby labour and capital, together with the government, set out the fundamentals of economic policy and bypassed Parliament or the electorate. Employers' leaders, the TUC and government ministers talked to each other (as they had done long before 1940) but they could not of themselves formulate policy (whether economic or political), order their members to follow it or even always persuade them to do so. Partly this was a matter of structure. Trade unions and employers remained decentralised and guarded their autonomy although they had developed national agreements in many industries. Nor could government ministers present the Cabinet, far less the House of Commons, with a policy arrived at in tripartite discussions and assume it would be rubber-stamped. But it was also a matter of attitude: the separation of politics and economics was an attractive doctrine to labour, capital and the state so long as each could take account of changed economic conditions. It allowed politicians to commit themselves to full employment and the Welfare State without having to elaborate just what political obligations that might place on employers or unions and securing legitimacy for the potential restrictions on economic freedoms it could imply. It also avoided drawing the government into too close a relationship with the complex and unpredictable affairs of industry. Similarly, employers were jealous of their economic freedoms and unions keen to rely on their own collective bargaining efforts rather than dependence on the state.

Thus 'voluntarism' and the concept of 'holding the ring' emerged virtually unscathed from the Post-War Settlement. The economic pressures forecast by

Keynes and Kalecki did emerge but were dealt with 'voluntarily'. The Labour government secured the support of the TUC from 1948 onwards for pay restraint. Moreover, the union leaderships were anxious to discipline any 'unofficial' rank-and-file resistance within their own unions. They performed their Praetorian Guard role at Party Conference. There was a 'community of outlook' between the TUC leadership and the Labour Party leadership. According to Morgan (1985, p. 78),

> On all aspects of policy the major union leaders regarded it as their moral duty to endorse the views of the political leaders ... At annual party conference the union block vote was notorious for its undemocratic, but automatic operation, to ensure a majority for the platform ...

Economic performance and the industrial relations system

While the post-war performance of the British economy was excellent in terms of historical comparisons and remarkable given Britain's immediate post-war position and loss of protected Empire markets, in comparison with the rest of Western Europe, North America and Japan, it was poor. As before the Second World War, British growth lagged behind other countries, but now it meant that British living standards started to fall below those elsewhere. Secondly, as productivity in industries producing for export lagged behind international competitors, so Britain's ability to export sufficient goods to pay for imports (which were increasingly imports of manufactured goods displacing British ones in home markets) was impaired. The result was successive balance of payments crises and stubbornly rising wage and price inflation.

Two major alternatives faced successive governments. They could deflate demand, hoping that this would reduce imports and domestic demand, thus indirectly stimulating exports. But as well as harming full employment, this could discourage investment, curb rises in productivity and therefore hamper long-term export performance and encourage greater import penetration. Alternatively devaluation of the currency could make exports more attractive, by cheapening them, but lead to inflation caused by the rise in costs of imported raw materials and foodstuffs. Were such inflation to be passed on in wages, then export competitiveness would be threatened afresh. Increasingly the problem of the British economy seemed to concern not deficient demand which a government might hope to rectify by Keynesian policies, but the failure of the 'supply side' of the economy to respond to demand dynamically enough to maintain employment and provide rising living standards. The result was stagflation: growing unemployment combined with rising inflation and continued balance of payments problems.

These circumstances made the separation between economics and politics more difficult to sustain for the poor performance of the economy was becoming a major political issue in terms which demanded more active government intervention. Attention was focused on the implications of full employment for power in the labour market. It had always been expected that full employment would lead to wage rises by giving unions greater bargaining power. In so far as this reduced the incidence of low wages, encouraged labour saving investment and transferred labour from sweatshop employers to high wage industries this was beneficial. But a full labour market could have other less beneficial effects on wage levels. Wages could be bid up to the levels which increased prices of finished goods, or diverted funds from investment, threatening long-run productivity or export competitiveness. Strategically powerful groups of workers might pursue high claims which others would try to follow. There might be a collective interest in holding money wage rises to a level which maximised long-term real wage rises (via increases in productivity and economic growth) but any individual section of workers could not be sure that others would feel bound to observe such a limit or that the resources freed by low wage claims would in fact be used for domestic investment growth. Thus, most Keynesians came to argue that full employment had to be matched by an incomes policy to be successful, as left to its own devices the labour market could produce wage and price inflation. Planning of employment implied the need to plan wages, too.

Conversely the ability of local groups within the British voluntarist system to bid up individual employers' wage rates well above nationally negotiated rates, often using unofficial action, seemed to encourage not only high wage inflation but also high levels of strike action and other disruption. In the 1960s observers started to blame industrial relations for Britain's poor economic performance. It was also argued that local collective bargaining placed a premium on developing restrictive working practices and resistance to technological change which could be 'sold' for higher wages. This slowed modernisation of industry and encouraged keeping employment in individual factories artificially high. Thus in 1965 the Donovan Commission was established

> to consider relations between managements and employees and the role of trade unions and employers' associations in promoting the interests of their members and in accelerating the social and economic advance of the nation, with particular reference to the law in affecting the activities of these bodies (Royal Commission on Trade Unions and Employers Associations 1968).

Its terms of reference implied that what was needed was some change in the way the state 'held the ring' between labour and capital, and that legal restrictions on unions would redress the balance of bargaining power in the labour market. However the Commission drew very different conclusions from the evidence presented to it. Instead of focusing on the workings of the labour market in general, it examined how the institutions of the labour market and collective bargaining worked in individual companies and workplaces. It concluded that wage drift, which fuelled wage inflation, and disruptive strikes were caused by the failure of industrial relations institutions to adapt to the changed economic power of the work-group on the shop floor brought by full employment. In particular it criticised management's behaviour and attitudes towards unionism.

Alan Fox and Allan Flanders, in their influential submissions to the Commission, argued that unofficial strikes were a function of out-of-date industrial relations institutions. If anything management was the real culprit in failing to develop or apply any comprehensive industrial relations strategy. Instead of legal curbs on unions, collective bargaining should be actively promoted in width (to unorganised industries and to white-collar workers) and depth (the range of subjects covered by joint regulation) and anti-unionism proscribed. They argued that management should face up to the fact of economic power enjoyed by the work-group on the shop floor by full employment. If it continued to try and ignore it, the result would be increasingly chaotic and irrational pay structures, restrictive practices and industrial disruption. Alternatively management could admit the strength of shopfloor organisation, formally recognise it, and, jointly with the shop floor's representatives, produce agreed rules concerning the extent of managerial prerogative, discipline, pay, job descriptions and many other matters to do with the organisation of production and distribution of rewards from it. Thus management would regain its lost legitimacy in the eyes of the workforce and 'regain control by sharing it.' In short, industrial trouble was a symptom of managements' denial of industrial rights to the workforce, rights which full employment gave workers the power to pursue. Management had to drop its *laissez-faire* approach to its workforce and develop rules jointly with trade unions about how labour was to be used and work organised.

To do this management should drop its unitarist attitude and approach: the idea that it represented the true interests of all in the company and that therefore unionism, because it was sectional, might be tolerated but never afforded legitimacy. Rather management should adopt a pluralist approach that in reality they shared power with a workforce which could have interests in conflict as well as in common with their employers. Management should seek to develop consensual 'high trust' relations with shopfloor union organisation, meanwhile unions would improve their image and regain their popularity by pursuing issues of workplace rights and industrial suffrage rather than simple wage claims.

Fox and Flanders certainly did not advocate management abdication of their responsibilities. Indeed their analysis could be seen as a demand for management to manage *more*. As well as all its technical functions it also had to calculate the social and industrial relations consequences of its managerial decisions and take these into account. It was management's duty to have good industrial relations because it determined the working environment which gave rise to workers' attitudes and actions. This would broaden, strengthen and deepen collective bargaining and mutual legitimacy and secure a proper balance between the need for industrial discipline and economic performance, and the autonomy of individuals and work-groups: their rights to pursue what they saw as their distinct interests. Such an extension of joint regulation should be encouraged by the state, but on a voluntary, not legal, basis. Meanwhile joint regulation should not go so far as trade union involvement in management or responsibility for its decisions (for example, via board level representation) because that would represent union collaboration rather than cooperation with management. Unions had to remain responsible to the distinct interests and wishes of their membership. This was both a defence of their members' freedom and a matter of realism: unions too closely identified with management would be deserted by disenchanted members.

The Commission took on board most of this analysis. It argued that the 'formal' system of industry-wide bargaining which had developed over the years had been overtaken, under conditions of full employment, by local 'informal' bargaining at plant level. Management had not recognised this and such bargaining had become reliant on restrictive practices and wildcat strikes. These produced chaotic settlements: voluntarism was turning into market-based and inflationary anarchy because there were no agreed norms nor proper procedure about how the system should work. Management should therefore formalise the informal, as it were. It should develop a comprehensive policy on industrial relations at company level, and develop procedures with trade unions jointly to regulate how industrial relations were to be conducted. Collective bargaining should extend to work organisation and other areas. This would restore the legitimacy of management, increase efficiency (through such initiatives as productivity bargaining) and remove the cause of unofficial action by incorporating the interests and attitudes of the workforce into the process of management. To help and guide management and unions a Commission on Industrial Relations would be established to encourage and spread good practice. Thus the voluntarist character of the British system was to be maintained, along with the separation of economics and politics. The state would still 'hold the ring' but within that ring labour and capital, by reforming their procedural relationships, were to be encouraged voluntarily to cooperate more effectively.

Donovan's analysis is testimony to the continued traditions of *laissez-faire* even within the Post-War Settlement. It focused on workplace industrial relations, as if these could be divorced from the context of the wider economic order. Leaving aside the moot point about how far poor productivity could be blamed on industrial relations as opposed to other factors which we cited earlier (factors which Labour's abortive National Plan and Department of Economic Affairs were conspicuously unable to tackle) it was surely utopian to reform the economic order in the workplace without also changing the wider context. Employers and workers were being invited to reach a new consensus on their mutual responsibilities at workplace level, while at the level of the economy as a whole, market forces would still play the leading role. There were no plans for industrial democracy, nor was there a coherent industrial strategy through which the state, capital and labour might agree on their longer term goals (what could be seen as the ends to which such closer workplace cooperation was the means) and secure the support of their members for them.

The next chapter examines the shortcomings of Donovan's analysis, and the continued failure of the Post-War Settlement to produce new institutions or social forces which could address the increasingly acute economic problems which Britain faced by generating higher growth and productivity. This failure ultimately resulted in the resurgence of a more resolutely *laissez-faire* approach to the economy and industrial relations that was Thatcherism. It proposed to separate economics and politics once more, by abandoning the commitment to full employment, abandoning any attempt by the state to modernize domestic industry, and instead rely on the fortunes of these sections of industry able to survive in a *laissez-faire* environment and on the profits of industry's international activities and the City.

CHAPTER 3

The 1970s: The System in Trouble

The collapse of voluntarism and failure of corporatism

In the 1970s the economic problems discussed in Chapter 2 came to a head, putting tremendous strain on the Post-War Settlement. Both Conservative and Labour governments intervened more directly in the economy and industrial relations in an attempt to combat rising inflation and unemployment as well as poor growth, productivity and export performance in industry. This undermined the tradition of voluntarism: governments felt they could no longer leave matters to employers and unions to sort out themselves but had to intervene directly either to determine procedures (how employers and unions bargained with each other) or substantive outcomes, especially earnings. This move was important in itself, but it also posed critical problems for other fundamental aspects of the British system. Once it intervened directly is was more difficult for the state to claim that it was merely a neutral referee 'holding the ring' for capital and labour. It was now getting involved in the fight. The separation of economics and politics was likewise eroded. Once the state intervened more directly in the economy and industrial relations these became more directly political issues. This posed problems for the traditional roles of all those involved. There was concern about how far state intervention could legitimately go in a democracy. Both employers and unions resisted state regulation of their affairs. For the Labour Party and the trade unions there was the special problem of the relationship between the union Praetorian Guard and the party leadership, now that the latter's economic policies posed problems for their own role.

If economic pressures meant that voluntarism, the separation of economics and politics and the state holding the ring were all relationships that could no longer be maintained, that did not mean that employers, unions or the state were able to evolve new more adequate sets of relationships. In many other countries there had been a move towards 'corporatism', whereby each of the parties meeting centrally agreed the basic framework of economic policy and its implications for their own members. Thus unions might agree to secure their members support for pay restraint, while employers offered to ensure a certain level of investment or employment and the state would propose various policies to complement the deal. A fundamental feature of corporatism was the agreement of the 'social partners' (as the unions, employers and state sometimes called themselves) to forego their autonomy and agree to act in concert for their mutual benefit. As we shall see moves in this direction in Britain foundered on the inability of any of the social partners to go very far down this road. In the wake of the failure of these moves monetarist ideas gained ground. They offered a very different solution to the problem: that the state should draw back from attempting to reconcile the competing claims of employers and employees and leave market forces (which could of course be influenced by the state) to restrain their demands.

The Donovan Report's commitment to voluntarism represented the twilight of that powerful doctrine. The Labour government accepted its recommendations but added in its 1969 White Paper, *In Place of Strife*, proposals legally to restrict unofficial strikes and enforce 'cooling-off periods'. This move strained the relationship between unions and the Party. The unions saw the proposed laws as unworkable. Their case was argued inside the government by James Callaghan, by no means a militant. In 1971 the new Conservative government under Heath introduced more widespread changes with the Industrial Relations Act. The aim of the Act was to revolutionise labour law in Britain by regulating directly the procedures employers and unions could follow. Trade unions would have to register with a National Industrial Relations Court. The Act also adopted Donovan's idea of a Commission on Industrial Relations (CIR). The CIR was very active, and produced a number of guides, codes of practice and investigations into problems of particular companies, all in an ethos informed by Donovan. But its work also showed that Donovan's emphasis on the virtues of good procedure could be utopian. It did not recognise the substantial substantive conflicts between the objectives of managers and workers, nor did it take enough account of the very different conditions facing workers in industries like shops, hotels, restaurants, public houses and business services where union organisation was weak and sporadic and management procedures informal and often arbitrary (CIR 1971; 1974). The Act was part of a wider strategy by the Heath government to escape from poor economic performance, the frustration of stop-go policies and rising inflation. There was to be free collective bargaining rather than an incomes policy, tax changes, a floating exchange rate and entry to the EEC. Meanwhile public expenditure was to be controlled and nationalised industries' prices held down (which implied a strong squeeze on public sector pay). These measures were aimed at stimulating competitiveness and the government was to draw back from intervention in the economy. If industry found the going tough in the short run it could not look for state aid. There would be no supporting 'lame ducks', in the words of John Davies, head of the new Department of Trade and Industry. Heath had 'very little patience with sluggishly accepted consensus values' (Butler and Kavanagh 1974, p. 10). His government wanted change. But its original policy aimed to maintain the separation of economics and politics but combine this with legally induced changes in the immediate relationship between labour and capital in industry: a sort of Donovan by decree, but with the emphasis on curbing militants as much as reforming management.

The policy fell apart on all fronts. Inflation accelerated while the balance of payments worsened. Unemployment grew by half between 1970 and 1972. The bankruptcy of Rolls Royce and Upper Clyde Shipbuilders forced the government to reverse its 'no lame ducks' approach. It introduced an Industry Act which provided extensive public support to companies in trouble. Days lost through strikes continued to increase, despite higher unemployment: over 13 million days in 1971 and nearly 24 million in 1972. The Industrial Relations Act became a dead letter. Most managers, aware of the likely trouble from such dramatic and unpredictable changes, colluded with unions to avoid it. It was also internally contradictory, seeking simultaneously to curb the power of trade unions, yet also to increase the authority of 'responsible' union officials over their members. The unions nationally ignored it, and government attempts to put it into practice quickly became spectacular and embarrassing failures. Public expenditure did not fall and the government, despite its efforts, failed to hold down public sector pay. In particular the miners, back in a better bargaining position for almost the first time since their crushing defeat in 1926, won not only a substantial increase from the public inquiry established to end their strike, but forced the government to improve on its recommendations. This episode revealed one of the Donovan Report's weaknesses. While its contrast between formality and informality and emphasis on procedural reform might fit privately owned manufacturing well, its analysis was less relevant to the problems of coal. The industry had well-developed collective bargaining procedures, little local 'informality' and extensive joint regulation of work through consultation procedures. The miners' problem, one which public opinion sympathised with, was that they did a dangerous job in hostile working conditions for poor pay.

In a virtually complete reversal of policy (the celebrated 'U-turn') Heath attempted to find a corporatist solution to the problems of industry. There was to be an export-led 'dash for growth' in an attempt to escape from balance of payments problems and bring down unemployment. And in the very month that the TUC killed off the Industrial Relations Act by suspending all unions which had complied with it, Heath invited the TUC and CBI to discussions about running the economy: 'an offer to employers and unions to share fully with the government the benefits and the obligations involved' (Butler and Kavanagh 1974, p. 23). This was not just the development of tripartism — discussions between ministers, employers, and union leaders about industrial relations which were as old as the century — but the offer to the TUC and the CBI to bargain directly with the government about its entire programme in return for commitments on pay and prices. This was a far closer and less informal avenue of influence on government than the TUC had traditionally enjoyed with Labour government ministers. The talks broke down because Heath was not prepared to repeal the Housing Finance Act and the

Industrial Relations Act: the price of the TUC's cooperation. A statutory incomes policy followed, but price inflation reached double figures and the balance of payments worsened. The 'dash for growth' boosted output by a remarkable 7 per cent in one year, but without solving the issue of competitiveness, and then ran into the brick wall of the huge rise in oil prices and other raw materials. The government entered the winter of 1973–4 facing a second miners' strike. It was forced to put industry on a three-day week to conserve energy supplies. The Prime Minister who had offered the TUC a probably greater role in the government of the country than at any time since 1945, held an election on the issue of union power and 'Who Governs Britain'. Heath lost. His experience showed that in the early 1970s both a 'hands off' approach to industry and a corporatist one faced tremendous difficulties. His 'U-turn' and ensuing defeat started some Conservatives thinking an entirely new approach was needed.

For the remainder of the 1970s the economic position continued to deteriorate relative to the rest of the developed world, with the added problem that the OECD countries were now also experiencing the first serious check in their virtually continuous economic progress since 1945. By 1976 the balance of payments position was poor enough to reduce the value of sterling by 25 per cent in six months and require a £3.5 billion loan from the IMF, which imposed various conditions about cutting public expenditure. Manufacturing output remained depressed. After falling dramatically from its peak during the 'dash for growth' to a low in 1975, it had still not recovered its 1973 level when it reached its next high point in 1979. UK unemployment passed the psychological barrier of 1 million in 1975 and peaked at 1.6 million in 1977. Inflation rose from 8 per cent in 1974 to over 25 per cent in 1975. Rising unemployment and ailing industry had helped push up the proportion of national wealth devoted to public spending, while the fall in manufacturing employment continued. This was the focus of an influential book published in 1976, *Britain's Economic Problem*, which argued that increasing state intervention in the economy was starving the private sector of investment and labour, leaving 'too few producers' in the economy (Bacon and Eltis 1976).

The Labour government's response to these problems arose from the formation in 1972 of a Liaison Committee between the Labour Party and the TUC. This proposed an annual agreement on a 'Social Contract' which would formalise relationships between the trade union movement and a Labour government. In return for trade union restraint on wages and industrial militancy they would be able to influence government policy in other areas. The Contract also allowed for the union leaders on Labour's National Executive Committee to continue to act as Praetorian Guard for the Labour leadership. It was increasingly at odds with its left-moving constituency membership, critical of the failure of Labourism to halt rising unemployment or expand public services.

The government pursued an interventionist strategy to begin with. The 1975 Industry Act established a National Enterprise Board and provided for planning agreements between employers, unions and the government in firms receiving state aid. British Leyland, the aircraft, aerospace and shipbuilding industries, which were all facing job losses, erosion of market share and bankruptcy, were nationalised. After a brief interlude free collective bargaining was replaced by a very tight pay policy. Control of public expenditure and of money supply was introduced from 1975 onwards, partly because of concern at the rate of increase of public expenditure, and partly because it was what the banks baling out Britain's balance of payments problems demanded. Answering criticism that by agreeing to the terms of the IMF loan his government was abandoning the Post-War Settlement, and the pursuit of full employment, Prime Minister James Callaghan argued at the 1976 Labour Party Conference: 'It used to be thought that a nation could just spend its way out of recession and increase employment by cutting taxes and boosting government spending. I tell you in all candour that that option no longer exists' (quoted in Feinstein 1983, p. 25). The unions' 'Praetorian Guard' role began to crack, however. The conference voted for increased spending. However, the 'Letter of Intent' sent by the Chancellor, Denis Healey, to the IMF to secure the loan outlined what was in effect a monetarist policy, leading the political editor of the *Financial Times* to comment later that 'If there has been a Thatcher experiment, it was launched by Denis Healey' (Riddell 1983, p. 59). It was not just the left of the Party and the trade unions which opposed the consequent public expenditure cuts, but 'social democrats' such as Shirley Williams and Tony Crosland. They argued that such cuts did little to help improve the economy: they simply pandered to bankers' political prejudices.

The Labour government continued the dismantling of voluntarism but in a way which stressed the positive rights and obligations of employers and employees while leaving unions and managements jointly to devise procedures to spell out just what form these rights would take. The Trade Union and Labour Relations Acts, Health and Safety at Work Act and Employment Protection Act gave workers protection against unfair dismissal, and gave trade unions greater involvement in health and safety affairs, rights to information, training and facilities for collective bargaining and provision for claiming recognition and fair wages from employers. The Advisory, Conciliation and Arbitration Service (ACAS) was established to implement some of the provisions of the legislation as well as to promote good industrial relations (the role of the defunct CIR) and a system of Industrial Tribunals was established to try to keep the jurisdiction and administration of the new laws as simple and accessible as possible. Many of the measures were unpopular with employers at first: they were seen as restricting management's freedom to manage. However, many managements came to value the regularisation of health and safety or discipline procedures which resulted, while unions came to complain that beyond the statutory procedures lay the ability of employers to flout the spirit of the law in practice while obeying its letter in principle. They still felt that proper legal rights were no substitute for bargaining power.

A further measure was to be legislation on industrial democracy, which was anticipated by the Bullock Report in 1977. It advocated union-based employee representation on the boards of large companies and consultation and information rights for trade union representatives on Joint Representation Committees — a sort of statutory combine committee. These proposals brought tremendous resistance from employers, who saw them as a potential trade union veto on their decision-making powers. Nor were trade unions unequivocally supportive. From disinterest in industrial democracy in the era of Donovan and relatively full labour markets, the economic climate of the 1970s had made unions aware of a 'gap' in the coverage of collective bargaining. While they might enjoy the right to bargain over terms and conditions of work, the circumstances under which such bargaining took place were really decided by earlier employers' decisions about products and marketing strategy, investment, and so on. It was not possible to negotiate good terms and conditions in a plant which a company was deciding to phase out in its longer-term plans, for example. However, the trade unions were divided in their response to this issue (Elliot 1978, Cressey at al. 1981). Many union officials, and even shop stewards, were worried about what they feared would be their incorporation into management ways of thinking and acceptance of joint responsibility for management decisions which could be unpopular with their membership. The Bullock Report was in effect advocating that both employers and unions should refashion their traditional arms-length adversarial stance and build new cooperative, closer and collaborative relations. Many union officials and stewards baulked at the prospect of abandoning their ability to withdraw and oppose management decisions when this would defend their members' interests. Their feelings towards Bullock were best articulated by Hugh Scanlon, leader of the Amalgamated Union of Engineering Workers (AUEW), who argued: 'We think that industrial democracy can best be strengthened by an extension of collective bargaining, to which we know no limit' (*Morning Star*, 27 January 1977).

From 1977 onwards the Social Contract fell apart. In July Jack Jones, leader of the Transport and General Workers' Union and major architect of the policy, failed to secure the backing of his union for further wage restraint. The strains between Labour government ministers and trade union leaders reached breaking point as each side felt that the other was expecting too much from the bargain. Union leaders found it virtually impossible to hold back their members' pay demands when 1976–8 had seen a real drop in living standards with apparently little government response: unemployment still stood at over 1.5 million, the 'social wage' of the Welfare State was being cut and the more interventionist aspects of government economic policy were being quietly dropped; for example, planning agreements were simply ignored or not enforced. For their part, ministers were hemmed in by the tight economic situation, angry that unions seemed to be willing to abandon their role of protecting the Labour leadership from a rank and file fiercely critical of its policies and exasperated by the weakness of the commitments union leaders could make. If they could not deliver support for the government's policies and pay restraint, where was their part of the bargain? Hence Lord Houghton's (at the time Douglas Houghton, a Labour minister) (1981, p. 149) bitter view of the Social Contract:

Following each unsuccessful election, however, it is the trade unions which have grumbled the most. They have wanted to guide, shape and possibly control the policies of Labour governments more than Ministers have been able or willing to concede ... [The Social Contract] contained clear commitments on behalf of the next Labour Government but of reciprocal assurances by the unions there were very few.

The end came with the 5 per cent pay norm proposed for the 1978–9 wage round. This dismayed union leaders, who saw it as quite unrealistic. The limit was not agreed with the TUC, simply announced in July in the government's White Paper, *Winning the Battle against Inflation*. At the TUC General Council one vote was cast in favour of the limit. The Congress in September voted for a 'return to normal and responsible free collective bargaining'. Worse, Callaghan's unilateral decision to postpone the election to 1979 placed public sector unions in a dilemma. A pre-election period was their best chance to claw back losses in comparability with the private sector which the government's pay policy had created. Yet they were clearly 'expected to behave' in order to enhance Labour's electoral chances. In the event the private sector breached the limit and the government failed to get support for sanctions against the companies concerned. The lorry drivers' strike and the 'Winter of Discontent' followed in which low-paid public sector workers in local government and the health service took militant action which, despite the low pay of those involved, aroused less public sympathy than the miners' strikes because of the effects on those who depended on public services. Prime Minister Callaghan, who ten years before had championed the unions' resistance to *In Place of Strife*, urged workers to cross picket lines, and spoke of 'free collective vandalism'. Meanwhile, Conservatives seized the opportunity to call for legal curbs on excessive union power. Sir Keith Joseph spoke of the state of relations between the unions and Labour as 'a militants charter' under which was proceeding 'the systematic destruction of law abiding, job creating, free enterprise in the name of Socialism' (*Glasgow Herald*, 6 February 1979).

By February 1979 a 'Concordat' was patched together on pay and industrial action, but in very general terms. Trade union leaders were well aware that it would be vain to promise more. In the May general election Callaghan faced a Conservative Party with policies reminiscent of Heath's early years. Under the slogan 'Labour Isn't Working' it promised to revive the economy by cutting public expenditure and state intervention, cutting taxes, abolishing price and wage controls and introducing legislation to curb the 'excessive' power of trades unions. Callaghan lost.

The system in 1979: Past achievements and future prospects

If we stop the historical clock in May 1979 and put aside for the moment what has happened since, it is possible to explore how far developments since 1979 have been 'inevitable': whether the 'system', such as it was, was falling apart anyway or whether it was moving in ways which could have led to further change and reform, or even an escape from the vicious circle of economic decline. Nowadays there is an established image of Britain in 1979 as a country in trauma, paralysed by trade union action, weakened by an ailing, over-regulated economy and governed by a divided Labour Party. This is far from the whole picture. A record number of days were lost through strikes in 1979. But the 'Winter of Discontent' accounted for only one-quarter of them. More than twice as many were lost in the national engineering stoppage which took place in the autumn, well after the general election.

The Labour government could claim to have had some success with the economy, too, in the face of severe international difficulties. Unemployment was moving down, albeit very slowly, jobs had been created. The share of public expenditure and taxation in the national economy had been reduced sharply from the rising levels of 1974–6. Keegan (1984) warns that not too much should be read into Callaghan's famous assertion in 1976 that spending one's way back to full employment was impossible. His main aim was to settle the markets. In practice the government combined monetary control with a recognisably Keynesian stance towards stimulating employment. Manufacturing output had grown from its lowest point in 1975. Price inflation was down to 8 per cent. The government could claim that the Social Contract had benefited those who did not have the strongest bargaining positions. Differentials between high- and low-paid workers and between men and women workers had narrowed, even if women's pay still remained substantially below that of men. Finally, North Sea oil was coming on stream providing both both tax revenues to the government and substantial exports. It held out the promise of escaping from the vicious circle of currency crises, deflation, poor productivity growth, low output growth, poor balance of payments and further currency crises. Posner (1986, p. 310) argues that the North Sea oil windfall could and should have been treated 'in effect as a rise in the medium-term path of productive potential in the economy, and in consequence to have allowed the path of effective demand itself to accelerate.'

Despite the problems over the 5 per cent pay norm, and immediate problems with the Social Contract, the government had presided over a fairly dramatic retreat from voluntarism with minimal disruption. Employers were clearly hostile to the government's plans for industrial democracy and even the unions had reservations, but such opposition and suspicion had also greeted the Health and Safety at Work Act and many aspects of the government's labour law reforms. Indeed there was evidence that British employers were losing some of their traditional hostility and suspicion of corporatism. The CBI had put forward the idea of a National Economic Forum to discuss pay and other economic issues with the TUC and government. It could well be that such a forum, or such version of the Social Contract as would emerge on the basis of the 'Concordat' between the Labour Party and the TUC in February would successfully blend the traditions of suspicion, fudge and compromise typical of British industrial relations in the past, with the more cooperative and wider ranging commitments that corporatism would require.

Moreover, these changes had been achieved by a Labour government when many of the elements of the system that was 'Labourism' were crumbling away. In their seminal work published in 1960, *Must Labour Lose?*, Abrams, Rose and Hinden argued that the Labour Party faced long-term political decline because of the direction of economic change. Heavy industry depending on large amounts of manual labour, was declining steadily. White-collar workers were growing in number instead. Full employment and economic growth created by the Post-War Settlement had led to a tremendous rise in working-class living standards and this was leading to a change in lifestyles. The counterpart of mass production was mass consumption. Workers and their families now had spending power and the ability to take part in the delights the capitalist marketplace had to offer. There was the prospect of the *embourgeoisement* of working-class lifestyles. This led to the third factor: the decline of a labour identity and image. This was particularly important if we bear in mind Hobsbawm's arguments about the importance of culture to Labour's electoral appeal.

There were still greater changes facing Labourism in the course of the 1960s and 1970s. Trade unionism embarked on a major period of expansion in the 1970s, organising many more white-collar workers both in the public sector and manufacturing. These workers brought new attitudes and traditions to the unions, as well as new problems. In some ways their position as paid workers could be little different to their manual colleagues. They could be subject to the same hierarchy and authority and face alienating or arduous work. Many of their fathers would have been manual workers (see Goldthorpe 1980) and so they could well be familiar with the older traditions of unionism. But there were other factors, too. Many exercised a degree of authority or enjoyed higher status. Many might look forward to the chance of promotion and responsibility in the future. In their relationship with their white-collar staff British employers have been less devoted to the principles of *laissez-faire*. They were far more likely to have policies for the training and career development of some of these staff, for example. For many white-collar staff in the public sector traditional modes of industrial action 'created enormous difficulties for people whose job [was] to care for others while working in, for example, health authorities who couldn't care less for them' (Beynon 1983).

As well as rising earnings and different jobs, the Post-War Settlement brought rising absolute but not relative social mobility. According to Goldthorpe (1980, p. 251),

> the increasing 'room at the top' created by the growth of professional, higher technical, administrative, and managerial positions could provide the occasion, in an analogous way to increasing national wealth, for inequalities in class life chances to be reduced, but without members of any class having to become less advantaged than before in absolute terms.

This increased the chances of upward mobility for the offspring of manual workers, without either increasing the mobility chances of manual workers (skilled or unskilled) *once* they were in work, or increasing the chances of other groups having to suffer downward social mobility. In turn, chances of advancement within white-collar jobs often hinged on individual careers and were seen by those concerned as 'essentially a matter of personal achievement' (Goldthorpe 1980, p. 264). Such an orientation might well be compatible with unionism, but would bring to it quite different traditions to that of Labourism. There would be no reason to expect white-collar workers to see Labour as 'their' party either. Most white-collar unions remained unaffiliated to the Labour Party, or were able to affiliate only moderate proportions of their membership.

Conversely the manual working class, as it declined in numbers, enjoyed increased living standards and better mobility chances for its offspring, nevertheless did not itself enjoy increased social mobility. Indeed, quite the reverse happened. It became composed increasingly of second-generation manual workers both because of the absence of downward social mobility and because 'green' agricultural labour had been exhausted as a source of supply much earlier in the process of industrialisation in Britain than elsewhere. Goldthorpe (1980, p. 260) estimates that in the 1970s three-quarters of the British manual working class were 'second-generation' workers, compared to just over a half for the United States and less than a half for France. This 'largely self-recruiting bloc' was composed of men who were, as Goldthorpe (1980, p. 268) says,

> aware of their actual lack of opportunity so far as their own lives are concerned ... the goals that it appears possible for them to pursue within work are narrowly restricted: in effect, to ones of a largely instrumental kind which centre on the wage-bargain ... ones to which individual initiative can be only of secondary importance and which must in their nature be primarily achieved on a collective basis.

These patterns could have been expected to undermine the entire system of Labourism. The fact that there had been no increase in relative social mobility was hidden from view. This, combined with the experience for many white-collar workers of absolute social mobility in terms of personal success, could have been expected to diminish the appeal of Labour both industrially and politically. Paradoxically, the lack of change, aside from increased earnings, for manual workers and their solid inter-generational homogeneity could have been expected both to fuel their disaffection from the system and to provide them with the organisational and ideological means to pursue their interests in the way trade unions had been doing for over a century: bargaining hard on wages. Labourism would thus have been squeezed on two fronts: politically by the decline of its voting base as the manual working class grew smaller and industrially as the economic demands of its natural constituency conflicted with its attempts to contain wage inflation in order to maintain full employment. In fact, Labourism dealt with these surprisingly successfully. Far from the Post-War Settlement inducing an individualistic orientation to the manual working class, it brought increasing numbers of the salariat and service-class workers to support Labour (Heath, Jowell and Curtice 1985). Had Callaghan won the 1979 election the Conservative Party would have faced two decades in which the unhappy years of the Heath government were its only experience of office.

Industrially Labour's record on controlling wage inflation also withstood scrutiny. Concern about the effects of the decentralisation of bargaining, economism and leapfrogging wage bargaining reached back at least to the early 1960s. The concerns expressed by Hobsbawm (1981), Ellman *et al* (1974) or Hirst (1981) were the same ones which had led before to the Donovan Commission. Long before Hobsbawm wrote *The Forward March of Labour Halted?*, Flanders (1961a) was drawing attention to the dangers of unionism that depended too much on the 'vested interest' role of economistic wage bargaining and not enough on their 'sword of justice' role; the 'spirit of materialism' had submerged 'the spirit of idealism within trade unions'. Flanders (1961a, p. 16) warned that their role as 'vested interest'

> has become accepted as their normal, natural image by the unions themselves. It is this, more than anything else, which has been ultimately responsible for their loss of sympathy. The trade union movement deepened its grip on public life in its aspect as a sword of justice. When it is no longer seen to be this, when it can no longer count on anything but its own power to withstand assault, it becomes extremely vulnerable. The more so since it is as a sword of justice rather than a vested interest that it generates loyalties and induces sacrifices among its own members and these are important foundations of its strength and vitality.

When we consider Goldthorpe's evidence on the patterns of occupational mobility and the reasons for the growth of white-collar unionism, the difficulties of the unions appear even greater. The main avenue through which their established manual membership might wish to pursue 'social justice' was precisely by reinforcing the 'vested interest' role of unionism and achieving the only improvement that new economic order of the Post-War Settlement held out for them: a share in rising living standards. Their newer white-collar membership, as we have seen, could have quite different views of what social justice might consist of. They could not simply be recruited to a Labourist world view through their union membership. But one of the forces propelling them into unions in the 1970s was price inflation and the concern to protect their own living standards (Bain and Elsheikh 1976). Both sections of the unions' membership were therefore concerned to emphasise the drive for higher wages and the 'vested interest' role at a time when the TUC, in order to promote the corporatist policy which the Social Contract represented, wished to emphasise wage restraint and pursue 'social justice' questions. Thus while commentators focussed on the implications which these changes had for the electoral success of Labour, they were no less important in determining the fortunes of a corporatist solution to the tensions in the Post-War Settlement.

Just as writers such as Hirst commended the pursuit of industrial democracy to the unions, so too had Flanders (1961a, p. 21) argued that unions should find renewed social purpose in the pursuit of workers' rights and status at work: 'The struggle for status has received scant attention ... At their place of work Britain's workers are still in many respects second class citizens. They are subjected to treatment which would be considered intolerable in any other walk of life.' The magnitude of such a task should not be underestimated. If we consider the traditions of British union organisation and British employers' attitudes to labour which we have reviewed, it can be seen that to take up the issue of rights at work through extending the range and changing the purpose of collective bargaining was a mammoth task. It was not a simple matter of swapping money wage gains for elements of control. In any case such an effort was running against the grain of union members' perception of their interests.

Yet in some ways this was a transformation which Labourism achieved with some success. Much of the labour legislation of the last Labour government can be seen as providing such a framework of industrial rights, with a careful mixture of government regulation and 'voluntarist' bargaining. Only legislation on industrial democracy remained to be achieved. It had proved by far the most difficult and contentious area of workers' rights, for both unions and employers. The 1970s was a period of change in British workplace industrial relations, most of it in terms of the procedural reform espoused by the Donovan Report. This was achieved while effectively containing real wage inflation. Indeed Labour governments appeared 'better' at holding down the real spending power of employers than Conservative ones. In this the Social Contract was very successful. Between 1975 and 1979 real earnings over the whole economy did not increase at all. They advanced some 4 per cent in manufacturing but fell back elsewhere.

Internal contradictions in the Post-War Settlement

But there were less auspicious signs, too, of the failing health of the Post-War Settlement which the international economic difficulties of the 1970s highlighted. While the Labour government checked rising unemployment and coped with the immediate currency crisis of 1976, it engineered only a sluggish recovery in manufacturing output and productivity. Only the progressive devaluation of sterling was holding back the steady deterioration of the international labour competitiveness of British manufacturing. Even its success in price inflation and wages were threatened by the pressures released by the slight easing of wage controls and reflation in the year before the election. By June 1979 the underlying rates of increase of money earnings and prices were both around 15 per cent.

Some commentators, particularly those who were disillusioned with Keynesian full employment policies and favoured monetarism as a solution to the problems of stagflation were very pessimistic indeed. They expressed a deeper current of disillusionment with the dynamics of the Post-War Settlement that embraced both fears of a slide into collectivism and a more powerful state and fears that the centrifugal force of the competing demands of different interests would precipitate economic and political disorder. Peter Jay (1977, p. 181), Economics Editor of the *Times*, argued that

> the operation of free democracy appears to force government into positions (the commitment to full employment) that prevent them from taking steps (fiscal and monetary restraint) that are necessary to arrest the menace (accelerating inflation) that threatens to undermine the condition (stable prosperity) on which political stability and therefore liberal democracy depend. In other words, democracy has itself by the tail and is eating itself up fast.

He argued that free collective bargaining, full employment and a 'usable currency' were incompatible, but democracy could not afford to abandon any of these. Samuel Brittan, a prominent journalist on the *Financial Times*, presented a paper to the British Association 1974 Annual Meeting entitled 'The Economic Contradictions of Democracy'. Democracy encouraged political parties to hold out excessive expectations of rising living standards to the electorate, and also held them back from adequately checking the power of sectional interest groups (i.e. the unions) to disrupt the economy in the pursuit of further economic gain. It had been assumed in the past that democracy in practice as opposed to principle worked by forcing parties (regardless of their detailed policies or means of formulating them) to win the consent of the electorate and of important interest groups; industries, regions, labour and capital, and so on. But now the problem was that there was overwhelming pressure on governments to promise more than they could deliver, while there were few constraints on electors (or unionists or members of other interest groups) to face up to that problem. Brittan (1975, p. 150) argued:

> These weaknesses have become more important than they were before because of the lack of any widely shared belief in the legitimacy of the present order, which might have held them in check. Nor, on the other hand, is there any commonly held conception of any feasible alternative social order in which democracy might operate in the future.

He concluded (Brittan 1975, p. 219) that

> on present indications, the system is likely to pass away within the lifetime of people now adult ... It may help to avoid misunderstanding if I emphasise right at the beginning that there is no such thing as historical inevitability. The point of saying a house is on fire is to alert the fire brigade, not sit back and enjoy the blaze.

These fears were exaggerated and alarmist, given the actual record of the Labour government, and their expression rather grandiose. They were further fuelled by mistaken central statistical office figures which put public expenditure at 60 per cent of GDP, some 11 percentage points higher than its actual level (Hadjimatheou 1987, p. 17), but they did point to real and fundamental problems for the Post-War Settlement and for Labourism.

The scale of the problem was not always so well appreciated by theorists on the left who were more inclined to view the strains and tensions in the Post-War Settlement and Labourism as evidence that these were part of a restrictive and outmoded social order whose disintegration would be welcome because it had failed to challenge any of the fundamental inequalities of capitalist society. Miliband (1978, p. 402) argued that a state of 'desubordination' had come about:

> people who find themselves in subordinate positions, and notably people who work in factories, mines, offices, shops, schools, hospitals and so on, do what they can to mitigate, resist and transform the conditions of their subordination. The process occurs where subordination is most evident and felt, namely at the 'point of production' and at the workplace in general; but also wherever else a condition of subordination exists, for instance as it is experienced by women in the home and outside.

Such 'desubordination' was of itself not enough to bring into being a genuinely socialist movement to challenge Labourism. As Miliband (1978, p. 409) put it:

> The great paradox of political life in Britain is precisely the existence of a strong and pervasive sense of desubordination on the one hand, and the absence of significant political agencies on the other which could give to that sense coherence and shape.

Miliband forecast increasing class conflict, political instability and state authoritarianism as the Settlement fell apart. Panitch (1986) went further. The 'Impasse of Social Democratic Politics' was that it had itself blocked the development of a socialist outlook in the working class by its appeals to such things as the national interest and its strictures on workers' economism. The way forward would entail the overthrow of the Labourist old guard in the Labour Party by genuine socialists from the constituency parties, or by the creation of a new party altogether.

What did seem to be true was that the Post-War Settlement was coming apart at the seams. Unemployment of around 1.5 million was no longer full employment. Nor, in Callaghan's words, which returned to haunt him, did the government appear to be able to do much about it. The Welfare State was threatened by public expenditure cuts. These would almost certainly reduce the ability of the state to promote genuine equality of opportunity. As we have seen from Goldthorpe's evidence on social mobility, and as other evidence on the continuation of poverty, differential achievements in education and inequalities in health demonstrated, the Post-War Settlement had fallen in practice far short of the hopes of its founders. Public expenditure cuts would simply mean greater comparative advantage in health care and education for those able to afford to avoid the state sector.

Nor had the Post-War Settlement been comprehensive in those who were included. It was not a settlement which offered equality to women, for example, despite their increasing role in the economy. For a start 'full employment' had different implications for women in families who continued to be responsible for the bulk of domestic labour involved in both rearing children and in feeding, clothing and servicing the adult workforce. Their earnings could be decisive for the household, particularly with the rapid expansion of married women in the workforce, yet they enjoyed neither equal pay nor public or employer-based child-care facilities nor even tax concessions on the costs of child care. Unions were not always keen to raise women's interests, on equal pay for example, which conflicted or cut across those of their male members. They were wedded to the conception of the family wage, which conflicted with the principle of equal pay and reinforced the view that women were 'not real workers'. Armstrong's classic quote from a union official — 'If it's only women it doesn't matter so much' (West 1982) — captures the attitude well. In so far as unions saw themselves as defending established job hierarchies against 'dilution' by less skilled workers, or opposing flexibility in employment, they could often be jointly responsible with employers for the exclusion or segregation of women in the labour market. The ways that trade unions organised, meeting at times when women face the demands of domestic labour, restricted women's ability to participate. The issues they took up were often focused on the interests of career employees. Yet breaks in employment for childbirth and employers' assumptions about women's familial and domestic orientation prevented them from reaching established career jobs. So, too, could the workplace union organisation be run by 'career' men and suffused with masculine and patriarchal ideology (Ellis 1981; Cockburn 1983a). For many women the experience of unions was an alien and remote one (Pollert 1981; Cavendish 1982; Beechey 1984) yet they joined at faster rates than men so that from 1951 the proportion of union members who were women rose from one-fifth to almost one-third. By 1984 the British Social Attitudes Survey confirmed that women workers were as likely to be union members as their male equivalents. Paradoxically women's occupational segregation helped them to organise independently and define their own priorities (Gardiner 1984).

In fact Labourism made some gestures towards women in the 1970s with the Equal Pay Act (1970) and the Sex Discrimination Act (1976). Both these measures were incomplete. For example, achieving equal pay usually required finding a male worker doing the same job when women's subordinate position in the labour market resulted in tremendous occupational segregation. However, between 1970 and 1977 women's hourly earnings rose from 63 to 74 per cent of men's. Their weekly earnings remained much lower, since many worked part-time, while men continued to work far more overtime. But the main reason for the difference lay in the concentration of women in jobs which were poorly paid.

Corporatism in the workplace

There is substantial evidence that, at workplace level, particularly in larger private sector enterprises, the procedural reforms urged by Donovan were carried through to some extent. The number of personnel specialists increased, as did the number with some sort of qualifications. The deduction by employers of union dues at source, and training and facilities for shop stewards, all became more widespread. Wage bargaining at plant and company level became more widespread and was more likely to be conducted through formally agreed procedures. Procedural agreements also spread to cover issues such as discipline, health and safety and to some extent the organisation of work and deployment of employees (see, for example Brown 1981; Daniel and Millward 1983; Brown 1978; Bain 1983, and Batstone 1984). However Donovan's conviction that procedural reform would institutionalise conflict and reduce the substantive disagreement between employers and workers about wages or work organisation proved uncertain in practice. It was an ominous portent for the future that, within months of the appearance of the Report, two of the academics who had exerted great influence on it were arguing that the substantive normative disorder of British industrial relations required an incomes policy (Fox and Flanders 1969). Donovan had sought to replace a state of affairs whereby attempts at unilateral managerial initiatives were followed in practice by the fact of union resistance and informal bargaining over substantive issues with a system whereby joint regulation of procedures between management and union beforehand then allowed management to proceed unilaterally so long as it kept to these procedures.

The crucial assumption here was that the right formal procedures would minimise or institutionalise substantive disagreement. But our survey of the traditions, structures and attitudes of British industrial relations might lead us to expect such an outlook to prove utopian, particularly in the area of work organisation and deployment of labour. Here employers would want procedures which maximised their freedom of action whereas unions would want to retain safeguards and guarantees. Since rules can only be general, and are made at a higher level but interpreted and applied in detail at a lower level, there tended to be what Terry (1977) termed 'an inevitable growth in informality'. Rules were sufficiently vague to require negotiation about their application in practice which was in essence little different to what had happened before. Indeed Batstone (1984, p. 298) even suggests that procedural reform may have legitimised and encouraged an increase in informal bargaining over work organisation:

> First, these rules and agreements often encourage the expansion of workplace union organisation and built up expectations of influence on the part of workers and shop stewards. When, for whatever reason, workers objected to management actions they were, therefore, more able than they had been in the past to challenge those actions. Second, in order to achieve joint agreement over new rules managements often extended rather than reduced the union role, and their formal recognition of that role. Thus agreements could in fact reduce rather than increase managerial prerogative. Third, the explicit statement of rules increased their visibility: it was now easier for groups to challenge management actions which were not consistent with the rules.

But there was a still more fundamental obstacle that went to the heart of the very role of management. In Donovan's approach it was assumed that, while there might be a pluralism of interests in the enterprise, there was little room for disagreement over management's essential role. Everyone had an interest in management being able to manage and direct work effectively, so long as workers' substantive interests in fair wages and working conditions were addressed. But it could be, as McCarthy and Ellis (1973) argued, and as the growing interest in industrial democracy registered, that it was this very process of management itself that most urgently needed legitimation. This too could be achieved by procedural reform, argued McCarthy and Ellis (1973, pp. 83, 96):

> New products and processes can create different kinds of grievances and disputes that need to be handled in a different way. Plants can change and their markets can decline ... Once one rejects attempts to insist on the right of management to decide unilaterally there can only be one alternative way forward; authority must be shared with workers through an extension of the area of joint regulation. This is the essence of 'management by agreement' ... This would entail a circumspection of existing unilateral rights and customs on both sides of the bargaining table.

The problem with such a line of argument was that it shared with Donovan an assumption that there would be little substantive disagreement between management and employees about what the goals of the process of management should be. Our review of British industrial relations traditions would lead us to expect the opposite: that employers would adopt a *laissez-faire* perspective and that unionists would emphasise employment security. Even here there might be scope to reconcile these aims, but there was another fundamental obstacle, unrecognised by those who emphasised the value of procedural reform. This was the importance of organisational pluralism, an idea developed by Burns (1981). MacInnes (1985) and Cressey *et al.* [(1985, ch. 10) pointed out that if the goals organisations pursued are variable, and these organisations are themselves heterogeneous and composed of sectional interest groups, it follows that different groups could have very great substantive conflicts of interest in what goals each organisation pursued and how. This meant that employers were liable to have little faith in the idea of 'management by agreement' because dropping managerial prerogative might force them into accepting both means *and ends* they did not want. Conversely, unionists were happy to distance themselves from any such process both because it would highlight differences within and between unions about what management objectives should and could draw them into carrying joint responsibility for unpopular management objectives. Cressey *et al.* (1985, pp. 170–2) reviewing six companies experiences of participation found:

> Participation never reached the stage of taking decisions, or reviewing jointly the range of information relevant to reaching a decision. It could not incorporate worker representations into management decision-making because nowhere were they allowed unfettered access to it. It could not educate worker representatives about the requirements of business life because the details of those requirements were rarely opened to their view. ... Managers ... insist on a

monopoly of management authority and the information on which management decisions rest. They may be concerned with authority and the legitimation of their power, but that legitimation has very definite limits to how far it can go ... management may not wish to recognise the legitimacy of conflicting interests, because there are real choices involved in how they are to be resolved and that they may be resolved in ways management does not want ... Once it is realised that there can be not only divergent interests in organisations but that these can also be accommodated in different ways, the contradiction between managerial prerogative and managerial accountability becomes irreconcilable. If managers lose the right to decide unilaterally when they cannot persuade by force of discussion, then what power have they left? Conversely, if they retain that right, how can the workforce and its representatives enforce their distinct priorities on a reluctant management?

Lane (1986, p. 326) notes how the trade union attitude to management in Britain remains ' "Get on with it but we'll tell you when you've got it wrong" ... Isolated instances apart it is *not* common for workers or their representatives to express concern about what is produced and how'.

The failure of participation or industrial democracy to develop at workplace level, and the negative reaction to the Bullock Report at national level, showed just how far Britain was from an industrial or commercial corporatist order in the 1970s. The procedural reforms produced by Donovan had not produced either a procedural or substantive consensus in the place of conflict.

Trade unions, the Labour Party and government

For trade unions, formalising unofficial workplace organisation and recognising the decentralisation of bargaining and representation also implied a corresponding shift of power downwards and less power and authority both for national union leaders and the TUC as a whole. Jack Jones, as leader of the TGWU, could never be a union baron in the mould of Ernest Bevin, nor did he aspire to be. He had risen through the union as an advocate of internal democracy and the rights of the rank and file. But this downward shift of authority severely limited the ability of the TUC to propose or deliver corporatist agreements on the shape of economic policy. Thus TUC General Secretary Len Murray informed the Liaison Committee developing the Social Contract in 1974 'that the greatest disservice that the TUC could do for the Labour Party was to "pretend it could do more than it could" (Taylor 1982, p. 204). Dorfman (1983) provides an extensive analysis of the real weakness behind the TUC's apparent strength which this decentralisation of power caused.

So, too, any desire the unions had to pursue 'social justice' and restrain economism was tempered by the fact that, while their membership (particularly their newer white-collar membership) had a variety of views and attitudes to the former, their prime commitment was to the latter. Thus Frank Cousins, General Secretary of the TGWU before Jones, argued:

If we do not fulfil the purposes for which members join unions, to protect and
raise their real standard of living, then the unions will wither and finally die.
We can give leadership, we can persuade, but basically we must serve trade
union purposes (quoted in Taylor 1982, p. 195).

This instrumental collectivism, organised and expressed sectionally, was, as we
have seen, a long standing feature of British trade unionism, but it made it very
difficult for unions to follow a corporate solution for three reasons. First rising
living standards and the general spread of unionism made it more difficult to
present wage struggles as part of a campaign for social justice — no matter how
genuine such a claim might be in fact. Second, these struggles were more likely to
be seen *by other unionists* not as part of some general labour movement campaign
but as hostile conflicts competing with them for a share of national economic
resources. Third, there was a general decline in mass involvement in unions: it was
up to them to 'perform' satisfactorily on the wages front, but few members felt a
wider commitment beyond this. The 1980 Workplace Industrial Relations Survey
(WIRS 1980) found that about one-fifth of manual union members attended
workplace branches and about one-twentieth attended geographical or multi-
employer branches (Daniel and Millward 1983, pp. 85–6). Nor was this low level of
mass involvement confined to 'new' unionists. Beynon (1983) reports how 'Mining
areas still vote Labour, but even here lodge officials talk of members who "are more
loyal to their families than their union", who "won't attend the lodge because they
can't be called out on a strike without a vote" '. The result of all this was that at a
time when more people than ever before were union members, these very members
were indifferent or hostile to the union's aims, while the sources of that hostility
could be quite contradictory. It might combine a desire for *other* union leaders to
exert more control and restraint over their members, while demanding that one's
own union leadership listened more to the demands and aspirations of the rank and
file. It could combine a sense that other unions were too powerful and undemocratic
with the feeling that in one's own workplace the union did a valuable and necessary
job. An opinion poll of unionists in 1973 found 73 per cent thought the unions had
too much power, 86 per cent supported the idea of outlawing secondary picketing,
while 91 per cent supported mandatory secret postal ballots before strikes.

In 1983 the British Social Attitudes Survey still found 59 per cent of those polled
thought unions had too much influence and this figure fell to only 48 per cent
among union members. But workers usually thought their *own* union did a good
job. Fifty-eight per cent of those with jobs in workplaces where unions were
recognised thought so (Harrison 1984, p. 57).

In this context developing their 'social justice' role was an uphill struggle for most
unions. It encountered the resistance not only of members' own aspirations but of
the structures of the unions themselves. The major avenue for unions' pursuit of
social justice was the link to the Labour Party and the prospect of corporatist trade-
offs between wages and social welfare policy. But as the strains on the economy
became greater so the bargaining between unions and Labour implied by such an
arrangement started to conflict with the 'Praetorian Guard' role of the unions in

ratifying whatever the Labour leadership decided. In addition, the form of the constitutional link between affiliated unions and the Party was particularly ill-suited to handle disagreements over policy

> since the unions' main business is industrial relations, their political positions may change as unintended by-products of industrial factors. Thus a slight change in leading personnel, determined by internal and often non-political criteria, can lead to a shift in several hundreds of thousands of votes at party conference (Crouch 1982, p. 180).

The Labour Party's structure was a poor vehicle for corporatism. There was a vacuum at its centre where policy formulation and discussion ought to take place. Policy was effectively laid down by the parliamentary leadership, protected from the more radical constituencies at Conference by the union Praetorian Guard. There was thus no direct need either for the parliamentary leadership to secure the allegiance and commitment of the mass membership to its ideas, or for the constituency membership (or once the Praetorian Guard role collapsed for the union delegates) to temper their policy objectives with political judgment and expediency. Instead the parliamentary leadership could talk radical to the Party conference while practising realism in office, while the membership became increasingly dissatisfied with their record in office and turned to accusations of 'betrayal' and still more radical policies in a vain attempt to bring the leadership to heel. As long as men and women of real ability, imagination and commitment found their way into the parliamentary leadership this vacuum might not be exposed. But there was no guarantee of this, as the unenlightened pragmatism of the Wilson years appeared to show. As Crick (1983, p. 348) commented after Labour's electoral disaster in 1983, 'If pure socialism is not going to win the next election, it was no socialism at all under Wilson that broke the heart of the party'.

In a corporatist order the internal democracy of a party becomes more important as the government seeks to do deals with interest groups outside Parliament, rather than simply respond to the legislature. The informality of Labour's ties to the unions then appeared as totalitarian. Corporatism ran against the grain of a society suffused with the importance of parliamentary sovereignty and individual autonomy. It did so all the more when it appeared to consist in the trading of political power with individuals rather than interest groups. Hence Jack Jones, leading architect of the Social Contract, was seen as 'the most powerful man in the country'. It appeared that Cabinet government had surrendered to union power. The reality behind these appearances was rather different. What was striking was the lack of influence of the unions over broader government social and economic policy. When it came to deciding on the need for public expenditure cuts, for example, the IMF had far more clout than the TUC.

CHAPTER 4

The Thatcherite Programme

The genesis of Thatcherism

Heath's experience led some Conservatives to draw two lessons. The first was that the logic of the Post-War Settlement in an era of increasingly severe economic and industrial problems was to draw the state further into the economy. Heath had started out with a policy of reinvigorating market forces and ended up with an incomes policy, talks with the TUC and CBI about the government's programme of legislation, and the nationalisation of prominent manufacturing companies to avert their bankruptcy. There was a feeling that a slide into corporatism would undermine the power of the private sector and become a slide into collectivism which the government could not contain. 'Names, targets, pay pauses, relativities commissions, special cases, sanctions against employers, flat rates, percentage rates, freezes, secret agreements at Downing Street, beer and sandwiches, NEDC negotiations — all had been tried and with lamentable success' (Holmes 1985, p. 15).

The second lesson drawn from Heath was a dread of union power, particularly in the public sector. This was not just borne out of the experience of the miners strikes of 1972 and 1974, but of the result of the 1974 election itself. The miners became the subject of particular concern, and by 1978 Nicholas Ridley had drawn up a report which outlined how the power of the NUM could be tackled through changes in the policing of strikes, changes in industrial relations law, increased reliance on alternative sources of energy (chiefly nuclear power) and the build up of greater coal stocks.

The discussion in Chapter 3 of the state of the British Post-War Settlement and its industrial relations in 1979 suggests that Thatcherism was almost an idea whose time had come: the old system was breaking apart, creating the circumstances for a new set of policies to be introduced by a radical government. However, the early development of Thatcherism suggests that this is far too neat an analysis. Many of the core elements of Thatcherism sit happily with many of the long-established features of the British industrial relations system which Chapter 2 identified. The separation of economics and politics, the belief that it was neither legitimate, effective or necessary for governments to intervene too far in industry, goes back to the industrial revolution itself. So, too, does the belief that the state ought only to take a minimalist role, that it does not embody directly a supra-individual national interest or consciousness. Thatcherism meshes well with the long-standing idea that government was at best a 'necessary evil'.

Its attitude to industrial relations law also had early antecedents, such as the pamphlet *A Giant's Strength* (Inns of Court Conservative and Unionist Society, 1958) which criticised union power and the evidence given by Geoffrey Howe to the Donovan Commission which favoured the legal curbs on unionism. The idea that Parliament should change the law to reduce union organisation rather than protect it from too great an interference from the courts was still consistent with the concept of the state 'holding the ring'. The difference was the idea of what would constitute a 'fair' ring. In the context of political concern about the extent of strikes and public hostility to what appeared to be excessive union power it was quite possible for Parliament to change its approach to the unions: it became possible to court public support for 'dealing with the union problem' rather than maintaining positive relations.

There were also other traditions of ideas to draw upon which were almost as old as the Post-War Settlement and critical of its implications for the balance between private and public power. The Austrian philosopher and economist Hayek (whose important work *The Road to Serfdom* was published as early as 1944) argued that any attempt by the state to promote full employment, especially if it went along with state protection for union activities, would eventually erode the market system altogether and lead to a collectivised centrally planned economy. Given that democracy was likely to encourage parties to promise voters that they would attempt to secure full employment, this established a dilemma. It was possible that democracy and the free market mechanism could be incompatible. It was thus conceivable that 'freedom', defined in terms of a market system, would have to be defended against 'democracy'. Hayek's view was that trade union action, by introducing an element of monopoly in the labour market and raising wages, drove up unemployment. State intervention to reduce unemployment simply caused inflation, as the response of the economy to government-stimulated demand would be increases in prices rather than output. Milton Friedman became the most prominent of a school of Chicago economists which focused on the argument that state intervention into the economy produced inflation. Friedman's theory of 'monetarism' argued that the crucial determinant of inflation was the increase in the supply of money. This in turn was caused by governments intervening in the economy in response to social or welfare demands and attempting to maintain full employment. This led to governments increasing public spending without restricting private consumption and so increasing the money supply. Important in this process were expectations and attitudes. Friedman was less convinced than Hayek about the ability of unions to intervene in the labour market and raise wages, but they could play a role through helping to generalise self-fulfilling inflationary expectations about rises in wages, prices and government spending.

In 1957 the Institute of Economic Affairs was founded. It was a research institute with a firm commitment to stressing the benefits of a strong role for markets. Nor was the idea that the Post-War Settlement was suffocating the market mechanism confined to private research institutes or academics. Shonfield's description of 'Operation Robot', a strategy for the economy devised within the Treasury in the 1950s, bears a remarkable similarity to what was to become the Thatcher government's economic and industrial policy:

> This was a plan which was intended to abolish in one move all the restrictions and arrangements governing the permitted use of sterling abroad, and at the same time to make both the volume and direction of economic activity at home subject to the unimpeded play of world market forces. The public authorities were to be allowed to exercise their influence on economic events by means of two instruments only. These were changes in the bank rate, which would raise or lower the level of interest payments on all forms of credit, and adjustments in the rate of exchange of the pound sterling, which through its influence on the money value of foreign exchange earnings and expenditure would keep the external balance of payments automatically in equilibrium. The aim essentially was to simulate in Britain something close to the conditions of the pre-1914 world. It was hoped to subject the economy once again to maximum international exposure, while the removal of all controls would ensure that there was no possibility of any response to the external pressure other than total internal discipline. Market forces would be relied upon to impose the necessary adjustments in domestic living standards or in the level of employment (Shonfield 1969, pp. 100–1).

The experience of the Heath government of 1970 brought these ideas to prominence with a small group of Conservatives, grouped primarily round Sir Keith Joseph, and invested them with an almost messianic power. The Centre for Policy Studies was established to promote the new ideas. Joseph, for example, wrote 'It was only in April 1974 that I was converted to Conservatism. I had thought I was a Conservative but I now see that I was not one at all' (Joseph 1975, quoted in Riddell 1983, p. 21). Margaret Thatcher was part of this group but there was little in her political behaviour as a minister in Heath's government that showed her to be more concerned about excessive public spending or economic intervention than her fellow 'Keynesian' ministers. Prior (1986) alleges that her inclusion in Heath's cabinet was a virtual accident: she was appointed because the team lacked a 'statutory woman'.

The theories of Hayek and Friedman gave these Conservatives an alternative route to the corporatist one and a political language to espouse it. Not only was government intervention in the economy troublesome and politically difficult (the troubles of economy became the misfortunes and electoral liability of the government), it was, according to the new theories, economically harmful, too. Thus not only could the government kick over the traces, as it were, leaving capital and labour to fend for themselves, this would be better for everyone in the long run, too.

These ideas were part of a wider reaction against the whole social order created in the Post-War Settlement. It was argued that the state's assumption of responsibility for ensuring minimum standards of subsistence, welfare and employment had led to a decline in individual initiative and responsibility, to the decay of family life and even to less respect for authority and the rise of permissiveness. At times these ideas reached alarming extremes. Sir Keith Joseph prevented himself from becoming Conservative leader by making a speech in October 1974 which suggested that irresponsible lower-class women were threatening 'our human stock' by 'producing problem children, the future unmarried mothers, delinquents, denizens of our borstals, sub-normal educational establishments, prisons, hostels for drifters' (Loney 1986, p. 44). However, Thatcher's election as leader certainly did not represent the triumph within the Conservative Party of these ideas. They were anathema to traditional Conservatism with its stress on consensus, reform rather than radical change, pragmatism and hostility to economic theory or political ideology. Thatcher received the support of many figures who were later prominent 'wets' because the party was keen to replace Heath and because no other suitable candidate with leadership qualities emerged. It was far from clear that Thatcher as leader would remain loyal to the ideas of Joseph and others. Her political language was not far out of step, since even the left of the Conservative Party clothed their interventionist policies in the rhetoric of markets and private enterprise. Indeed as the discussion in Chapter 3 showed, pessimism about the future of the Post-War Settlement, worries about hyperinflation and enthusiasm for monetarist ideas were also held by academics and journalists. Nor did the Conservatives have a monopoly of the commitment to 'monetarism'. Since 1976 a Labour Chancellor of the Exchequer had been following monetary targets and trying to control public expenditure.

It was not clear how far the monetarist ideas would be carried out in practice. For example, Joseph supported state aid to British Leyland by the Labour government. This was difficult to reconcile with monetarist theory, but pragmatically understandable because many marginal constituencies were found in the Midlands where British Leyland-related employment was concentrated. James Prior, shadow spokesman on Employment, told the Commons in a debate in early 1978 that the next Conservative government

> would not undertake sweeping changes in the law ... neither unions nor management wished for another great upheaval in industrial relations law ... successful industrial relations policy was even-handedness achieved through full consultation.
>
> Coercion would not work in the modern day and age ... The Conservative Party were not trying to take sides. They realised the desperate state of industrial relations. They recognised that this country had not achieved in the past few years the success and prosperity that other countries had managed to achieve. They did not just blame the unions for it. They recognised the part

government and management had had to play as well ... there ought to be even-handed changes to the law (*The Times*, 28 January 1978).

In the course of the 1979 election, Thatcher promised to honour any public sector pay awards made by the Pay Comparability Commission, the so-called 'Clegg awards'. This was hardly the stance of a government really intent on rolling back the frontiers of the state.

It was only after her election victory, and even then after a period of some months that it became clear that there was policy substance behind the rhetoric, combined with the determination to see it through despite formidable opposition both from the Party in the House and the Cabinet itself. Riddell (1983, p. 10) described Thatcher's victory in the Conservative Party as a *'coup d'état'* and Keegan (1984,p. 33) quoted one 'dissident' Conservative minister who described it as the 'hijacking of a political party'. This perhaps understates the way in which the Party's disaffection with Health was allied to its alarm at what it saw as the dangers of union power and corporatism. But it is an accurate description in that her election as leader did not signal any groundswell of changing political outlook in conservatism. Nor did all of her right-wing supporters have much knowledge of, or enthusiasm for, monetarism as such.

Conservative policy in practice

'The Conservative Party decided that the elimination of inflation should take priority over all other economic objectives, and the development of policy since 1979 is a relection of that decision' (Wass, quoted in Riddell 1983, p. 57). Reducing price inflation was the government's overriding goal to which other macroeconomic aims (such as low interest rates or higher PSBR) were sacrificed. This was because it was taken to be symptom and symbol of the frustration and blockage of enterprise capitalism and the market system within the Post-War Settlement. It represented both the rise of bargaining power with full employment and the economic costs of greater state activity to promote social welfare. Attacking inflation, it was argued, meant undermining the political and institutional constraints on markets (such as the trade unions or managements who were too 'soft' on them and state obligations to social welfare spending). It meant 'making markets work better' and allowing the market mechanism freedom to sort out the competitiveness of the British economy by forcing workers and managers, labour and capital, fundamentally to change the way they behave. The inertia of too much state control, the lack of commitment to enterprise, the assumption that extra wage demands or profits or public spending could be passed on through higher prices or taxes and mopped up by general inflation; all these would be 'squeezed out' of the system along with inflation. Thus the stress was laid on the medium and long-term benefits rather than short term results: the government, through reconstructing the social and political order as much as the economic, saw itself as laying the foundations for future growth. The

'Medium-Term Financial Strategy' announced in 1980 was significant in this sense not just because it firmly abandoned any commitment to traditional macroeconomic management of the economy but because it was monetarist in the way it expected the resultant economic changes to take place. Firms and trade unions would have to alter their private economic behaviour on the market (for example, in setting wage and price levels) in line with the monetary constraints outlined, or real reductions in output and employment would follow. Its 'strategic' nature was confirmed by the refusal of the government to revert to traditional macroeconomic management to stem the alarming falls in output and employment which followed. Its political character, too, provides clear confirmation of the abandonment of consensus. Not only the TUC but the CBI and indeed the 'wets' in the Conservative Party itself, were removed from any influence over economic policy.

Targets were announced in the March 1980 budget for the control of the money supply ('sterling M3'). These targets were the basis of the government's plans to cut public expenditure. The 1980 budget planned a 4 per cent reduction in real terms by 1983-4. In November an extra £1 billion of expenditure cuts was announced. The March 1981 budget cut PSBR drastically by one-third. This was accompanied by a shift to indirect taxation to finance government expenditure. VAT was virtually doubled to 15 per cent in June 1979, and £2 billion was to be raised by higher national insurance contributions. Reduced subsidies to nationalised industries also implied higher prices there. By 1986 these and other government controlled prices had risen at double the rate of inflation (Labour Research 1986). The lower rate of income tax was abolished, higher rates reduced substantially. Unemployment benefits were made taxable and earnings-related benefit was abolished. By 1986 the unemployed were receiving £2.8 billion less in benefits than they would have been entitled to in 1979. Various duties and charges, including NHS prescription charges, were raised.

The main effects of these central measures in the first two budgets of Sir Geoffrey Howe were to restrict the money supply and create a 'tight money' regime (as evidenced by the unprecedented rises in the exchange rate for sterling and interest rates). It was also a complete break with the traditions of Keynesian macroeconomic management of the post-war years in that the macroeconomic effects of both the 1980 and 1981 budgets were to depress demand and output at a time when both the British and the world economies were moving into recession. It was estimated that the measures in the March 1981 budget alone would have cut output in the economy by 2 per cent.

There could have been no clearer signal of the government's intention to create a new economic order than its refusal to put the behaviour of other economic factors such as interest rates, exchange rates, output employment or the balance of trade before its determination to control sterling M3, and, through it, inflation. Economic policy in 1979-82 was severely deflationary. The only comparable period, both in terms of the government's economic posture and the performance of the economy was the post-war crash of 1920-2. The slump in output and employment which was precipitated was worse than the recession of the 1930s, as

Chapter 5 will show. It alarmed even members of the Cabinet and prompted the chair of the CBI to promise a 'bare knuckle fight' with the government over its economic policy. By December 1981 support for the Conservative party was recorded at 28 per cent by a Gallup Poll.

Restricting the role of the state

The second dimension of the government's programme along with the control of money supply and government spending, was to 'roll back the frontiers of the state' and pull back the state from intervention in the economy. Along with controls on prices and wages, all control on the movement of foreign exchange was abolished, leaving companies and investors free to move capital and revenue abroad if they wished. A new Industry Act repealed the provision for planning agreements and cut public subsidies to industry. There would now really be 'no lame ducks', despite record levels of bankruptcies, closures and redundancies. Regional aid was reviewed, made more selective and heavily cut. By 1986 the budget of the Department of Trade and Industry (DTI) was virtually half its 1979 level. Not only did the government not have an 'industrial strategy', it saw this as a positive achievement, hence Paul Channon, Secretary of State at the DTI in 1986, argued that 'We want government to get off the backs of industry — that is the only policy that works' (*Guardian*, 9 October 1986).

Enterprise Zones were established in several depressed regions. The zones were to have a tax and rates holiday for businesses, and simplified planning regulations to encourage business to develop free from 'red tape'. Lord Young, as Secretary of State for Employment in 1985, announced that 'governments do not create a single job'. Privatisation, the transfer of state-owned assets to the private sector, was another feature of this policy, but one which became more important only in the government's second term, and for a variety of motives. As well as reducing the size of the public sector it had three other benefits. Asset sales could be geared to small investors, providing them with significant windfall gains as well as a lesson in the virtues of a property-owning democracy and an incentive (if they held on to their shares) for not voting Labour in future. They were particularly troublesome for a future government to reverse both because of the political difficulties and the economic problem of financing their return to public ownership. Thirdly, they provided a very useful one-off source of revenue for the government, while, because of an accounting quirk, they counted as negative public spending. Hence Lord Stockton, the former Conservative Prime Minister Harold Macmillan, argued that the policy amounted to 'selling off the family silver'. Privatisation was also supposed to reintroduce market forces and competition into the industries concerned, and shake up labour relations. Where the state was a direct employer and privatisation was not envisaged an effort was made to replicate market forces by the use of cash limits instead of incomes policies and the enforcement of 'competitive tendering'. Comparability with the private sector was to be replaced by ability to pay as determined by the cash limit. Subsidies to the nationalised industries were cut, and the aim of restoring them to profitability (regardless of the cuts required to do this) announced. The state's experience as an employer is reviewed in Chapter 6.

The state was to withdraw more from the labour market. Many industry training boards which operated by receiving a levy from relevant companies and oversaw training needs and standards were abolished. However, the government became more involved in training in other ways, particularly through the Youth Training Scheme, which became a virtual bridge between school leavers and proper employment (or in many cases unemployment). The Scheme was one of the few concessions by the government to the much bigger than expected falls in output and employment that its policies precipitated. By 1986 over one-third of a million young people were on YTS places, and the throughput of youngsters was probably about half-a-million per year.

The Labour government's incomes policy was of course abolished, and free collective bargaining returned, but within the new economic environment which ministers expected would erode unions' bargaining power and reduce the level of wage settlements. The government also moved to rescind the 'Fair Wages Resolution' originally passed by the House of Commons in 1891 which required the government and its contractors to pay the 'going rate' to employees. It also abolished several Wages Councils, and restricted the jurisdiction of others to adult workers. The Councils were statutory bodies covering employees in poorly organised, low-paying industries which were aimed at securing a minimum floor of pay rates for workers otherwise liable to find themselves in sweatshop conditions. Both these measures meant 'denouncing' relevant International Labour Organisation conventions which Britain had signed (Wedderburn 1986, pp. 348, 353).

Some aspects of the Labour government's employment protection legislation were abolished. The right of unions to claim recognition from employers and to claim the going rate from employers who were paying below the 'recognised' or 'general level' of terms and conditions in an industry was scrapped. The length of service needed before a claim for unfair dismissal could be brought was increased from six months to two years. Minimum compensation was abolished, burden of proof was removed from employers (so that tribunals could ask employees to demonstrate that a dismissal was unfair), and tribunals had now to take the firm's size and administrative resources into account in deciding if the employer had acted reasonably. Women's rights to return to work after maternity leave were made more complex. Small employers could claim it was not reasonably practicable to re-employ women, while larger employers could offer alternative (but not substantially less favourable) jobs. But there were also some positive changes for women. They won a new right to time off for ante-natal care, the Sex Discrimination Act was extended to small employers and the Equal Pay Act was amended to allow women to claim equal pay for work of equal value rather than simply similar work done by men. The two last improvements came directly as a result of pressure from the

EEC, and there was considerable criticism that the government's drafting of the 'equal value' measures severely weakened their potential impact. The government lobbied energetically to stop EEC directives on the rights of part-time workers, which would overwhelmingly have affected women.

After initial resistance the government accepted a House of Lords proposal that companies with more than 250 workers should include in their annual report what measures they had taken to involve and consult employees. Meanwhile it vigorously opposed draft EEC legislation on industrial democracy both in the form of reforms to Company Law (the Fifth Directive) and on rights of workers in larger companies to information and consultation (the Vredeling proposals). The government published a highly critical discussion document on the proposals and effectively vetoed them within the EEC Council of Ministers, despite widespread support for them elsewhere in the Community. In September 1983 John Selwyn Gummer, a Minister at the Department of Employment, stated that the measures 'failed the key test of whether [they] would help recovery from the recession'. Ministers came to see 'employee involvement' as a way of boosting productivity and tempering pay demands. In his Stockton lecture in April 1986 Lord Young argued that 'the idea of bosses and workers doesn't really fit the facts' and that employees true interest lay in high profits plus profit-sharing (Young 1986).

Strengthening market forces

The third major strand of the government's economic and industrial policy was to 'make markets work better' and thereby to promote what it saw as an 'enterprise culture' once more in the British economy. Since one of the government's contentions was that the monopoly power of trade unions acted to block and frustrate the free and efficient working of the market mechanism, it is unsurprising that most of its measures to 'make markets work better' focused on the curbing of union power through restricting the circumstances under which unions had immunity from prosecution in undertaking industrial action, limiting the extent of the closed shop and determining how unions should organise themselves internally. With all these measures it is important to distinguish between the detail of the law, how it has in fact been implemented and used and its other more general effects.

The 1980 Employment Act was drafted and enacted while James Prior, a prominent 'wet' who had earlier promised 'no sweeping changes' in employment law, was Secretary of State. As well as abolishing the trade union recognition procedures and restricting unfair dismissal and maternity leave rights as outlined above, it made secondary picketing (i.e. picketing other than at one's own place of work) unlawful and opened secondary industrial action (i.e. sympathetic action) to claims for damages by removing immunities. Secondary action could only be lawful if it was taken by employees of a customer or supplier of an employer in dispute who had a current commercial contract with that employer, and the action was aimed at preventing or disrupting supplies to or from the employer and likely to succeed. An associated code of practice on picketing (which courts could take into account) laid down a maximum of six pickets as being reasonable. The closed shop was restricted by giving Industrial Tribunals power to decide if exclusion from a trade union was 'reasonable'. Unions would be liable to pay compensation up to £16,000. The 'conscience' clause permitting non-membership on grounds of religious belief was widened to include 'deeply held personal belief'. New closed shops would require the approval of 80 per cent of the workers concerned (not just those voting) in a ballot, and non-members at the time of the agreement would not be compelled to join. The Act also made state funds available to unions to finance the cost of secret postal ballots.

The 1982 Act, drafted under the new Secretary of State, Norman Tebbit, went further. It increased the amounts of compensation payable for dismissal on account of a closed shop to up to £250,000 for the largest unions and made liability to claims retrospective to 1974. Current closed shops now needed periodic ballots to validate them. It narrowed the definition of a trade dispute to one between workers and their employers 'wholly or mainly' about terms and conditions of employment, and opened up union funds to suits for damages where action was not covered by immunities. It outlawed industrial action against non-union companies, and clauses in contracts requiring the use of union labour. Employers could also selectively dismiss strikers without notice, without this being unfair. The Act opened up unions to injunctions restraining them from 'unlawful' industrial action. This made unions liable to large fines for being in contempt of court, as well as sequestration of their assets. By 1986 unions had been fined over £1 million for various contempts.

The 1984 Act was the responsibility of Tom King: it was aimed at the internal workings of trade unions. It required secret ballots for the election of union executives at least every five years, secret ballots before industrial action if immunities were to be preserved and on political funds maintained by trade unions which finance campaigning and lobbying, and the contributions to the Labour Party of its affiliated unions. After talks with the TUC, Mr King drew back from requiring members to 'contract in' rather than 'contract out' of paying into political funds.

Alongside these Acts were a number of other measures related to trade unions. The law on social security was amended deeming all unions to pay strike pay to strikers, regardless of whether they in fact did so. Indeed the provision applies to strikers who are not members of any union, or are members of unions who are unable to pay strike pay because their funds have been sequestrated. By 1986 this meant that £17 per week was deducted from the benefits payable to the dependents of strikers. (Strikers themselves have never been eligible.)

In some way these measures went further than might have been expected in 1979. The extent of the removal of trade union immunities from prosecution over industrial action was dramatic. Many employers' organisations voiced disquiet over the extent of some of the proposals, particularly those concerning the closed shop and secret ballots before strikes. But neither were the proposals as far as the government could go. It drew back from any attempt to outlaw strikes in 'essential' public services although it did ban union membership at GCHQ, an intelligence gathering centre, as a security risk. Nor did it attempt to make agreements between unions and employers legally binding, as the 1971 Industrial Relations Act had attempted. It did not replace 'contracting out' of contributions to union political funds with 'contracting in' which would almost certainly have brought a dramatic fall in the number of unionists paying into these funds. In February 1987 Kenneth Clarke, a minister at the Department of Employment, announced a Green Paper on a set of further measures entitled *Trade Unions and their Members*. The proposals in effect outlawed the closed shop by giving full legal protection to non-membership for any reason, and making industrial action to enforce one unlawful. The ballot-approval mechanisms of the 1982 Act would simply be repealed: making 'approval' impossible and any dismissal automatically unfair. On industrial action, it proposed that individual union members (rather than employers) could require unions to hold ballots and prevent any action in advance of the ballot. Once a strike was called no union member should be obliged to obey it: 'no member should be penalised by his trade union for exercising his right to cross a picket line and go to work'.

Ballots for union executives were no longer to be permitted in the workplace, but were to be fully postal. Union trustees would be appointed who would have a duty in law to prevent funds being used in contravention of court orders. Union members would have the right to inspect accounts and would have the help of a new 'Commissioner for Union Affairs' who could help individual union members take court action against their unions and pay for it. The proposals were partly a reaction to the tactics used by the NUM, SOGAT and NGA in the coal dispute and in the News International dispute, and partly potential vote-catchers in a general election. However, it was perhaps significant that they were not announced by the Secretary of State for Employment, Lord Young, and it was known that some cabinet members doubted their value. The deputy general secretary of the National and Local Government Officers Union (NALGO) called the proposals a 'scab's charter' but in general the response of the TUC was muted. They certainly appeared to be based on the realisation that the willingness of dissident union members to challenge their leaderships offered a way out of the problem of employers' reluctance to use injunctions for fear of upsetting good relations with a union. Legal restraints on their activities could now be presented as an internal squabble to be adjudicated by the courts.

Under the rhetoric of 'making markets work better' the government had a firm view that unions had little or no positive contribution to make to how markets operated, and therefore ought to be weakened. The tenor of its legislation was 'anti-union' both in its purpose and method: little account was taken of the unions own views. In terms of the governments' overall strategy this had to be so. Since it believed that unions retarded efficiency and profitability in industry, and it intended industry, shaken by market forces, to engineer its own recovery, it followed that the power of the unions had to be undermined. Making markets work better effectively meant removing union influence from the labour market.

There were a number of other measures aimed at 'making markets work better'.

Tax cuts were introduced in the 1980 budget which brought the highest rate down from 83 per cent to 60 per cent. Thresholds were also increased which reduced the number of people paying tax, and the number paying the highest rate was virtually halved. Unemployment benefit was reduced by phasing out earnings-related benefit, and was made taxable. These measures were supposed to encourage 'enterprise' by rewarding high earners more, while increasing the incentive to find jobs, no matter how poorly paid, by reducing the income of those without jobs. However, as Chapter 5 examines, the tax burden actually increased from 1979 as the government did not raise allowances in line with inflation. It had to raise substantially more taxes in order to pay for the increased public spending on benefits for those who became unemployed as a result of its policies.

The rise in unemployment, of course, was itself a measure to make markets work better. Nicholas Ridley, one of the less tactful of the cabinet, announced in March 1981 that 'the high level of unemployment is evidence of the progress we are making'. If the government refused to take responsibility for the level of employment, it was argued, then employers and employees would have to face up to the impact of their bargains over wages and productivity for the demand for their goods and services and the demand for labour. If the government refused to stimulate demand (by greater public borrowing or higher public capital spending) then employers ought to respond by becoming more competitive and reducing prices, while labour ought to respond by accepting lower wages to maintain the demand for labour. High unemployment, in this scenario, represented delays in people adjusting their market behaviour to the new conditions. This was a major way in which inflation would be 'squeezed out' of the system through the market mechanism working more efficiently again.

There were relatively few moves directly to increase competition. Critics of the way public monopolies like British Telecom, British Gas and British Airways were privatised pointed out that there were very few consumer safeguards or measures to introduce competitive pressures. These could, of course, adversely have affected the valuation of the new corporations, and brought the government less revenue from privatisation. The laws on conveyancing and opticians were changed to increase competition and banks and building societies were allowed to extend and overlap their range of services. Bus transport was deregulated, evoking controversy over whether lower prices and more services on popular routes outweighed the loss of unprofitable services to rural communities or in off-peak hours. In this sense the government's commitment was not to competition as such, but to the private sector, whether 'competitive' or not.

The Enterprise Allowance Scheme was introduced to encourage unemployed people to become self-employed. There was also much emphasis on the importance of flexibility in the labour market. The term 'flexibility' was used ambiguously to cover everything from non-standard hours of work, part-time work, temporary work, to contracting out, self-employment and even decentralisation of wage bargaining. In its 1984 White Paper on Employment the government argued that 'New working arrangements must be mainly a matter for employers and employees.

Government cannot impose these without destroying the flexibility that makes them attractive' (DE 1984, p. 18). However, the evidence reviewed in Chapter 6 casts doubt on the real extent of moves towards 'flexibility'.

Finally, the government hoped to reform indirectly the workings of wage determination in the labour market. As we have seen, it eschewed incomes policies, believing that a sufficiently strict monetary regime would force both capital and labour to adjust expectations and alter their bargaining behaviour. But from the outset the level of pay settlements did not fall as much as ministers had expected, and they felt the need to help adjust expectations by arguing forcefully that wage increases caused higher unemployment. Between 1979 and 1981 ministers repeatedly made public statements that they would not print money to finance wage increases. But the White Paper on Employment in 1984 admitted 'There is little evidence despite expressions of concern that employers and unions negotiating for those in work have yet appreciated the effect of wage increases on the chances the unemployed have of finding jobs' (DE 1984, p. 19).

The level of pay settlements continued to be a problem and became progressively more visible as price inflation fell to lower levels. From 1982 onwards real wage inflation reached record levels and stayed there as the economy began to recover from the monetarist shock treatment of 1979–81. This led ministers to argue on two fronts. They argued that the institutions of the labour market prevented greater flexibility and greater differentials between wages in different parts of the country or between more or less profitable industries or companies. Ministers attacked the idea of national and even company-wide pay bargaining against great hostility from the TUC and no open support from employers. In a remarkable speech in February 1987, Kenneth Clarke argued that annual pay rounds and ideas about the going rate ought to be scrapped. National and company-wide pay bargaining was 'remote and destroys jobs'. Job evaluation was a 'bogus science' in so far as it purported to be an 'exact science which can determine the worth of a job'. Comparability was a 'dangerous delusion' because it failed to take sufficient account of different employers' circumstances. The only form of pay determination of which Mr Clarke approved was local bargaining by single employers geared to the individual's performance and merit: 'It is only right to pay more to those who bring to their job enthusiasm, enterprise and initiative than those who are prepared to idle along' (Clarke 1987, p. 19).

In addition, Mr Clarke advocated profit-related pay. This was the second component of government thinking. 'The divide between earners and owners' was 'divisive and self defeating'. A 'stake in an enterprise' provided by relating earnings to profits would make earnings more flexible and break the rigidity of the labour market. The government made tax concessions for various forms of employee share ownership in the Finance Acts of 1980 and 1984. This followed similar but less extensive measures by the Labour government in 1978. If employees received company shares and held them for a certain period, they were exempt from capital gains tax. By 1987 the Inland Revenue had approved nearly 1,300 schemes covering all the employees in a firm (as opposed to executive share option schemes). In July

1986 the government went further by proposing in a Green Paper that

> profit related pay (PRP) be eligible for tax relief. PRP would vary according to
> the profitability of the workers' employer. Nigel Lawson described it in his
> 1987 budget speech as a 'tool' to help business to overcome one of Britain's
> biggest national handicaps: the nature and behaviour of our labour market.
> (*Financial Times*, 18 March 1987)

The hope was that PRP would make employees identify more with their employers'
aim of maximising profits, and also avoid redundancies when business was slack by
automatically reducing pay. As long as 5 per cent of pay was in PRP, half of it
would be free of income tax.

These proposals met criticism from employers organisations, who were
unconvinced about the benefits to motivation. While employees might wish to share
increased profits, managers were unconvinced that they would be prepared to suffer
losses with equal enthusiasm. They were also worried about the possible demands
for disclosure of information which profit-related pay could generate.

The government's frustration at the level of pay settlements was evident from its
castigation of both employers' and workers' behaviour in the labour market. But
true to its market-orientated outlook it refused to consider any form of pay policy.
In a speech to the Institute of Directors in December 1986, Lord Young affirmed
that the general exhortation to people to curb wages 'for their own good and the
good of the country' did not work and that statutory incomes policies were 'futile'.
The government was convinced that further decentralisation of bargaining and the
injection of a closer dependence on immediate market forces was the solution. To
bring this about it was advocating measures which found little response from
employers in any sector. Chapter 6 examines the behaviour of the labour market
and casts doubt on the internal logic and empirical evidence for the government's
thinking on pay.

A new social order?

The remainder of this book considers the effects of the government's policies on the
economy and industrial relations, comparing the actual results with what the
policies were supposed to produce and examining why there have often been
substantial differences between intention and result. But first there remains the
question of how coherent the government's programme as described here was. Did
it really represent a monetarist attempt to restructure the social and economic order
and thereby escape the restrictionism and poor performance of the later stages of the
Post-War Settlement?

The government has proclaimed that its policies have been coherent and based on
clear economic theories about its policies' effects. However, as Tomlinson (1986, p.
7) puts it, 'we should not accept this rhetoric at face value — it is itself part of the
policy and requires assessment'. In fact the government's behaviour has been less

than consistent. While arguing that public spending restrictions and PSBR cuts are vital to control inflation and promote economic recovery, it was found possible to give significant reflationary boosts to the economy prior to the election years of 1983 and 1987. Milton Friedman, leading academic light of monetarism, has been keen to distance himself from some of the government's actions. Nor is it always clear that the government itself has had an articulate picture of its own strategy. Christopher Huhne (1985) has pointed out the remarkable ignorance Mrs Thatcher displayed of the central monetarist concept of a 'natural' rate of unemployment in a television interview with Peter Jay. This is not simply a matter of terminology. The idea of a natural rate of unemployment caused by the failure of firms and workers to adjust behaviour so as to minimise unemployment and inflation was at the heart of the government's economic policies, yet the Prime Minister simply did not know what Mr Jay was talking about. Such a state of affairs lends some weight to those who would argue that the elaborate theories and rhetoric of monetarism have really been a rationalisation of more basic and cruder aims such as deliberate deflation to teach the labour movement a lesson.

Nor does the Prime Minister's espousal of 'Victorian values' fit well with the history of the development of British industrial relations outlined in Chapter 2. As Riddell (1983, p. 8), among others, has commented, the Victorian Age was one where the Conservative Prime Minister courted the growing union movement and gave it unprecedented legal protection from prosecution under common law. It was also an age where general economic prosperity and expanding markets abroad gave unions a much better bargaining position and encouraged employers to tolerate their existence rather than try to avoid them. But the intellectual coherence of the rhetoric of the government's strategy is not paramount. As Crick (1983, p. 349) comments:

> Mrs Thatcher developed a *popular ideology*, going back to where Edward Heath began, but with much greater vulgarity, tenacity and empathy — a suburban version of Hayek's political economy as mediated by Sir Keith Joseph. She had no doubt that most people are more worried about inflation than about unemployment. It is no use arguing that this new ideology is as full of holes as a sieve. Austerity, frugality, hard work, self-interest, value for money, getting government out, freeing capital, grandmother's virtues and licensed xenophobia make a psychologically compatible popular ideology for those in jobs.

Insofar as this ideology was important, the triumph of Thatcherism after 1979 was facilitated by its consistency with many of the attitudes and institutions which originated early in Britain's industrialisation and which fitted ill with the increasingly corporatist measures needed to maintain the Post-War Settlement. Free collective bargaining and the reigning back of state intervention could appeal both to a working class frustrated by incomes policies and employers fed up with state regulation. The message that markets worked best and that state intervention had actually lowered economic progress rather than maintained full employment could strike a potent chord in a country which in the era of *laissez-faire* had been a dominant world power and workshop of the world. De-regulating economic activity (especially the abolition of exchange controls) might cause grave difficulties for the domestic sector of industry, but the City and profits from overseas would not suffer. On the contrary the City would welcome a policy which rejected the view that the requirements of Britain's domestic industrial base should determine economic policy. Thus far from representing an entirely new approach to the British economy and industrial relations, the Thatcherite programme borrowed monetarist ideas to inform an approach which was similar to the early nineteenth Century: a minimalist role for the state, reduction of the National Debt, free trade, tight money and *laissez faire*. It represented the attempt to revert to precisely the economic order which the Post-War Settlement has to some extent reformed. What was different to the nineteenth century was its concern to undermine unionism, and its sensitivity to the popularity of some of the Post-War Settlement's advances in health and education. These forced the government to adopt a more pragmatic approach to public spending than it wanted to.

CHAPTER 5

Economic Change and Economic Performance, 1979–1986

Introduction: examining economic change

Economic change is important to examine carefully for four reasons. First the performance of the economy as a whole, and manufacturing in particular, is central to the debate about whether or not the Post-War Settlement and its industrial relations was indeed responsible for Britain's poor economic record and how far Thatcherism has transformed it. Because of this it is at the centre of political controversy and debate. All the main political parties and interest groups have seized upon statistics which appear to support their version of events so that it is necessary to try to produce a clear and comprehensive account. Second we need a detailed picture of the changed economic environment in which industrial relations operated. This is particularly important because, as we saw in Chapter 4, it was through changing this environment (as well as by more direct methods like new legislation) that Thatcherism aimed to transform industrial relations and thereby improve the supply side of the economy. Examining the effects of these policies tells us not only whether they worked but also how they worked: what their mechanics were. Third economic data such as wages or labour productivity figures give valuable clues about the outcome of that process; about the state of industrial relations directly. Finally economic change in the sense of the restructuring of the economy was an important element in the arguments we outlined in Chapter 1 that long run economic trends were undermining the unions' power base presenting the labour movement with problems even without the Thatcherite challenge. The rest of this chapter examines the economic record in detail drawing attention to the significance of the material for each of these arguments along the way. But first we consider some of the caution that must be exercised in using economic evidence of this sort.

Comparisons of economic performance, in order to contrast Labour and

Conservative economic and industrial policies for example, are complicated by the cyclical nature of economic activity — one government may preside over a boom, another over a recession — and by longer-term trends, such as the switch from manufacturing to services or the discovery of North Sea oil. However, the shape of cyclical activity or speed of these trends is itself subject to the influence of the government. Thus manufacturing employment and output were going into a cyclical decline after 1979, but the severity of the decline was affected by the Conservative government's monetary and fiscal policies. There is also the question of the period over which a government is assumed to bear responsibility for its policies, so that the first year, for example, of a term of office might be seen as subject to the influence of the previous government. Indeed, the Thatcher government argued that most negative aspects of Britain's economic performance were attributable to past government interference and an accumulation of 'anti-enterprise' institutions, social relations and attitudes which it would take many years to erase. A fourth factor is the international economic environment – whether other developed countries are in a period of boom or recession and trends in the terms of trade or relative cost of raw materials.

The effects of these factors make it possible by the selection of appropriate base years or relevant indicators to produce figures which give wildly different accounts of economic progress. A second dimension is added to this by the availability of statistics of varying definitions from different sources. For example, estimates of employment are obtainable from the Census of Employment, Census of Population and Labour Force Surveys. Each of these gathers the information in different ways and produces slightly different answers and trends. This problem has been aggravated by changes in the definition of statistics which make comparisons over time difficult. Some of these changes are necessary in order accurately to reflect economic change itself. But others are more a question of political convenience. The definition of unemployment used to produce the monthly totals by the Department of Employment changed no fewer than 17 times between 1979 and 1986. The approximate effect of this (it is difficult to measure precisely) was to reduce the total UK unemployment count by 635,600 persons by 1986: about one fifth of the total. (Labour Research Department 1987, p. 24).

A final problem for analysis is that of identifying mechanisms of cause and effect in economic change. Governments naturally claim credit for the good aspects of economic performance while attributing problems and failures to their predecessors or to international conditions beyond their control. Thus, while the government disclaimed responsibility for rising unemployment between 1979 and 1983, because 'governments do not create a single job', it nevertheless claimed credit for the creation of 'one million new jobs' between 1983 and 1986 — a claim we will investigate later.

However, these problems are not insurmountable. This is particularly so in recent British economic history because of a fortuitous coincidence between changes in government and the business cycle. The last two troughs of manufacturing output were in 1975 and 1982 and the last peak in 1979. We can therefore compare the periods 1975–9 and 1982–6 and contrast the 'performance' of Labour and Conservative governments and measure the changes Thatcherism has wrought upon the Post-War Settlement. The years 1973 and 1979 are taken by the OECD as marking roughly equivalent phases of economic activity in OECD countries so we can use the periods 1973–9 and 1979 onwards to compare the UK's performance with that of the rest of the OECD before and after the 1979 election. This allows us to take account of changing world conditions. This chapter looks first at the scale of the economic recession from 1979 to 1982 and then examines aspects of the recovery from 1982 onwards. It considers whether the process of economic 'restructuring' was speeded up or slowed down by the government's policies, and examines some of the factors behind 'deindustrialisation': the rapid decline of the manufacturing sector. Finally, it looks at the international and historical comparisons of Britain's economic performance in this period and asks just how 'monetarist' Thatcherism in practice proved to be. For the sake of consistency, all figures on employment and unemployment used in the chapter refer to Great Britain rather than the United Kingdom except where comparative OECD statistics are being cited.

The crash of 1979–1982

The government's intention, as we saw in Chapter 4, was to 'squeeze' inflation out of the system by reducing the money supply, and reducing the share of public expenditure. In order to reduce the rise in interest rates which it was expected this would cause, public borrowing was to be sharply reduced. This meant that despite the fact that the Thatcher government came to power at a time when the rest of the OECD countries were moving into recession, it produced new monetary, PSBR and public spending targets, which were sharply deflationary. Table 5.1 compares the government's money supply, spending and borrowing targets with their eventual

Table 5.1 Government targets and outturns on money supply, public borrowing and expenditure 1980–4 (per cent)

	1980–1	*1981–2*	*1982–3*	*1983–4*
Growth of £M3				
Target	7–11	6–10	5–9	4–8
Outturn	19	13	11	10
PSBR as % of GDP				
Target	$3\frac{3}{4}$	3	$2\frac{1}{4}$	$1\frac{1}{2}$
Outturn	6	4	3	3
Public expenditure as % of GDP				
Target	42	41	40	under 40
Outturn	46	$46\frac{1}{4}$	$46\frac{3}{4}$	$45\frac{3}{4}$

Source: Treasury Economic Progress Reports

outturn. It can be seen that in practice the government 'overshot' virtually all its targets, and in particular the decisive (in its own eyes) money supply target, defined as 'sterling M3'. However, this did not mean that the government was preaching monetarism while practising profligacy, because a major cause of the overshoots was the much larger than expected slump which its tight money policies produced. In turn the scale of the slump made the relative tightness of these policies even greater. Faced with such a slump in economic activity all previous post-war governments would have acted to loosen the controls, increase the money supply, reflate public spending and borrowing in an attempt to reduce interest rates and stimulate domestic demand. Riddell (1983, pp. 90–1) shows that in this period the fiscal regime was some four times tighter than elsewhere in the OECD. Evidence of the real tightness of money policy, as compared to the vast overshoot on the sterling M3 target, was provided by the 30 per cent rise in the sterling exchange rate and the jump in interest rates during 1979 from 12 to 17 per cent. This increased both domestic costs for producers and raised the price of their goods abroad, while simultaneously demand at home was cut back. Leys (1985) notes that exchange rate rises alone cost ICI half-a-billion pounds in 1981. As a result international UK manufacturing competitiveness declined by almost half in 18 months, an unprecedented slump. Table 5.2 describes the slump which followed, and follows the main indicators of economic activity through to 1986. There was a fall in manufacturing output of 17 per cent between 1979 and 1981, while total gross domestic product (GDP: that is the total wealth of goods and services produced) fell by 4.5 per cent over the same period. Redundancies and closures reached record levels as producers found it impossible to trade profitably. In manufacturing, average profit levels fell by half, capital investment fell by over one-third and from 1981 onwards net capital investment became negative as plant closures reduced the stock of equipment in use dramatically. Meanwhile investment flowed abroad where companies now found trading conditions relatively more attractive. The total of UK investment overseas rose from £38 bn at December 1978 to £177 bn by December 1985.

Real wages in manufacturing fell by about 3 per cent in 1980 and 1981 despite increasing in money terms by over 30 per cent. Living standards fell with falling wages and reduced employment. The reduction of price inflation was the overriding object of the government's policies but at first it rose sharply from an annual rate of 10 per cent in May 1979 to a peak of 22 per cent in May 1980. This was a combination of a rising underlying trend left by the Labour government, and boost added by the switch to indirect taxation in the first Conservative budget and the cost of the Clegg Commission's comparability-based public sector pay awards. It then fell away steeply, reaching 4 per cent in April 1983.

As a result of these changes employment in manufacturing fell by 21 per cent, shedding 1.5 million jobs between December 1979 and December 1982. Total employment fell by 2 million (9 per cent) in the same period. As a result unemployment grew from 1.2 million in June 1979 to 2.9 million in June 1983. Employment fell for both men and women, checking a rise in women's employment

Table 5.2 Main economic indicators 1979–80

	1979	1980	1981	1982	1983	1984	1985	1986
GDP (Index) 1980 = 100	102.3	100	98.8	100.3	103.7	106.6	110.2	113.1
Manufacturing output (Index) 1980 = 100	109.5	100	94.0	94.2	96.9	100.7	103.8	104.1
Manufacturing rates of return (per cent)	4.5	3.6	2.7	3.9	4.9	6.1	7.2	NA
Manufacturing investment (£bn 1980 prices)	7.5	6.5	4.9	4.7	4.8	5.8	5.9	5.8
Export of capital (£bn 1980 prices)	8.1	8.1	9.4	9.3	9.5	11.9	18.5	24.1
Retail price index (annual percentage change)	13.3	18.1	11.9	8.7	4.6	5.0	6.1	3.4
Sterling effective exchange rate (1980=100)	90.8	100	100.5	95.6	88.1	83.9	83.3	77.2
Interest rates (per cent)	13.7	16.8	14.0	12.4	10.1	10.0	12.2	11.0
Redundancies (thousands)	187	494	532	400	327	245	235	225
Manufacturing employment (millions)	7.1	6.8	6.1	5.8	5.4	5.3	5.3	5.1
Total employment (millions)	22.6	22.5	21.4	20.9	20.6	20.7	21.0	21.1
Unemployment (millions)*	1.2	1.4	2.3	2.7	2.9	2.9	3.0	3.1
Unemployment rate (per cent)*	4.2	4.8	8.2	9.5	10.6	10.8	11.2	11.5

Definitions: All figures are annual averages, except those for employment and unemployment which are for June, seasonally adjusted, excluding school leavers.

GDP: Average estimate, 1980 prices at factor cost, seasonally adjusted.

Manufacturing Rates of Return: Net return of capital employed on UK operations, before interest and tax at current replacement cost.

Unemployment rate: Unemployed as percentage of total working population (including self-employed)

* Figures for unemployment from 1983 are on the new basis, which revises figures downward: see text.

Sources: Economic Trends; Department of Employment Gazette; Treasury Economic Progress Report; Pink Book 1986; British Business 27 February 1987, 10 October 1986; Department of Trade and Industry.

that had continued despite the gradual rise in unemployment through the 1960s and 1970s. The slump also dragged down employment in the services sector, checking another long-run trend. There was not a region of the country which did not have lower employment and higher unemployment in 1982 than 1979. The size of the rise in unemployment, especially for teenagers who faced unemployment rates of over 20 per cent, prompted the government to introduce special employment measures, principally the Youth Training Scheme. The rise in unemployment would have been even steeper, but the scale of the recession checked the growth in the 'working population' (the total of those in the economy either working or looking for work): high unemployment meant that people who might previously have sought work did not do so. The collapse in output and employment was the worst ever (Singh 1981, p. 12), outstripping that of 1920–2, and far worse than that of the 1930s. Between 1929 and 1931 0.8 million jobs were lost, but by 1936 over 2.5 million new jobs had been created and manufacturing output was one-third higher than its 1929 level (Stewart 1985).

Aside from causing the government to exceed its own targets on money supply, spending and borrowing, the slump had various other effects. In contrast to the government's pledge to reduce the burden of taxation and government spending, both rose. Between 1979–80 and 1982–3 the share of taxation in GDP went from 39 per cent to 45 per cent, while the share of public expenditure grew from $43\frac{1}{2}$ per cent to 47 per cent. Direct taxes on earned income increased for virtually all except those on the greatly reduced top rate of taxation. The composition of public spending changed. More was spent on unemployment benefits and special employment schemes for the expanding numbers of unemployed. Spending on defence and law and order also rose but spending on housing, industry, education and industry fell. In effect oil revenues, which by 1981–2 were running at £6.5 billion a year, plus an increased tax take, paid for the large rises in the cost of unemployment benefit, social security and housing benefits. Between 1979 and 1985 the government received £52 billion in oil revenues and spent £33 billion on unemployment benefits. Oil exports performed another valuable function by keeping the balance of payments in surplus as the balance of manufactured trade decreased. Only in 1984 did the volume of manufactured exports regain their 1980 levels, by which time the volume of manufactured imports had risen by one-third.

Whatever government was in power, employment and output would have fallen in the wake of the world recession. Given the relative weakness of Britain's manufacturing performance, particularly in the 1970s, it is also possible that the slump would have been greater in Britain than elsewhere. But the scale of the world recession itself was in part attributable to the British slump. In the international economy severe deflation in one country spread round the system through a reduction in international trade. In addition, Britain's bonus of North Sea oil, which by 1985 was contributing 6.2 per cent of GDP, should have allowed Britain to play a positive role in the world economy, since alone amongst the major OECD countries it did not face balance of payments difficulties caused by the second large oil price rise.

The slump in Britain came earlier and was much deeper than in the OECD countries as a whole, or in the EEC. GDP in the OECD as a whole grew 3 per cent while it was falling in Britain, and slipped back 0.5 per cent in 1982. Between 1980 and 1982 manufacturing output slipped less than 2 per cent in the OECD and 3.5 per cent in the EEC compared to Britain's 17 per cent collapse. While Britain's employment was falling, that of the OECD actually rose 0.4 per cent. Over the same period unemployment rose 124 per cent in Britain, 59 per cent in the rest of the EEC and by the same amount in the OECD as a whole. From a rate close to the OECD average throughout the 1970s, Britain's unemployment rate was nearly half as much again by 1981, and continued to increase thereafter. Only on inflation was Britain's record a little better. From an average of 18 per cent in 1980 it reached 4.6 per cent in 1983, compared with a fall in the OECD from 12.9 per cent to 5.2 per cent. Other countries' inflation rates continued to improve after this so that by 1986 British inflation was close to the OECD average again. Meanwhile West Germany and Japan had reduced inflation to less than 1 per cent.

The government argued, however, that the real cause of the scale of the slump was weaknesses in the economy, particularly overmanning in manufacturing, which had simply been obscured by government intervention in the 1970s. Higher employment totals in earlier years had not been 'real' jobs but the artificial (and ineffective and uncompetitive) result of state subsidy and protection. Its policies had created the basis for an economic recovery which would be faster and longer lasting because of the new competitive and enterprising environment in which they would take place. At the same time it dismissed the considerable alarm voiced by both the opposition and industry itself about the collosal falls in output, employment and exports in manufacturing industry. It argued that these were part of a long-term trend covering all industrialised countries, and also part of the unavoidable effects of North Sea oil on the exchange rate. As oil exports declined market forces would push down the exchange rate so that the level of manufactured exports would recover again to take their place. It argued that recovery would be stronger when it came because its tough policies had made the 'supply side' of the economy more efficient and that no special measures for industry were necessary. Replying to a very critical report from the House of Lords Select Committee on Overseas Trade, which examined the recent fortunes and future prospects of manufacturing, Lord Lucas, Under Secretary for Trade and Industry, commented in 1985 that 'the problems that continue to beset British industry do not amount to a crisis and do not require an action plan' (*Financial Times*, 3 December 1985).

The government was undoubtedly surprised at the level of unemployment its policies precipitated. Monetarism in its original form as propounded by Geoffrey Howe, which underlay the first two decisive budgets, simply stated that control of the money supply was a necessary and sufficient means to control price inflation and to adjust the behaviour of all the other markets in the economy as employers and workers were forced to adjust their expectations. It was accepted that other rates — whether interest rates, the exchange rate or indeed wages — should be left to find their own level as determined by market forces. This policy was relaxed as early as 1981 as it became clear through the alarming rises in interest rates and rapid appreciation of sterling that, despite a large overshoot in sterling M3, monetary policy was in fact very tight indeed. From this point on the Treasury was to take other factors such as the exchange rate into account in setting its targets. This was more than a technical adjustment to policy. It represented an admission in practice that the link between money supply, market forces and people's behaviour in the markets was more complex and obscure than monetarist theory asserted, or that the time lags or levels of unemployment needed made the policy politically impossible. In other words the basis of the way the policy worked could be seen not as the moulding of new expectations and market behaviour by the government imposition of monetary targets but the adjustment of expectations and market behaviour by adjusting the state of the markets themselves. Crudely the government encouraged a dramatic rise in the level of unemployment and a sharp worsening in the trading conditions facing companies. It was hoped that this would force employers to be tougher with their workforces and more enterprising in the marketing, while it would force workers to lower their wage expectations, cooperate more effectively with management and work harder in order to avoid unemployment. The length of the dole queue and sharper product market competition were the means by which the government would produce 'new realism', not the publication of monetary targets which employees and unionists would use to guide their bargaining in the market.

The response of the economy was more understandable in 'Keynesian' than in 'monetarist' terms. The government had in effect engineered a dramatic deflation by its restriction of public borrowing and public capital spending combined with increases in taxation. This dampened economic activity sufficiently to reduce inflationary pressures, but at the cost of a large drop in output, slower growth and much higher unemployement. The latter could only be sustained because over £50bn of oil revenue was available to the government to help pay the annual exchequer cost of keeping an extra two million in unemployment. It is not the case that Thatcherism 'caused' an extra two million unemployed since unemployment would have risen in 1980 anyway, as world trading conditions and the business cycle took effect. Both monetarist and Keynesian economists would attribute perhaps half of the rise to the government's policies, but no firm figure is really provable. What can be said is that collapse in output and employment was directly caused by the government's actions, and that the mechanics of the change were certainly not those envisaged by the monetarists at the start of the process. By 1982 the economy was certainly leaner, but not necessarily fitter. Whether the economy now performed differently depended on the effects of the destruction of less productive plant in the slump, and the behaviour of surviving employers and workers in the new economic environment of high unemployment and lower inflation.

The recovery of employment: 1983–1986

The Conservative manifesto of June 1983 argued that 'the foundations for recovery have been firmly laid'. Output in manufacturing bottomed out in mid-1982 and took employment with it from the spring of 1983 onwards. Inflation rose in 1984 and 1985 but fell back to a record low of 3 per cent in 1986, helped substantially by falls in raw material prices. GDP rose by 13 per cent between 1982 and 1986. The growth of manufacturing output was less, however, at just under 10 per cent. Exports of manufactures increased, but imports of manufactures continued to increase at a faster rate, leading to an increasing deficit on manufactured trade. Employment in manufacturing continued to fall, but at a slower rate than during the recession. From March 1983 to September 1986 it fell by 300,000 or 5.5 per cent. However, employment in services rose by 1.2 millions or 9.3 per cent. Taking account of seasonal variations, there was a rise in employment of 570,000 over this period. In addition the number of self-employed rose substantially from about 1979 onwards. Between March 1983 and September 1986 their number increased by 445,000 to nearly 2.6 million. This led the government to claim that it had created an environment which had led to over 1 million new jobs which it argued was more than the rest of Europe put together.

Such claims were open to doubt, however. The favourable comparison with Europe arose partly because there the recession came later and because fewer jobs were shed to start with. Thus in 1986 compared to 1980 (a base year more favourable to Britain than 1979) total UK employment was 3 per cent lower, EEC employment 2 per cent lower and OECD employment 5 per cent higher and US employment 10 per cent higher. Half of the new jobs were 'self-employed'. In one sense this was a real contribution to job creation, providing 'real' jobs in the sense that most of the self-employed worked considerable hours. It could be argued that the expansion of self-employment reflected the success of 'enterprise culture', but the fact that the last major rise in self-employment took place in the last major recession in the 1930s casts some doubt on this. There are little data as yet on the earnings of the self-employed, or the length of time their self-employment lasts, or what they actually do. One-third describe themselves as 'managers', but what they manage is obscure. Self-employment is concentrated in the service sector, agriculture and construction: less than 10 per cent of jobs are in manufacturing. It is not clear how far the rise in self-employment is simply a response to the high level of unemployment, and the availability of measures such as the Enterprise Allowance Scheme, and how far it is a response to other factors. Furthermore, the data on self-employment come from a 'soft' source: the annual Labour Force Survey. This is based on a survey of a sample of 60,000 households with interviewees themselves responsible for defining their economic status. They may often be mistaken. For example, a Department of Employment survey of homeworkers found a very strong tendency for respondents to classify themselves as self-employed when in fact they were employees. This source is thus more prone to error than the comprehensive Census of Employment which provides estimates of the number of employees in the economy. Thus the 1986 Labour Force Survey caused the Department of Employment to revise its estimate of the growth of self-employment between June 1985 and 1986 from 122,000 to 17,000, a drop of 86 per cent. Even if the Labour Force Survey were providing inaccurate estimates of the absolute number of self-employed, it should still provide a reliable guide to trends in self employment, which were clearly upward but prone to large fluctuations. There is therefore room for speculation about the size of the rise in self-employment and its significance.

The rise in employment of employees is more problematic. Of the 570,000 increase, about 144,000 were accounted for by an increase in the number of those who held second jobs (for example a clerical worker working in a bar at weekends) and were thereby counted twice. Gregory (1987) has calculated that 237,000 of the increase represented people on special government programmes for the unemployed, such as Community Programme, YTS and EAS who had contracts of employment and were therefore counted in the Census of Employment. If these people were discounted (in the government's own terms they clearly do not hold 'real' jobs) then the employment rise over the period becomes 189,000: a growth in employment of under 1 per cent. Moreover this rise in total employment has accompanied a fall in full-time jobs and rise in part-time jobs because of the shift in employment towards the service sector. Between March 1983 and September 1986 the number of part-time jobs increased by 288,000 for women, and something over 100,000 for men (no exact figure is available for March 1983). This suggests that the number of full-time employees (if we assume that second jobs are all part-time) in the economy actually fell by over 50,000.

The rise in employment and self-employment did not bring down unemployment levels, however. From 2.9 million at March 1983 it rose to 3.1 million by September 1986, even on the government's own statistics. This led the government to claim that only an unprecedentedly fast rise in the number of those seeking work was preventing unemployment from falling: many jobs were being taken by those who had not been on the unemployment register and who had not been looking for work. But much of the speed of the rise in the working population was a function of the way the depth of the recession checked its earlier growth. A more accurate way to look at trends in the working population is to measure changes between cyclical peaks, rather than just looking at the upturn or downturn. The growth in working population from its previous peak in December 1980 to September 1986 was just under 1.1 million. This was a similar growth to that faced by the Labour government. From its peak in March 1973 to its December 1980 peak the working population grew by just under 1 million. Moreover, the government itself checked the growth of the working population by changing its definition so that those seeking work but ineligible for benefit (mostly married women) were not included. It could hardly complain when these same people, finding new jobs, failed to depress the unemployment count.

By 1987 the government was making a concerted effort to reduce the unemployment statistics, if not employment itself. The programme of 'Restart' interviews for the long-term jobless was expanded to encourage the long-term unemployed to take up places on special employment schemes such as the Community Programme (only 1% of 'Restart' interviewees were placed in 'real' jobs). It was also expected that interviews would encourage some to deregister. By December 1986, 195,000 claimants had had their benefit suspended because of failure to appear, but this total includes many who would have left the register anyway to take up jobs. There were 843,000 on special employment schemes by March 1987, nearly double the number in 1983. The National Institute for Economic and Social Research estimated that these measures, rather than any underlying economic change, were responsible for the slight fall in unemployment towards the end of 1986. Layard and Clark (1987) estimated that while the expansion of these measures and of other jobs was stopping unemployment rising further as the population of working age expanded, this could not explain why unemployment started to fall from July 1986. They found that the answer lay in the contraction of the working population (those actually working or looking for work) which matched the fall in unemployment. It appeared that Restart interviews, plus tighter tests on 'availability for work' were leading people who previously would have done so, to stop claiming benefit and being counted as unemployed. In aggregate terms then, the Thatcher governments presided over a fall in employment of just over 2 million, followed by a recovery of less than one-quarter of a million jobs (but with more part time jobs in the economy) and half-a-million self-employed jobs. The recovery, therefore, did little to reverse the rise in unemployment which its policies had encouraged. We turn now to look at the nature of the recovery in more detail.

The industrial and geographical distribution of recovery: restructuring

The recovery was not evenly distributed across regions. The South-East, the South-West, East Anglia and East Midlands lost 136,000 jobs between 1979 and 1986 — just over 1 per cent of their 1979 stock of employment. However, the West Midlands, Yorkshire and Humberside, the North, North-West, Wales and Scotland, lost 1.43 million jobs — over 12.5 per cent of their 1979 stock. The northern half of the country was both hit hardest by the crash and had the weakest recovery from it, as Table 5.3 shows. Between 1982 and 1986, once output was picking up, the four southern regions gained 670,000 service sector jobs and lost just over 200,000 manufacturing jobs, while the other regions gained only 300,000 jobs in services, but lost almost 400,000 manufacturing jobs. The distribution of gains in self-employment was similarly skewed.

The rapid collapse of manufacturing employment in 1980–2 focused attention on the issue of 'economic restructuring', that is the change in the patterns of production and employment in the economy. This includes the relative rise in importance of the service sector compared to manufacturing, the increase in white-

Table 5.3   Regional employment, 1975–86 (percentage change)

	1975–79	1979–82	1982–86	1986 stock (millions of jobs)
South-East	2.1	−4.4	2.8	7.3
East Anglia	4.6	−3.3	12.2	0.8
South-West	4.9	−4.6	2.8	1.6
West Midlands	1.3	−11.6	2.0	2.0
East Midlands	4.6	−6.6	4.5	1.5
Yorkshire & Humberside	1.3	−10.1	−1.6	1.8
North West	0.1	−11.4	−4.6	2.3
North	−1.4	−12.4	−1.5	1.1
Wales	3.5	−12.3	−5.3	0.9
Scotland	1.3	−7.2	−3.2	1.9

Source: Dept of Employment Gazette, Historical Supplement, 1987.

collar jobs, in part-time jobs and in women's employment. It also includes changes within manufacturing from older heavier industries to newer lighter ones, often in new geographical areas away from urban centres, often in newer smaller premises, or as part of large and heterogeneous enterprises with global production strategies. Restructuring is of twofold significance to economic change and industrial relations. First, it is directly relevant to the debate on economic performance. Critics of Thatcherism claimed that 'deindustrialisation' and the attrition of Britain's industrial base was proof of the failure of the government's policies. Conversely, the government argued that the fall in manufacturing employment was part of a trend throughout the developed world away from manufacturing to services caused by rising living standards. The service sector would be the focus of employment in the future. Kenneth Baker, in an interview with the *Sunday Times* which appeared on 15 April 1984, (quoted in Carr 1984, p. 24), said:

> I know some will sneer and say that the British will become a nation of hairdressers, waiters and video salesmen. I would reply to that by saying that it is all part of the process of continuous adjustment, and that these jobs are no less worthy or noble than those who make scissors for the hairdressers or grow vegetables for the restaurant or make the electronics for the video machine.

Restructuring is also directly related to industrial relations, since almost all the trends in economic change seem to be *away* from areas where unions are fairly strongly organised to areas where they have been weak. Moreover, when such restructuring is accompanied by an environment of high unemployment and government hostility to union organisation this could be expected to worsen the problems faced by the unions. Any economic change means that unions have to recruit new members and organise in new plants in new industries, so that there is always a flow of members through unions. In a sense they always have to run in order to stand still. But this process becomes much harder if economic change means that the sorts of workforce available for unions to recruit are those where unions have found organisation difficult in the past, whether because of employee disinterest or employer opposition or size of workplace or working time arrangements of the employees. Traditionally the core of trade union organisation has been full-time male workers in production industries, chiefly mining and manufacturing. Male union density (the proportion of actual to potential union members) has been higher, not necessarily because they have been more militant, but because unions' policies and organisation have been aimed at and cater for men and because the jobs they hold are easier to organise. Density in the public sector and manufacturing has been much higher than private services, higher amongst manual than white-collar workers and higher amongst full-time than part-time workers. Yet it is the more poorly organised groups which are increasing their share of employment in the economy. The labour movement feared, and Thatcherites hoped, that economic restructuring, which would be quickened by its economic policies, was eroding the unions' power base in the traditional areas of the economy, leading to their long-term decline.

But restructuring is a contradictory process. We tend to think of the factories, shops and offices in the economy as a relatively static population and of restructuring as a one-off process of change: the closure of plants in old industries and the opening of plants in new ones. Moreover, we are most conscious of it when the net changes it gives rise to in the aggregate level of employment are large. Hence the collapse in employment after 1979 focused interest in restructuring. But once we look more closely we can see there is no necessary relationship between the overall visible net change, and what are called the gross components of change: the totals of closures and openings of plants, and contraction and expansion of employment that result in the net change.

The existence in Scotland of the Scottish Manufacturing Establishments Record, a database covering the employment history of Scottish plants since 1950, enables us to look in detail at the real dimensions of restructuring over time. Even when unemployment was low and growth was higher many plants were closing and many jobs being lost: but at the same time new plants and jobs were also being created. Throughout the period, roughly 1 per cent of employment was in establishments under one year old. New plants which survived (about one-third close in the first five years) roughly doubled their employment by maturity. Hence the pattern shown in Tables 5.4 and 5.5. By the late 1970s nearly half the employment in Scottish manufacturing was in plants opened since 1950: jobs in new plants were being created all the time, and were not confined to 'sunrise' industries. Conversely, new expanding industries lost plants and jobs too. Electronics in Scotland 'lost' the equivalent of 98 per cent of its total employment between 1968 and 1978 through closures and redundancies. In other words, restructuring was not synonymous with recession. The proportion of jobs in new manufacturing plants has always been fairly small, and became progressively smaller in the 1970s as plants employed fewer people to start with and also tended to grow less rapidly after they opened. It was also the case that new plants suffer higher closure rates than old plants (Henderson 1980).

Table 5.4 Restructuring in Scottish Manufacturing, 1950–80: the experience of establishments opened up to 1950.

	1950	*1960*	*1970*	*1980*
Number of survivors (thousands)	4.9	3.5	2.3	1.5
Average employment size	134	167	199	186
% of total manufacturing employment	100	88	69	55

Source: SCOMER

Table 5.5 Gross components of manufacturing employment change Scotland 1968–77 (changes calculated on an annual basis)

	Jobs gained in openings and expansions as % 1968 stock	*Jobs lost in contractions and closures as % 1968 stock*
New towns	131	98
Electronics	101	98
All manufacturing	63	77
Greater Glasgow	49	81
'Staple' industries (shipbuilding steel, railway engineering)	46	74

Source: SCOMER

There was therefore no reason why the slump of 1980–2 should promote restructuring in manufacturing. Indeed there is evidence to suggest that it slowed it down, by decreasing the level of new openings, further decreasing employment growth in new plants and by increasing the closure rate for all plants. In Scotland, for example, the average age of manufacturing plants and jobs increased from 1979 onwards as did the share of traditional industries in employment! The relative shift of jobs away from urban centres appeared to stop and the Scottish new towns lost jobs faster than the rest of the country (MacInnes 1987). 'Restructuring' in manufacturing was progressing much faster in the 1960s and 1970s, within high overall levels of employment and, as Chapter 7 will show, alongside increasing levels of union organisation. It was neither the product of Thatcherism nor has it all been accentuated by it.

But what of the net results of restructuring in changing the structure of the economy and types of job in it? Here, too, the factors are long-term ones, and again were operating most strongly in the 1960s and 1970s when union influence was increasing. Table 5.6 describes some of the main trends. The share of manufacturing employment has been falling since the early 1960s, that of traditional industries since the 1950s. The shift of industrial employment away from the cities also dates back to the early 1960s. The rising share of women workers in employment is as old as the century. The number of men in work has

Table 5.6   The changing nature of employment, UK 1951–84 (per cent)

	1951	1961	1971	1981	1984
Workers employed in manufacturing	39	38	36	29	26
Manufacturing workers employed in 'staples' (1)	24	22	18	12	10
Women workers	33	34	35	43	44
White-collar workers (2)	31	—	44	48	52
Part-time workers	4	10	16	21	22

(1) Metal manufacture, shipbuilding, locomotives and carriages, textiles; figures are for 1948, 1960, 1968, 1981, 1984.
(2) Figures are for 1948, 1973, 1979, 1984.

Source: Department of Employment Gazette, Abstract of Historical Labour Statistics and Labour Force Surveys.

been falling since 1965 when it stood at 14.6 million. Twenty years later there were 3 million fewer men in employment. The rising share of white-collar workers is also a long-term trend. Part-time work has been expanding since the 1950s. The expansion of both women and part-time workers has been caused not by a change in the share of these workers within manufacturing, but by the expansion of the service sector, both public and private, and the role of women part-time workers there. The following description of the effects of restructuring on the labour force, and therefore in the labour movement seems up to date:

> Modern industry is so complicated that it cannot get along without great numbers of managers, salesmen, engineers, chemists and technicians of all kinds ... More important than this is the spread of middle-class ideas and habits among the working class ... now better off in almost all ways than they were thirty years ago ... [Before] every human being in these islands could be 'placed' in an instant by his clothes, manners and accent. That is no longer the case ... in the new townships ... the southward shift of industry ... in light industry areas ... the old pattern is gradually changing into something new.

In fact it is George Orwell, writing in 1941 (Orwell 1982, pp. 66–8). Economic restructuring is a permanent process and we should be cautious about assuming too easily that at any point in time it leads to faster social change or transforms industrial relations.

Small businesses, however broadly defined, may be large in number but are only of negligible impact in terms of output and employment. Even if we define small businesses as firms with up to 100 workers they continue to represent only a small proportion of employment in manufacturing. The main reason this proportion increased after 1979 was because job losses in medium-sized firms reduced their size. The government emphasised the role that small firms could play in generating jobs. It is the case that small firms produce proportionately more job gains, and large firms shed absolutely more jobs. But this proves little about their relative ability to provide employment because most new firms which grow are small to start with while established large firms are older. There is also little connection between small size and high-technology plants. In fact the latter are usually bigger plants which in turn are part of giant enterprises (MacInnes 1987; Stewart 1986). Storey and Johnson (1987) studied job changes in Durham and Tyne and Wear and found that in periods of recovery larger plants were better at generating jobs. The rise of self-employment also started in 1979 but, as the previous section argued, this rise was one whose significance was not yet clear. Giant enterprises continue to be important, as Table 5.7 shows. The largest 30 enterprises account for as much employment as all small firms put together. The development of these giant enterprises was fastest in the 1950s and early 1960s. Between 1949 and 1963 the share in output of the top 100 firms increased from 22 per cent to 37 per cent, but after 1979 their share fell back. Average plant size (which is strongly related to many industrial relations characteristics) is now falling and this does reverse a previous trend. However, this fall dates back to the early 1970s. The average size of establishment is a misleading figure because there are so many very small establishments. In 1983 36 per cent of employees still worked in plants with 500 workers or more.

Table 5.7 Large and small firms in manufacturing

	1958	*1963*	*1970*	*1979*	*1983*
Firms with less than 100 employees:					
Percentage of all firms	87	88	91	94	95
Percentage of all employment	18	14	16	18	22
Firms with more than 20,000 employees:					
Absolute number of firms	32	38	38	34	23
Percentage of employment	17	22	24	24	19
Mean number of establishments per firm	44	55	58	59	67
100 Largest firms:					
Share of net output	27	37	41	42	40
All firms:					
Mean size of establishment	87	92	86	61	32

Source: Census of Production, appropriate years.

One aspect of restructuring the government was keen to promote directly was the switch from public to private sector employment, but as Table 5.8 shows, the proportion of civilian employees in the public sector declined by only 5 per cent by 1985. If the public sector corporations are excluded where privatisation reduced the number of public employees dramatically by transferring them to the private sector, then the proportion of public employees actually increased, because of the fall in employment in private industry.

Only one feature of restructuring appears to have intensified after 1978: the transfer of employment from manufacturing to services (Table 5.9). Job loss in manufacturing accelerated: even after output started to recover, job loss was running at three times the level of 1975-9. But the expansion of service sector jobs did not accelerate correspondingly. Between 1980 and 1982 service sector employment fell for the first time in many years. Once it started to grow again it did so about one-third faster than previously. In fact the Labour government presided over a greater absolute increase in jobs in services.

Table 5.8 Private and public sector employment 1975–85

	1975	*1979*	*1982*	*1985*
Employees (thousands) in:				
Central government (civilians only)	1965	2073	2076	2034
Local authorities	2917	2997	2865	2964
Public corporations	2035	2065	1756	1262
Private sector (including self employed)	17786	17948	16891	17828
Percentage of employees in:				
Private sector (including self-employed)	71.03	70.67	70.64	73.02
Private sector (excluding self-employed and forces)	69.54	69.19	68.70	70.84
Public sector (excluding self employed, forces and public corporations)	23.24	23.68	24.75	24.35

Source: UK National Income and Accounts, 1986

Table 5.9 Manufacturing and services employment 1975–86

	1975	*1979*	*1982*	*1986*
Manufacturing employment:				
Absolute level (thousands)	7351	7107	5751	5148
Change over previous period (%)		−3.3	−19.1	−10.5
Services employment:				
Absolute level (thousands)	12545	13260	13117	14119
Change over previous period (%)		5.7	−1.1	7.6

Source: Department of Employment Gazette, Historical Supplement 1987.

Thatcherism, therefore, did not produce intensified restructuring. Rather it drowned its effects by a recession. Its policies appeared to have stifled rather than stimulated economic change in the sense of restructuring. It proceeded much faster in the era of the Macmillan, Wilson and Heath governments than that of Mrs Thatcher. Relatively full employment and consensus politics coexisted with rapid economic change. We cannot simply equate 'restructuring' with 'Thatcherism'. There is therefore little evidence that Thatcherism has transformed the economic environment of British industrial relations through changing the nature of economic activity and therefore the institutional environment in which unions operate. Most of the changes in the composition of the workforce and the sorts of workplaces in which they are found have been developing for some time. But what stands out is the dramatic increase in unemployment caused mainly by the collapse of manufacturing. Should we see this as a process of restructuring too?

Deindustrialisation

The issue of deindustrialisation is a more complex one. The government claimed that the fall in manufacturing employment was simply part of a global process of restructuring. It is true that employment in manufacturing is falling in the OECD countries as a whole. But this is not true for all: Japan is one notable country to have bucked this trend. But the fall in employment has been faster in Britain — both before 1979 and after. Between 1960 and 1984 the proportion of employment in manufacturing in the UK shrank by 12 percentage points, a decline of one-third. This was nearly double the decline experienced by the United States, over three times that of West Germany and more than double that of the OECD as a whole. In terms of output, in the OECD as a whole the proportion fell one-fifth from 30 per cent to 24 per cent of GDP between 1960 and 1984. In the UK it fell one-third from 32 per cent to 22 per cent. In 1987 British manufacturing output was still below that not only of 1979 but of the three-day week in the first quarter of 1974. Nor was this low output a function of shift in demand in Britain towards services as living standards increased. For imports of manufactures continued to rise while the balance of trade in manufactures deteriorated. Gershuny and Miles (1985) cast doubt on any long-run trend for the share of services output to increase in advanced economies. Historically, as Chapter 2 pointed out, the role of Britain's manufacturing industry was to generate sufficient exports to pay for the amounts of raw materials and other goods needed to sustain the economy at a high enough level to promote full employment. By 1983 Britain's manufacturing industry was no longer able to export enough even to pay for the manufactures which were imported. Exports of oil bridged this trade gap, but it seems very unlikely that services could replace the past role of manufacturing as an export industry, simply because many services cannot be traded internationally. It is impossible to export haircuts, for example. Moreover, the service industries themselves are cautious about their ability to generate more exports in the future.

Thus the British Invisible Exports Council argued before the House of Lords Select Committee on Overseas Trade that it did 'not see this growth (of invisible earnings) as being to a major extent a substitute for decline in general industrial activity' (Aldington 1986, p. 7). The Committee estimated that because value added in manufacturing exports was higher, a 1 per cent drop in manufacturing exports required a 3 per cent rise in services exports to maintain the same level of economic activity. This seemed an unlikely scenario when Britain's share of invisible exports had 'fallen in the last twenty years in percentage terms by *more* than the share of world trade taken by our manufactured exports' (Aldington 1986, p. 8). The chair of the Committee summed up its conclusions on the government's view that manufacturing would recover 'automatically' via market forces:

> Services cannot substitute for manufacturing. The decline of manufacturing output was not an inevitable consequence of North Sea oil. New industries and new products require a long time-scale. Lost capacity will take time to restore. Lost markets at home and abroad will take time to regain. Recovery from the present base is not just a matter of improvement. You cannot improve what has gone (Aldington 1985).

Thus far from creating a new 'service economy', the legacy of the 1979–82 slump was to hasten the decline of manufacturing in Britain, worsening what had already been a poor record. This constituted 'restructuring' only in the negative sense that the government's policies effectively put the interests of the City first; it was not harmed by high interest rates or a high sterling exchange rate: on the contrary abolition of exchange controls, deregulation (the 'Big Bang') and a government which was prepared to sacrifice domestic industry to its monetary objectives gave it a stronger role than ever.

Perhaps the strongest evidence of the way in which the government's policies hastened deindustrialisation by worsening the domestic environment for industry was the response of industry to the abolition of exchange controls. A Labour Research Department survey of the 40 largest UK manufacturers showed that between 1979 and 1986 these firms reduced employment in Britain by 415,000 while *increasing* employment abroad by 125,000 (Wintour 1987). This does not mean that 125,000 new jobs were created abroad which would otherwise have come to Britain. But it does demonstrate that British companies found the environment of other countries less hostile: most of the new investment was in Europe and the United States.

Earnings, taxation and inequality

Critics of Thatcherism at first saw it as a programme to use high unemployment to force down wage rates and therefore labour costs in order to boost profits and increase competitiveness. Put in rather different terms, this was also what the monetarists expected. Squeezing inflation out of the system through controlling the money supply would force employers and unionists to bargain down wages in order to maintain production, profits and employment. By making money tight, and making it clear that it would not intervene to stop unemployment rising, the government would force workers to price themselves back into jobs. Thus the vicious circle of rising income expectations fuelling an inflationary spiral would be broken.

Table 5.10 shows the main results for manufacturing and for the whole economy.

Table 5.10 Average Gross Weekly earnings 1975–86 (April)

	1975	1979	1980	1981	1982	1983	1984	1985	1986
£ current: whole economy	54.0	89.6	110.2	124.9	136.5	147.4	159.3	171.0	184.7
£ current: manufacturing	53.6	92.5	110.9	122.5	135.9	147.0	160.8	174.7	188.6
Retail Price Index (1974=100)	129.1	214.2	260.8	292.2	319.7	332.5	349.7	373.9	385.3
Index of real earnings: whole economy (1975=100)	100	100.0	101.0	102.2	102.1	105.0	108.9	109.3	114.6
Index of real earnings: manufacturing (1975=100)	100	104.0	102.4	101.0	102.4	106.5	110.8	112.5	117.9
% change on previous period: whole economy	—	0	1.0	1.1	-0.1	3.8	2.8	0.4	4.8
% change on previous period: manufacturing	—	4.0	-1.5	-1.4	1.4	4.0	4.0	1.6	4.8

Source: New Earnings Survey

The only period when wages appeared to be checked by unemployment was in manufacturing industry when the *rise* in unemployment and rate of redundancies was at its height around 1980–1. Thus while real earnings in the whole economy continued to increase over the whole period, in manufacturing they fell back slightly first. In the face of closures and redundancies unionists were not able to increase money wages enough to cover the rise in price inflation. Studies by Gregory *et al.* (1987) and Nickell (1987) confirm that absolute high levels of unemployment had little effect on wages: only *increasing* that unemployment appeared to have much effect. But any period of restraint was more than made up for from about 1982 onwards. From 1983 onwards the underlying increase in money earnings stuck at between 7.5 and 8 per cent, and did not fall below this level even when the rate of price inflation dipped below 3 per cent. As a result real earnings inflation from 1983 to 1987 was probably at its highest ever level in Britain. Earnings increases were not evenly spread however, as Table 5.11 shows. Women full-timers did rather better than their male counterparts, but occupational segregation meant that their increases were from a lower base. Earnings for part-time women workers rose less than for women full-timers, and manual women part-timers did particularly poorly, partly because their average hours of work decreased. White-collar workers did rather better than manual workers.

Table 5.11 Change in gross weekly real earnings 1979–86 (per cent)

	Males full-time	Females full-time	Females part-time
All: average	13.8	21.1	8.1
Manual: average	4.2	8.3	−1.6
White-collar: average	20.5	22.7	13.6
All: lowest decile	0.1	9.9	6.5*
All: highest decile	21.1	26.0	23.5*
Public sector: average	13.2	19.2	NA
Private sector: average	14.1	23.0	NA

* Gross hourly earnings

Source: New Earnings Survey

As Tables 5.11 and 5.12 both show, differentials increased markedly between 1979 and 1986. As well as the gap between manual and white-collar workers widening, differentials within each type of worker in each sector tended to increase. The top 10 per cent of earners increased their earnings by over one-fifth in real terms, while men on the borderline of the bottom 10 per cent of earners had virtually no increase. The bulk of the bottom 10 per cent therefore suffered a real cut in their earnings. In 1979 differentials were higher in the private sector for non-manual male workers and (to a lesser extent) manual female workers. Between 1979 and 1986 they increased in all sectors, but generally faster in the private sector and

Table 5.12 Earnings differentials 1979–86. Highest decile gross weekly earnings as percentage of lowest decile gross weekly earnings

	1979	1986	% change
Public sector:			
Males manual	217	230	6
non-manual	230	263	14
Females manual	195	215	10
non-manual	214	238	11
Private sector:			
Males manual	217	245	13
non-manual	276	338	22
Females manual	203	216	6
non-manual	214	254	19

Source: New Earnings Survey

for non-manual workers. Male non-manual workers in the private sector saw differentials increase by nearly one-quarter in seven years.

Workers in the private sector, who did not face cash limits, did better than those in the public sector, but the effect was strongest on white-collar workers here. Despite the attempt to abandon comparability, public sector workers pay stayed above the private sector, except for non-manual males. While manual workers in the public sector improved their relative position, that of non-manual workers fell back. Since several groups of public sector white-collar workers achieved 'catch-up' deals in the course of 1986 after the April date on which these figures are based it may be that by April 1987 some of their comparability was in fact restored (Table 5.13).

There were substantial shifts in the distribution of wealth and income in the economy besides the increase in differentials which dramatically increased inequality. First, those who became unemployed suffered a large drop in their income. The incidence of unemployment was not shared equally. Disney (1979) estimated that 70 per cent of unemployment was borne by 3 per cent of the

Table 5.13 Public sector workers pay as percentage of private sector workers' pay

	1979	1986
Males		
manual	100.0	101.4
non-manual	99.0	95.4
Females		
manual	99.8	102.9
non-manual	125.8	116.5

Source: New Earnings Survey

workforce at the time of his study. Second, income tax cuts and the move to indirect taxation overwhelmingly favoured the well-off. In 1986 the Low Pay Unit calculated that the richest 7 per cent of tax payers had received 43 per cent of tax cuts. All except the top-band tax payers experienced an increase in the level of taxation from 1979 until the 1987 budget tax-rate reductions. As a result, inequality in income increased more than the figures on earnings differentials alone suggest, while the higher incidence of unemployment brought down incomes substantially for those experiencing it. Evidence for this comes from data on the distribution of household income. Table 5.14 shows the average estimated final income for each decile of households (ranked according to amount of final income). 'Final' income is the household's income minus taxes paid (both direct and indirect) plus benefits received (including both money benefits such as social security payments and collective benefits, such as education). Since retail prices rose 67 per cent in this period, average household real income rose by about 4 per cent over the period but the top twenty per cent of households did very much better. The bottom thirty per cent also appear to have done well, but the Labour Research Department (LRD 1987 p. 30) argues this represents the move to higher council house rents and housing benefits, so that the real final income of this group fell by about 5 per cent.

Table 5.14 Estimated household final income 1979–86
Average for each decile

	£ per annum 1986	% increase on 1979
Lowest decile	2,565	71
2nd decile	3,582	68
3rd decile	4,535	70
4th decile	5.451	64
5th decile	6,623	63
6th decile	7,767	67
7th decile	8.994	68
8th decile	10,288	70
9th decile	12.434	76
Highest decile	19,171	90
Average	8,141	73

Source: Economic Trends, January 1981; November 1986.

The relatively rapid rise in share prices helped the wealthiest 1 per cent of the population to increase their share of wealth from 11 to 12 per cent by 1983, reversing a trend fall in their share of wealth which had been occurring since the 1920s. The extent of poverty increased markedly. By 1986 the Low Pay Unit claimed that government figures showed that 10½ million people in Britain had incomes at supplementary benefit levels or less: over two-thirds more than in 1979.

A 'Leaner, Fitter' Economy?

In order to evaluate the claims made for the nature of the recovery since 1982 it is useful to compare the recent economic performance with the corresponding period of Labour economic management between 1975 and 1979. The periods are directly comparable in that both start from the trough of manufacturing output and follow its subsequent rise. The comparison flatters the earlier period in that output peaked in 1979 whereas it looked set to continue to rise after 1986: the second period of recovery has been longer lasting. However, it flatters the later period in that, given the depth of the 1979–82 slump, there was correspondingly more scope for recovery to take place. Table 5.15 shows the main comparisons.

Table 5.15 Employment change and associated factors 1975–86 (percentage changes over second quarter figures)

	1975–79	*1979–82*	*1982–86*
Manufacturing employment	−3.3	−19.1	−10.5
Services employment	5.7	−1.1	7.6
Manufacturing productivity (output per employee)	12.7	2.9	21.0
Manufacturing output	7.9	−15.5	9.1
Manufacturing average adult earnings	4.6	−0.7	15.1
Effective exchange rate	−16.3	5.3	−15.7
International labour competitiveness	−6.2	−21.2	2.4
Absolute change in balance of manufactures trade (£bn 1980 prices)	−7	−3	−7
Total employment	1.8	−7.3	0.8
Unemployment	31.9	126.9	22.6
Total output (GDP)	13.6	−4.0	13.0

Sources: Economic Trends; Department of Employment Gazette; Department of Trade and Industry.

Under the Conservatives growth was about 0.5 per cent more over the four-year period. Manufacturing output rose rather faster, but from a very depressed base. Manufacturing employment fell faster, linked to much bigger rises in productivity. There were two important factors behind the rise in productivity. The first was compositional. It is reasonable to suppose that it was the least productive operations which manufacturing companies tended to rationalise and close during the slump. This boosted average productivity without necessarily generating any change in the productivity in surviving plants. Thus the flattering comparisons between manufacturing productivity growth in Britain and the EEC in the 1980s are doubling misleading. They overestimate underlying productivity growth in Britain and compare it with that of countries which were experiencing recession later and less severely than Britain. Productivity was probably not being boosted by rapid investment, since even by 1986 it was still below the level for 1979. Nor were companies devoting more money to research and development. By 1985 industrial R and D spending was just below its 1981 level (*British Business*, 27 February 1987) and it employed 38,000 fewer staff — a drop of one-fifth in four years. Thus while other countries expanded their R and D spending, both absolutely and as a proportion of GDP, in Britain it fell further back. Meanwhile, military R and D reached an all-time high and was still rising. Further worrying evidence came from a report which suggested that the improvement in Britain's manufacturing performance was concentrated in low-technology sectors where there was little research and innovation (Midland Bank, 1986).

The second factor was the very large real earnings increases in manufacturing. At 15 per cent these were over three times the figure for the earlier period and probably the highest real gains ever made. As a result unit labour costs in industry increased faster than elsewhere, so that despite a 16 per cent devaluation of the pound over the period, international labour competitiveness improved by only 2.4 per cent. While this reversed previous trends, it did little to reverse the massive fall in competitiveness experienced during the slump, and was dependent on devaluation outstripping wage increases: an unlikely long-term trend. In turn only falling world raw material prices prevented devaluation causing increases in price inflation. The balance in manufactured trade continued to deteriorate at about the same rate as before the crash, but this was now a rising deficit, rather than a falling surplus as before. This indicated British industry's continuing failure to compete in either foreign or domestic markets. Manufacturing productivity growth after 1979 was well over 3 per cent per annum: roughly comparable to performance in the 1960s. Then much the same level of productivity growth was accompanied by significantly lower real earnings growth. And this was in the height of the Post-War Settlement with the sort of industrial relations problems that the Donovan Commission, for example, was established to investigate! Employment growth was faster in the earlier period — a rise of 425,000 jobs compared to 157,000. Unemployment also climbed faster in the earlier period, but from a much smaller base. In June 1975 it stood at 722,000 compared to 2.7 million in June 1982, even using the government's changed definitions. Other aspects, too, of the government's performance were surprisingly similar. Labour's record on reducing public expenditure and halting the rise in taxation was rather better than the Conservatives'. Between 1975–6 and 1979–80 the share of public spending in GDP fell from 48½ per cent to 43½ per cent. Between 1982–3 and 1986–7 it fell from 47 per cent to 44½ per cent (excluding privatisation proceeds).

It is also possible to compare the government's performance with the rest of the OECD nations. This is rather more difficult as Britain experienced recession and recovery in advance of other countries, so that comparisons year for year can be misleading. What can be done, however, is to compare relative British performance before and after 1979 to see whether it has changed. Table 5.16 gives the main results. It shows that growth and manufacturing output and employment continued to be worse than elsewhere, as did employment growth in services. Of the main

Table 5.16 Employment change and associated factors UK and OECD compared 1973–84 (average annual percentage changes)

	1973–9 UK	1973–9 OECD	1979–84 UK	1979–84 OECD
Manufacturing employment	−1.3	−0.4	−5.4	−1.3
Services employment	1.4	2.5	0.8	1.8
Real GDP	1.5	2.7	0.6	1.9
Real value-added manufacturing	−0.7	2.2	−1.7	1.7
Real value-added manufacturing per person in employment	0.6	2.5	3.9	3.0
Real hourly earnings manufacturing	0.9	2.0	2.2	0.5

Source: OECD

industrialised countries, only the United States suffered a significant deterioration in the manufactured trade balance and by 1985 Britain was the only major OECD country where manufacturing output remained below its 1979 level. The British share of the volume of world trade in manufactures fell from 11.25 per cent in 1976–8 to 8.5 in 1982–4, showing the impact of the over-valuation of sterling (Huhne 1986). One area of substantial change was again manufacturing productivity, where Britain not only improved its relative position, but went from well below the OECD average to well above it. But because this improvement was in a shrinking sector of the economy it did not translate into such a wonderful improvement in the performance of the whole economy, as Huhne (1986) points out:

> The average annual growth rate of the British economy between 1979 and 1985 was 1.2 per cent, compared with 2.2 per cent for the OECD area. But surely then it compares favourably with the past mismanagement of both Tory and Labour governments? Over the previous seven-year period from 1972 to 1978 the average annual growth rate in Britain was 2.4 per cent compared with 3.5 per cent for the whole OECD. During the Thatcher years Britain's growth lagged on average by 1 point compared with 1.1 point previously.

There was, however, a corresponding reversal in rate of earnings growth: from half the OECD average to more than double. The other area of improvement was inflation, which in Britain fell from 13.4 per cent in 1979 to 6.1 per cent in 1985 compared with a fall from 9.9 per cent to 4.6 per cent in the OECD.

These comparisons are made still less encouraging when account is taken of the contribution of North Sea oil. Every year between 1982 and 1985 it contributed an average of over £16 billion to the balance of payments, provided the Treasury with £10 billion in tax revenues and added about ½ per cent to the growth rate. Without it the government could not have afforded benefit payments to the unemployed and would have faced a serious balance of payments crisis. It does not appear that the recovery since 1982 has been characterised by a markedly superior economic performance to that produced by the last years of the Post-War Settlement, either in terms of a historical comparison within Britain, or a comparison of Britain's performance relative to other developed countries. In contrast to the government's public optimism about the future, its report in 1986 to the EEC Regional Development Fund projected that unemployment would remain above 3 million in 1990. Moreover, economic performance in the 1970s was poor compared to the 1950s and 1960s, so that a comparison of the Conservative government's performance, even after 1982 when it was claimed the foundations for recovery had been laid, with that of the 'Butskellite' governments of the classic years of the Post-War Settlement is still less flattering. The evidence from the economic indicators does not suggest that Thatcherism has revolutionised Britain's economic performance. This suggests that we re-examine the mechanics of the changes Thatcherism ushered in.

Monetarism and economic recovery

The recovery was accompanied by some loosening of the original monetarist squeeze. Although interest rates remained high, the pound was allowed to devalue quite substantially, making markets easier for exporters. PSBR continued to fall, but privatisation, which counted as negative public spending but in some ways acted like public borrowing, allowed some relaxation of public expenditure limits. Indeed, compared to the OECD the money supply in Britain expanded faster in the 1980s, as Table 5.17 shows. The reason for this was that along with high real earnings increases for those in work there was a credit boom with rapid growth in private borrowing. This kept interest rates high and also sustained a substantial consumer boom from 1982 onwards. This boom, along with North Sea oil production (whose revenues as we have seen paid for unemployment benefit)

Table 5.17 Money supply (M1 plus quasi-money) (average of annual percentage changes)

	1979–84	*1973–9*
UK	16.4	10.9
OECD	10.2	12.3
OECD Europe	11.1	14.1

Source: OECD

boosted GDP, but did little for domestic industry. Its continued poor international competitiveness meant that manufacturing output stayed depressed: fewer and fewer people were producing less than in the 1970s. Meanwhile imports, paid for by the export of North Sea oil, increased their market share. By 1986–7 the growth of earnings and company profits was providing the Chancellor with increased tax revenues, too. In both 1983 and 1987 the government relaxed public spending limits to provide some pre-election reflation. By 1986 public spending as a proportion of GDP was still above its 1979 level. It was projected to fall by 1988–9, but such projections had failed to materialise in the past. What had changed more dramatically was the composition of public spending; far more was being spent on transfers to the unemployed, much less on industry or housing. And such spending was financed more by taxation than borrowing.

Rather than the frontiers of the state being 'rolled back' state spending had changed its role. It was being used less to intervene in the economy, whether by funding infrastructure, aiding industry in strategic areas, guiding investment or redistributing incomes. It was being used more to pay for a much higher level of unemployment. The objective of economic policy had changed. It was no longer full employment, nor was it maximum growth. The management of price inflation still took precedence over other goals, so that, for example, in 1985 when domestic inflationary pressures increased, the sterling exchange rate was allowed to appreciate, and little was done to secure any reduction in interest rates, when industry would have benefited from lower interest rates and a more realistically valued pound. The government also continued to abhor public spending, so that in the 1987 budget, when the Chancellor had rather greater room for manoeuvre than usual, precedence was given to tax cuts, rather than any job-creating public expenditure. Monetarism, in its original guise of control of the money supply became less relevant. This process reached its logical conclusion in 1986 when targets for sterling M3 were dropped altogether. At that point, while price inflation had dipped below 3 per cent for the first time in two decades, money supply as measured by sterling M3 was growing at an annual rate of 19 per cent — its fastest for some years. By this time it was possible for the retiring Economic Director at NEDO to argue (Posner 1986, p. 305) that

> despite the monetarist ideology that still clutters some Ministerial speeches, the generally agreed macro-policy mix is back now where the brightest and best establishment economists — the Government's own top advisers and the blue chip financial journalists — wanted it to be in the mid-1960s. A managed float for sterling, a firm grip on pay, a tight fiscal policy, a cautious and rather restrictive eye towards monetary expansion.

The continued poor performance of Britain's manufacturing industry (despite the substantial increases in labour productivity recorded since 1979), as revealed by low output, declining competitiveness, continued rising import penetration, falling share of world trade and rising balance of trade deficit is a major factor to be considered when assessing how much Thatcherism has altered Britain's economic performance. Thatcherism charged the Post-War Settlement with the throttling of enterprise and wealth creation, squeezing the private sector and leaving 'too few producers'. However it has not, so far, been able to arrest the relative decline of Britain's manufacturing industry. It is not clear that 'getting off industry's back' or 'rolling back the frontiers of the state' (in so far as these objectives have proven to be obtainable) has in fact improved Britain's manufacturing base or the rest of the economy. Chapter 6 looks more closely at some of the reasons for this.

In this context, it is worth briefly examining Britain's economic record before the 1970s. Its poor performance since 1945 compared to other OECD countries was complemented by a very good performance after 1945 compared to Britain's dismal record before that. Feinstein (1983, pp. 5ff) shows that from the 1870s until the 1940s productivity in the British economy grew at about 1 per cent a year. In the 1950s this became 2 per cent and in the 1960s 3 per cent a year. The balance of trade was in deficit from the 1870s to the 1940s to the tune of 5–6 per cent of GDP each year. In the 1950s and 1960s this was reduced to a deficit of around 1 per cent. Until the Second World War, Britain's international economic position was maintained by income from foreign assets: from the profits of Empire. These protected British industry while it failed to modernise as effectively as Germany or the United States. These foreign assets were sold off to pay for the Second World War. The growth in industrial output achieved in the Post-War Settlement, while inferior to other countries, was nevertheless much better than Britain's precarious position in 1945 and its previous economic record might have been expected to lead to. Thus a seminar of senior economists brought together by the National Institute of Economic and Social Research mostly concluded that the 'deindustrialisation' faced by the British economy 'was an 1870s rather than a 1970s problem' (Blackaby 1978, pp. 263–4).

Barnett (1986) has argued that the creation of the Welfare State took precedence over developing a more dynamic enterprise culture. There was insufficient attention paid to technical education. There was little idea of an industrial strategy. Whitehall was geared to thinking in terms of stability rather than innovation. Keynesian deficit financing obscured structural problems with the economy which were not addressed. The result was that the 'New Jerusalem' of the Welfare State began to disintegrate as British economic performance fell behind and 'turned to a dark reality of a segregated, sub-literate, unskilled, unhealthy and institutionalised proletariat hanging on the nipple of state maternalism' (Barnett 1986, p. 304).

But Barnett's argument assumes too readily that the Post-War Settlement and economic progress were mutually exclusive alternatives. Certainly other European countries found it possible to create both. Britain's recovery after the Second World War was certainly preferable to that after the First World War when policies of balanced budgets and fiscal stringency presided over the 1920–2 slump and enduring mass unemployment. It could surely be argued, as Beveridge did, that low unemployment and the Welfare State, by increasing the economic security of the working class, could also contribute to productivity as well as bargaining power. Indeed, given the shape of public feeling in 1945 and the climate of a European world where the old political order was compromised and the legitimacy of the newly emerging one depended on its ability to espouse popular and national interests, it is difficult to see how any government could have done less and maintained its legitimacy. Anderson (1986) suggests that a more plausible reason for the technical and economic deficiencies outlined by Barnett was the dominance, from the onset of industrialisation, of City interests over industry. Not only was modernisation neglected. The economic policies it would have required would have conflicted with those of the City.

What is striking, in this context, once we recall our discussion of the origins of Britain's economy and industrial relations in Chapter 2, is how far developments since 1979 have brought back elements of the nineteenth century regime from which decline commenced. We have on the one hand a domestic industry with a declining ability to compete in international markets, or with foreign competitors in the domestic market. In contrast to the Thatcherites' professed aim of reforming the 'supply side' of the domestic economy, we have seen little evidence from its performance to suggest this has been done. We examine some of the detailed aspects of change in the supply side of the economy in Chapters 6 and 7, but we could note meanwhile that its ills, as in the nineteenth century, appear to be related to an over-reliance on short-term horizons. There is too little spent on investment, research and development, training. Just as a strong currency (in the interests of the City) damaged industry after World War One, so it did from 1980 to 1982. Currency fluctuations, high interest rates and a takeover boom focussed attention on maximising short-term profits and made long-term investment risky. The domestic sources of inflation such as wages and interest rates remained high. Price inflation was helped down (as in the rest of the OECD) by falling oil and commodity prices. On the other hand, we have a booming City, and a flood of overseas investment, both direct and indirect, which has restored a prime role to income from foreign investment in bridging what is not yet a trade gap (because of the contribution of North Sea oil) but is already a large and growing deficit on manufactured trade. By 1986, income from foreign assets was running at £4.3 billion per annum. The challenge which the economic changes engineered by Thatcherism posed to industrial relations had therefore relatively little to do with altering the structure or behaviour of the economy. Its main impact was to increase unemployment greatly, principally by wiping out large sections of manufacturing industry.

CHAPTER 6

Management and Industrial Relations in the Workplace, 1979–1986

> Managers for twenty years have had a buffeting and beating from government and unions and we have been put in a can't win situation ... we have an opportunity now that will last for two or three years. Then the unions will get themselves together again; and the government, like all governments, will run out of steam. So grab it now. We have had a pounding and we are all fed up with it. I think it would be fair to say that it's almost vengeance.
>
> Len Collinson, Managing Director and Management Consultant, *Financial Times*, 5 January 1981.

> All over British manufacturing industry, managers are celebrating their return to life and power, like eunuchs miraculously restored to wholeness and to potency.
>
> Turner (1981)

An employers' offensive?

There is a widespread assumption, shared equally by those who support and oppose Thatcherism, that it encouraged employers to mount an anti-union offensive in the workplace, sweep away restrictive practices, intensify and reorganise work, marginalise unions and forge a new more direct relationship with their weakened workforces who gave their consent to these changes and came to identify with the fortunes of their employer. As well as high unemployment and legal changes, economic restructuring further undermined trade union power by shifting the economy away from areas of union strength (see, for example, Beaumont 1987 for a discussion of these views.) There are examples, too, which fit this scenario. In British Leyland, in 1979 Michael Edwardes successfully sacked the senior convener Derek Robinson effectively for opposing management's policies for the company. He then pushed through wide-ranging changes in working practices and several very low wage deals. In British Steel, the workforce was reduced by nearly two-thirds by 1986. At Wapping, News International were able to relocate the production of their newspapers, introduce new technology using a non-union workforce (recruited with the help of the EETPU in anticipation of a single-union agreement) and sack their existing employees. In the *Stockport Messenger* dispute the attempt by the National Graphical Association (NGA) to enforce a closed shop was beaten by the failure of mass picketing, the imposition of fines and the sequestration of the union's assets. And, of course, there was the miner's strike. After a year-long strike to reverse pit closures, the National Union of Miners was left bankrupt, its members demoralised and desperately poor, many made redundant or sacked, its influence with local and national management gone, and facing a breakaway union in the Union of Democratic Mineworkers.

These are important examples, but there are others which could be cited. It is too easy to remember Wapping or Stockport and forget that in March 1980 the NGA won its dispute with the British Printing Industries Federation hands down. The steel strike of 1980, the longest national dispute since the war, ended in a deal worth around 16 per cent, compared to the original offer to the workforce of 2 per cent plus 4 per cent with strings and local bonuses. However the dispute left the union too exhausted to resist the closures which followed. Derek Robinson was sacked but a threatened dispute in May 1981 forced Ford to withdraw a tougher disciplinary code it had proposed. In September 1980, the dock employers withdrew attempts to abandon their policy of 'no compulsory redundancies' in the face of a threatened strike. The traffic was not all one way.

The cases where employers have gone on the offensive appear to be of two types. First, where the government is the ultimate employer, the pressures on management to change policy towards unions have been direct. But even here the government had to prepare its ground carefully. Thus in February 1981 (despite the fact that the Conservatives had been planning their assault on miners' power even while in opposition) the government granted extra subsidies to the National Coal Board to avert pit closures which provoked a vote to strike in the Yorkshire and Wales areas. Private sector employers would have found it very difficult to sustain the cost of the set-piece battles which took place in coal and steel and the disputes in the civil service: it was an option which only potentially limitless public funds could sustain. Second, in Fleet Street printing, car plants and the coal and steel industries the bargaining position of employees was particularly weak, because employers had high levels of unsold stock and low levels of demand, because there was a readily substitutable labour force available, or because the employers wanted to close down large sections of their operations. These conditions were not widespread in the economy as a whole except during the height of the slump when the government's economic policies meant that closure was a danger for many manufacturing plants.

Nor should we assume a community of outlook between employers and the government. It was, after all, a government offensive against employers, in the shape of increased interest and exchange rates and lower public capital spending and borrowing, which was supposed to initiate the whole procedure. For the Thatcherites, employers were as much to blame as unions for acceding to 'soft' deals which restricted efficiency and fuelled wage inflation. Thus employers had good reason to be hostile to a policy of drastic deflation which slashed their profits and forced them to cut back production. The evidence of many large manufacturing employers to the House of Lords Select Committee on Overseas Trade showed their frustration (Aldington 1985). That is why Sir Terrence Beckett, then Director General of the CBI, called in November 1980 for a 'bare knuckle fight' with the government over its policies. But the reaction to Beckett's speech showed that, whatever the reservations of manufacturing employers, most agreed with the Prime Minister's claim that there was no alternative to her policies. According to Leys (1985, p. 13):

> Beckett was obliged to disown his militant position when a number of major companies whose chairmen were close to the Conservative leadership left the CBI and others threatened to follow suit. Thereafter the CBI offered no further public criticism of the government's policies.

This partly expressed the continued absence of any real employer solidarity or institution capable of representing the collective interest and outlook of either employers in general or manufacturing employers in particular. The CBI might venture opinions on a range of issues, but it had virtually no ability to act as a collective instrument of employer interests, or as a body capable of organising and shaping the perception of that interest. For example, a plan to establish a strike insurance fund in 1980 proved abortive. CBI members welcomed the principle but baulked at the costs involved. Kellner (1985, p. 9) has argued that the CBI is a feeble and marginal organisation, lacking the involvement of Britain's major employers:

> each of the three words that comprise the initials 'CBI' is misleading. It is not a complete confederation ... Nor is the conference truly British [in 1985 the] third biggest delegation with seven [members] came from ... the British subsidiary of an American hospital chain ... Nor does it properly speak for industry. Of the ten largest delegations, three came from the banks and three from the service sector ... By contrast many of Britain's major manufacturing companies sent just one delegate each — usually from second tier management — with the apparent aim of keeping an eye on the proceedings rather than contributing to them.

One factor prompting employers to throw in their lot with Thatcherism was their anxiety about where corporatism and tripartism could lead as the pressures of Britain's poor economic performance grew. This anxiety had also been decisive in persuading Conservatives to tolerate Thatcherism. In the course of 1980 the CBI moved decisively away from tripartism. As late as June it produced the document *Jobs: Facing the Future* which proposed tripartite discussions about unemployment and productivity. In 1978 it had supported the idea of a national Economic Forum as a basis for influencing pay and salary negotiations. But by September 1980 it was withdrawing endorsement of the joint statement on new technology it had drafted with the TUC. Relations deteriorated and by July 1981 the TUC announced it had broken off all informal links with the CBI. The latter became more vociferous in its calls for cuts in public sector spending and public sector pay and pensions, in order to free up more resources for the private sector. In 1982 its conference reversed its previous policy and rejected the idea of a national Economic Forum in principle.

Leys (1985) argues that the Bullock Report on industrial democracy crystallised employers' anxiety about a corporatist future, and gave the CBI an issue which its diverse and divided membership could agree on. In 1979 a 'Steering Committee on the Balance of Power' was established which focused on the issue of reducing union power and establishing employers' independence from state regulation:

> During these years much of the CBI leadership, not just the small business membership, came to believe that (as one industrialist expressed it) 'Mrs Thatcher's government is all that stands between [us] and a rapid slide into a down-market version of the German Democratic Republic'. In the mid-1970s a majority of manufacturing executives had come to feel that the survival of capitalism was at stake. They judged that unless trade union power was drastically reduced, control of capital would pass out of owners' hands and profits from manufacturing would progressively disappear. Consequently short-term business interests, and even the long-term interests of individuals or firms, had to be sacrificed. Even those who were unconvinced by the Thatcherite project saw no realistic political alternative (Leys 1985, p. 17).

Such fears about where corporatism could lead hark back to the reliance on market forces and the absence of any development of closer relations between the state or finance capital and industry which we examined in Chapter 2. There were also other long established features of British industry which help explain its reaction to Thatcherism. The weakness of the CBI and divisions within employers reflected the absence of any organisation able to represent the district interests of British domestic manufacturers, as against the service sector or the City. In turn since many domestic manufacturers also had a strong international base, the abolition of exchange controls meant they could adjust to adverse trading conditions at home by expanding investment and employment overseas: Chapter 5 showed how important this was. Finally most employers were attracted by a government that appeared to promise to take responsibility for dealing with union power itself, rather than exhorting employers to act. In this context it was possible for industrialists to tolerate economic policies which in the short term worsened their trading position and profits.

However, a public retreat from tripartism nationally — in the face of a government set on such a course anyway — does not prove that employers proceeded to throw over their previous labour relations policies in their own workplaces. There are three main considerations which should be borne in mind when we proceed to examine the empirical evidence of how employers actually did respond to Thatcherism. First, however much employers might welcome a workforce in a weaker bargaining position, they also have an interest in maintaining good relations with their workforce. They desire order, predictability and trust. Just as in the nineteenth century employers wanted the state to take the initiative in undermining union organisation, in the 1980s employers had good reasons to emphasise the responsibility of their local union officials and members and to maintain their goodwill. Indeed their need to do this probably grew and was if anything enhanced by the recession. As Bendix (1956, p. 251) puts it:

> In modern industry the cooperation needed involves the spirit in which subordinates exercise their judgment. Beyond what commands can effect and supervision can control, beyond what incentives can induce and penalties prevent, there exists an exercise of discretion important even in relatively menial jobs, which managers of economic enterprises seek to enlist for the achievement of managerial ends.

Employers might rail against the effects of unionism and union members themselves believe that unions have too much power, but both managers and workers tend to believe that their own unions are different and more 'realistic'. For many employers 'the unions' are simply their own workforce. To mount an offensive against them as union members, while maintaining their morale and commitment as workers, would be very difficult to do. It would also mean introducing a far more elaborate personnel policy than British employers had evolved in the past and taking on functions previously performed by the union.

Second, while the economic difficulties which employers face may put a premium on cost control and competitiveness, this need not lead them to identify industrial relations or even the organisation of labour as the area where their problems could be solved. There is a major debate about how far the British workforce or workplace industrial relations are in fact responsible for Britain's poor economic performance (Nichols 1986). It is beyond the scope of this book to resolve this debate but the uncertainty and lack of good evidence surrounding this proposition at least makes it clear that employers themselves might believe that their most important priorities lay elsewhere: in marketing, in new products or design, in management reorganisation, in changing the location or sector of production. All these decisions might have longer-term implications for how labour was treated, but they certainly did not start out from that. It is too easy and very misleading to assume that employers or their managers see labour as 'the' problem or the main objective of their activity. It is not. It is but one element in a process of management that includes many others. Moreover, as we saw in Chapter 2 British employers paid little attention to the deployment of labour. Fidler (1981) found that most senior management does not have much background in production. Thus, while Michael Edwardes or Len Collinson might represent one strand of management opinion, there were other more cautious voices to be heard. Paul Roots (*Guardian*, 19 August 1985), industrial relations director of Ford UK, argued that 'the only useful result of weakening unions was that it had removed management's excuse for Britain's thirty years of relative inefficiency. Low productivity "has never been a problem of British trade unions" '.

Third, British management's attitude to labour and labour relations, as outlined in Chapter 2, would make an offensive against labour unlikely. If labour is viewed as a cost to be minimised rather than a resource to be developed then a crisis in revenues is surely more likely to lead to redundancies than a whole new approach to the organisation and deployment of labour. The high level of redundancies reported in Chapter 5 suggest this was indeed the usual response. A new strategy towards labour embracing participation, anti-unionism and the fostering of a new 'enterprise consciousness' in the workplace would require not just new resources, but the overthrow of long-established methods of management. Such a change might be in the objective interests of British capital and the economic crisis precipitated by Thatcherism might have made it urgent for British capital to pursue these interests more single-mindedly, but that does not mean that individual employers therefore had either the resolve or the resources to revolutionise their industrial relations. It is therefore necessary to study the empirical evidence of what change did in fact take place.

Procedural and institutional change

There are a number of surveys which provide evidence on whether employers did in fact use the economic and legal changes fostered by the government to change industrial relations in their firms. In 1983 Eric Batstone conducted a small survey of large manufacturing plants, which could be compared with the Warwick Industrial Relations Research Unit study done in 1978 (Batstone 1984; Brown 1981). In 1984 Warwick conducted a further survey of manufacturing (Edwards 1985a) and in the following year a survey of industrial relations arrangements at enterprise level including the service sector (Marginson *et al.* 1986). All these surveys provide useful information, but the most comprehensive data are provided by the two Workplace Industrial Relations Surveys (WIRS) carried out in 1980 and 1984. As well as providing data on establishments with 25 or more employees in all sectors of the economy, the 1984 survey included a small panel of about 200 workplaces which were surveyed in both years, allowing a direct account of change over the four years in these workplaces. These surveys give us a much broader view of industrial relations change than accounts of individual employers' actions or the course of particular disputes, but they neither obviate the need for case studies nor provide evidence which is necessarily more 'scientific' or 'objective'. Surveys are limited in the sort of data they can reliably collect and measure, are dependent on the accuracy of the information provided by the respondents and the quality of the questions devised by the social scientists who design them. Thus there is always substantial room for debate about just what survey results *mean*. Case studies have these drawbacks, too, but at the cost of greater amounts of researcher time and greater problems of representativeness of results they provide more qualitative information about processes and change over time.

Surveys are especially useful for providing data on industrial relations institutions and procedures. It is useful to consider what changes have taken place in these first, and then to look at the evidence about whether the way these institutions and procedures have been used is changing and therefore what the substantive outcomes have been, in terms of earnings, working methods, disputes, and so on. Despite the common assumption that change has been widespread, the overwhelming message provided by all the surveys on almost all aspects of procedure is that things have stayed pretty much the same. There is evidence of lower levels of union organisation in private manufacturing but most of it is explicable by the patterns of employment change there. Conversely, in private services union organisation seems to have increased. If there has been an employer offensive it has left remarkably few traces, whether in terms of existing employers changing their approach or new employers adopting a different one to their counterparts of five or ten years ago.

Union recognition and representation
The study in 1984 by Edwards (1985a) of manufacturing establishments with more than 250 employees covered three-fifths of the total manufacturing workforce in a sector where union power was concentrated in 1979 and where we might expect procedural change to be concentrated. He found that only one plant in five had made any change in bargaining arrangements over the previous two years, and most of these were described as 'encouraging awareness of the need for change'. None had ended their closed shop or removed facilities for stewards, and only 3 per cent had reduced the number or influence of stewards or conveners. Compared to the 1978 survey there had been a small drop in manual union recognition but half the plants still reported 100 per cent union membership for manual workers. However, the number of plants with full-time shop stewards for manual workers had fallen from a quarter of all plants to one-sixth. Batstone's (1984) survey reached similar conclusions, although he identified a very small number of plants where unions had previously been powerful and there was evidence of management attempts to reduce their influence. Batstone and Edwards's findings are significant because they concentrate on the sector where an employer's offensive should have occurred — in large manufacturing plants — and in the period when it should have occurred — in 1981–2 as the commitment of the government to its policies and the depth of the slump they precipitated had become clear to employers.

Comparisons of the two Workplace Industrial Relations Surveys provides evidence on the whole economy for the period between 1980 and 1984. Evidence from the 181 'panel' plants showed only three cases where it looked as if management had withdrawn union recognition since 1980 compared to nine where it had been granted. After examining these cases, Millward and Stevens (1986, p.

68) concluded that any changes in recognition in established workplaces must have been rare. In terms of net changes between the two surveys there appeared to be a substantial drop in recognition in private manufacturing, but a rise in both the private services and the public sector. Overall there was a slight rise in the proportion of workplaces in the economy which recognised unions from 66 to 68 per cent. There was also a small fall in the proportion of workplaces where there were union members but no union recognition: an anti-union drive would tend to produce the opposite result. Millward and Stevens concluded that the bulk of the change in recognition in manufacturing was explained by employment change: average union density (which was closely related to recognition) was three times higher in plants which had reduced employment substantially than in those which had grown substantially. This finding does not mean that changing employment patterns were rolling back union organisation overall, rather that job losses were concentrated in the sectors of manufacturing where unions were strongest, such as large plants. More extensive recognition in private services suggests that unions were still coping well with structural changes in employment, in the way they had done in the 1960s and 1970s. Coverage of the closed shop did contract, perhaps by about $1\frac{1}{4}$ million workers, or about one-quarter of those covered. Again the main explanation was the pattern of employment decline in manufacturing and the public sector, but this is unlikely to have been the only cause (Millward and Stevens 1986, p. 105). Despite the publicity given to single-union agreements, there seemed to be little change in multi-unionism either, both in terms of the number of unions employers recognised and the number of bargaining units they dealt with.

It seems, too, that collective bargaining with unions has also survived intact. As Chapter 2 pointed out, recognition and collective bargaining in Britain has been strongest in the public sector. In the private sector it has been less universal and it has been more extensive in manufacturing than in services and for manual rather than white-collar workers. In 1980 five-sixths of manual workers in private manufacturing had their pay determined by collective bargaining, compared to about half in private services. The corresponding proportions for non-manual workers were three-fifths and two-fifths. Table 6.1 shows the changes by sector and type of employee between 1980 and 1984. Again the only area of decline in bargaining was private manufacturing, and was mostly attributable to changes in plant size. The proportion of workplaces where pay was decided by collective

Table 6.1 Percentage of workforce whose pay is determined by collective bargaining: 1984 (1980)

	Private manufacturing	*Private services*
Manual	79 (84)	53 (53)
White-collar	79 (63)	40 (37)

Source: Millward and Stevens (1986 ch. 9)

bargaining increased except for manual workers in manufacturing (Millward and Stevens 1986, ch. 9).

As we might expect from the continued growth of union recognition and collective bargaining in the workplace, the shop-steward system remained intact. Estimates produced by the WIRS researchers shown in Table 6.2 show that the number of stewards increased between 1980 and 1984 despite the overall fall in employment. There was a large fall in private manufacturing, particularly of full-time stewards, but as with recognition and bargaining, a large part of this fall is attributable to employment change: the number of stewards in manufacturing fell more slowly than the numbers employed in manufacturing. The number of stewards increased by nearly one-fifth in private services and by almost one-third in the public sector. The numbers also showed that 'the stereotype of the trade union representative as a manual shop steward in manufacturing industry evidently needs revision' (Millward and Stevens 1986, p. 86). Less than a quarter of stewards were representatives of manual workers in private manufacturing industry and there were almost as many white-collar stewards as manual ones. There were no dramatic changes in the way these stewards organised. They were as likely as before to be involved in a multi-plant 'combine' committee but perhaps slightly less likely to meet as a joint stewards committee in multi-union plants.

Table 6.2   Numbers of trade union representatives (thousands)

	TOTAL	Private Manufacturing		Private Services		Public Sector	
		Manual	White-collar	Manual	White-collar	Manual	White-collar
1980	317	95	35	26	14	62	86
1984	335	72	23	23	24	77	116

Source: Millward and Stevens 1986, p. 84.

These results suggest that the basic institutions of workplace trade unionism survived the economic and legal assault of Thatcherism. Edwards (1985b, p. 35) concluded from his results that 'managements in large firms have not been engaged in a systematic attack on unions'. He was surely right. When we consider the impact of economic restructuring the results suggest that workplace trade unionism did rather well in this period. The unions appeared to be increasing their organisation in areas of the economy in which they had been weaker such as private services and in white-collar jobs and which were the expanding areas of the economy. To this extent the unions were continuing their successes of the 1970s. But there are two qualifications to this picture. First, it could be argued that given what we know about the pattern of economic change in manufacturing the unions could have been expected to maintain an even stronger position. When we attribute declining union strength in manufacturing to the dramatic fall in plant sizes recorded in Chapter 5 it is because many studies have shown that union organisation is stronger in bigger plants. But we know from our analysis of economic restructuring that the major cause of the fall in plant sizes in manufacturing was not the growing weight of new smaller plants in the economy but the shedding of jobs in existing plants and closure of large plants. The closure of large and well-organised plants lessened the average overall level of union organisation. But in some plants which shed jobs union organisation must have weakened so that the level of organisation overall became similar to that existing in comparable smaller plants of a few years ago, and was not simply the same level of organisation that existed in these plants *before* they grew smaller.

A second qualification is that plant-based survey evidence on the private services sector provides us with a less complete picture than it does of either manufacturing or the public sector because there are many more small businesses in the private services, especially in sectors like shops, hotels, catering and business services. The cut-off point in the WIRS surveys is 25 employees. In manufacturing this excludes less than one-tenth of employees, even with the recent fall in average plant size. But in private services it excludes up to a half or more of employees in some sectors. It would be reasonable to assume that union organisation is much lower in these small shops, offices, pubs, and so on. Evidence from this is available from the 1985 New Earnings Survey. It gives estimates of the proportion of employees covered by collective agreements in each industry: a figure which is roughly equivalent to those for bargaining we have examined from WIRS. Only 28 per cent of employees were covered by a collective pay agreement in retail and wholesale distribution, hotels, pubs and catering, and business services. This compared with 64 per cent for all industries and services. The figure of 28 per cent may still overstate union strength as it refers to full-time workers on adult rates: union coverage of youngsters and part-timers would be lower. In 1984, the British Social Attitudes Survey estimated that in workplaces with less than 25 employees, 27 per cent were union members. What the data from surveys such as WIRS therefore tell us is how the relatively larger employers in private services were behaving. It seems reasonable to assume that in small business in private services, which was a substantial and expanding area of the economy, trade union organisation was much weaker. This was not a new phenomenon: union organisation has always been very weak in this sector, as Chapter 2 pointed out, and the growth of employment in this sector has been going on for decades, as we saw in Chapter 5. But it is a phenomenon which may increase in importance with increased unemployment, as we discuss later on in this chapter.

Personnel and industrial relations management
Any employers' offensive would have changed or downgraded the role of personnel or industrial relations management compared to line managers since the latter have usually been assumed to have a less close relationship with unions, and be more concerned with production and profit than employee relations. In fact evidence from all the surveys suggests that the opposite happened. Fifty-eight per cent of chief executives surveyed by Edwards thought that the personnel function had become more important. Nearly a half of head office personnel managers in the

Warwick enterprise-level study thought the influence of their function had increased. The WIRS 1984 survey confirmed this finding for other sectors as well as manufacturing, and also suggested that changes in industrial relations law and issue of employee involvement were two of the main reasons for the change that managers identified. Of course, this leaves open the question of just what personnel managers were doing with their increased influence and on what terms it was being offered to them.

Employers had at their disposal the new industrial relations laws but here, too, the evidence suggests that they did not rush to avail themselves of them for the same reason that there was no rush after the Taff Vale case in 1901, and for the same reason that employers had been reluctant to invoke the law for the last two centuries. Using the law threatened to disrupt established relationships of trust and good will with trade union officials and members which would need to last long after any particular dispute had finished. Evans (1985) found only 34 cases where injunctions had been used in industrial disputes between 1980 and 1984, half concerning picketing, about one-third concerning unlawful secondary action. In this period there were over 5,000 strikes. A project on the use of the law on picketing confirmed employers' traditional approach to the law. They used it according to Evans (1985, p. 134)

> to reinforce rather than undermine the 'rules of the game' with the union. They used the threat of legal penalties to demoralise strikers and pickets into handing over control of the dispute to the senior ranks of the union ... Injunctions were more likely to be used where managements could clearly see that those taking the unlawful action lacked cohesion and were isolated from other would be supporters and carried little influence with union officials.

The Industrial Relations Director of Ford argued that 'in many areas of industrial relations the law was irrelevant, having more to do with political exigencies and public opinion than industrial reality' (Edwards 1986, p. 5). It could, of course, be argued that, in contrast to their public protestations of defiance, in practice the economic situation forced unions to knuckle under the law and avoid taking action which ran foul of it, but evidence of such a course of action was not widespread. Far more important has been the ability of the law to hamper unions contending with a divided workforce or one in a very weak bargaining position. As we discuss below, that is probably the lesson of the two encounters which have dominated public discussion of Thatcherism and industrial relations: the miners' strike and the News International dispute at Wapping.

Bargaining structure

It has also been widely assumed and asserted that Thatcherism encouraged employers to hasten the decentralisation of bargaining in Britain, rendering national bargaining less important, and making bargaining within individual plants, usually by shop stewards rather than full-time officials, more important. Before considering the survey evidence it is useful to bear two points in mind. First, decentralisation is a long-established feature of British industrial relations, particularly in manufacturing. As Chapter 2 showed, the Donovan Report concentrated on the issue of formalising local bargaining which had been growing since the 1950s. Second, decentralisation has always been much weaker in the public sector and in private services, as we discussed in Chapter 2. Because of this it would be reasonable to expect restructuring in the 1980s to have reduced the process of decentralisation as enterprise- or industry-wide bargaining in private services covered more workers. This is indeed what the WIRS 1984 results, reproduced in Tables 6.3 and 6.4, show. There were not dramatic changes in bargaining levels within sectors. If anything there was a slight shift towards company rather than plant bargaining in private manufacturing, and a shift towards company bargaining from national bargaining in private services. In 1984 about half of the workers covered by bargaining in manufacturing bargained primarily at plant level. Conversely, about five-sixths of workers in private services had their pay bargaining based at national, industrial or company level.

Table 6.3 Percentage of workforce whose pay is determined by plant-level collective bargaining: 1984 (1980)

	Private manufacturing	*Private services*
Manual	35 (41)	8 (6)
White-collar	35 (36)	6 (5)

Source: Millward and Stevens (1986 pp. 228–237)

Table 6.4 Most important level of collective bargaining for most recent pay increase in establishment: 1984 (1980)

	Manual Employees	*White-collar Employees*
National/regional	40 (32)	36 (29)
Company/divisional	13 (12)	13 (11)
Plant/establishment	7 (9)	4 (4)
Other	1 (1)	1 (2)
Not result of collective bargaining	38 (44)	46 (53)

Source: Millward and Stevens (1986 p. 226)

Participation, involvement and industrial democracy

A final area of procedural change to consider is that of participation. As we noted in Chapter 1, it was possible that rather than mounting an attack on union organisation, employers might instead try to change the basis of industrial relations by using their increased bargaining power to develop closer, more cooperative relations with their own workforces and promote enterprise unionism and consciousness. This is clearly what the government and the CBI both hoped for. An additional factor was the threat of European legislation on participation in the form of the Fifth Draft Directive on Company Law and the Vredeling proposals from the Social Affairs Committee of the Commission. These measures raised the spectre of Bullock for British employers. There was also great public support for the principle of industrial democracy and participation and other European governments were sympathetic to the EEC proposals. The government's response was twofold. It sought to draw a distinction between 'genuine' industrial democracy which was based on employee involvement, developed voluntarily and flexibly according to the needs of each company, and 'rigid', 'inflexible' workers' control promoted by legislation which simply interfered with efficient management. It argued that the former was in everyone's best interests, and that British management was now developing such initiatives on a large scale because the government's policies had removed the barriers to such an approach caused by militant unionism and had encouraged a 'new realism' in the attitudes of both employers and employees. Tougher trading conditions meant they had to work together to survive. This upsurge of voluntary developments, the government argued, obviated the need for legislation which it effectively vetoed at the EEC in 1984. Behind the scenes ministers lobbied hard for the CBI, the Engineering Employers Federation (EEF) and other bodies to exhort their members to develop participation and employee involvement in visible ways. There was a considerable publicity effort, and many employers and management organisations produced guidelines, codes of practice and such like (see MacInnes 1985; and Cressey *et al.* 1985.) There were waves of enthusiasm in particular approaches, such as quality circles, briefing groups, team briefings and the use of video to promote employee communications.

Secondly, the government advocated profit sharing through employee share ownership schemes or profit-related pay as a practical form of employee involvement which would ultimately remove all barriers between manager and worker, so that Kenneth Clarke (1987, p. 21), Paymaster General, argued:

> I would like to see people moving away from a total reliance on wages towards sharing profits ... I see the divide between owners and earners as divisive and self defeating. People without a stake in the enterprise may believe they have little to lose from its failure and nothing to gain from its success.

However, the results of WIRS 84 suggest that this exercise resulted in very little change on the ground. Probably the main institutional avenue for employee participation continued to be joint consultation. Yet its overall coverage remained about the same, and possibly fell between 1980 and 1984. Edwards found evidence of new committees and upgrading of committees in his survey, but MacInnes (1985) argued that such a finding was to be expected: joint consultation tended to be marginal or unstable so that new or stronger committees arrived while older ones declined or petered out. Indeed it is doubtful whether the incidence of joint consultation has changed much in Britain since the Second World War. A small survey by Marchington and Armstrong (1985) confirmed this trend. They revisited 18 firms in 1984 which they had studied in 1980:

> What struck us was the lack of uniformity in development in consultative arrangements. Some have been revitalised whilst others have collapsed. ... On the direct employee involvement front, it is the range of techniques rather than the similarity which is most apparent.

A longitudinal study of six companies by Cressey *et al.* (1985) reached more pessimistic conclusions about the fate of participation. They concluded that the effect of the recession was probably more likely to undermine than promote participation, because managers and employees had very different approaches to it.

The WIRS 1984 survey produced results on wider participation initiatives which must be interpreted carefully. They found that managers in over a third of workplaces reported some initiative to increase participation, compared with just under a quarter in the 1980 survey. 'Structural' changes, such as new joint meetings or committees, had stayed about the same or declined: they were reported in less than a tenth of all workplaces. The biggest increase was in 'two-way communications' and a miscellany of other initiatives. This is reminiscent of companies in the Edwards survey which reported 'creating awareness of the need for change' as the way in which they had changed bargaining arrangements. However, when stewards were asked the same questions, only just over half as many reported participation initiatives. They reported the same pattern of initiatives as managers, but at a consistently lower level. For example, 8 per cent of stewards compared to 14 per cent of managers reported that there was 'more two-way communication'. Millward and Stevens (1986) note that the pattern of steward and manager responses is similar and a third of all responses about initiatives happening concerned 'two-way communication'. Because of this they argue that

> the qualitative change reported by managers is validated by the representatives of those affected, giving perhaps the clearest possible indication that there has been a change in the *type* of initiative that managements have been taking on employee involvement in the early 1980s as compared with the late 1970s (Millward and Stevens, 1986 p. 167, emphasis in original).

Such a conclusion would have been stronger had the authors shown that it was in the same workplaces that stewards and managers reported participation initiatives, but this was not investigated. 'Two-way communication' could hardly have been a new focus of employer initiative in participation when less than one in ten of stewards (who are presumably usually supposed to be part of such an initiative) report its occurrence. The WIRS 1984 survey also found that 'systematic use of the management chain' was the most frequently reported means of communication used by management, ahead of meetings between managers and employees, and newsletters (Millward and Stevens 1986, pp. 151–3). It is reasonable to conclude from this pattern of response that managers, especially senior managers aware of the political and public pressure for participation, have in some cases made some effort to communicate more with employees, usually using the line-management chain. However, their subordinates did not necessarily prioritise it to the same extent (they were perhaps under other urgent pressures to cut costs or throughput times, increase efficiency and such like which conflicted with the desire to communicate), nor did they necessarily feel they were as well trained in the art of communication or adept at handling queries or controversy as their superiors who in any case did not need to face the workforce direct.

Further embarrassing evidence for the government came from the results of the statements of employee involvement produced by companies in their annual report and accounts which was required by the Lords amendment to the 1982 Employment Act (which the government opposed). Not only was the absolute level of response low, the statements produced were vague and general. Despite continued efforts by employers' associations and the Department of Employment, the second round of reports proved worse: many companies simply repeated their original statement rather than reporting on practical developments over the course of the year.

The evidence is overwhelming that Thatcherism did not change the institutions and procedures of British workplace industrial relations. It is worth emphasising this point because the opposite has so frequently been asserted or assumed: as much by the proponents of Thatcherism as by its opponents. Unlike the United States, where particular industries or particular regions have become no-go areas for unions, there has been no such assault on unionism in Britain. Unlike the 1920s and 1930s, when the post-war slump followed by employer hostility and unemployment sent union density crashing to half its former level, workplaces of the same sort had just about as many union members in 1984 as in 1980. The extent of non-unionism has been exaggerated by accounts which fail to consider the overall incidence of the phenomenon they investigate. For example, Beaumont (1985) and Cairns (1985) found high levels of non-unionism in high-tech plants in Scotland, especially in new town greenfield sites. But these surveys, like many others, were overwhelmingly of very small new companies where union organisation in Britain has never been strong. Moreover, the trend of economic change in manufacturing throughout the 1970s and into the 1980s has been to *lessen* the amount of employment in such new, small, growing firms (MacInnes 1987). A survey at the end of 1984 of Scottish electronics firms in fact found levels of union recognition similar to those in other sectors of manufacturing industry. It also confirmed that multi-unionism was the norm, in contrast to the well-reported signing of single-union agreements by the

EETPU in electronics in Wales (MacInnes and Sproull 1986). Bassett's (1986) study of no-strike agreements and single-union deals is a similar case in point. Bassett himself is careful to point out that the arrangements he describes cover only a tiny proportion of the British workforce, perhaps 9,000 workers altogether.

This is all the more striking because the scale of the slump unleashed on British manufacturing was unprecedented: a 50 per cent fall in its international labour competitiveness, a fall in output of one-sixth, a fall in employment of one-third, a fall in average size of plant of over one-quarter. Despite this economic carnage there was not much weakening of the unions' formal position. In the service sector of the economy, which was spared the more dramatic effects of the government's policies, union organisation probably increased. The final section of this chapter discusses why this happened but first we examine a second dimension of the evidence: how these institutions and procedures worked and what substantive results they produced. It could be argued that employers kept procedures intact because they could afford in practice to ignore or circumvent them, that beyond an unchanged formal system lay the reality of new working relationships and weaker union influences.

The breakdown of procedure: strikes and industrial action

The Conservative government made much both of the industrial 'turmoil' represented by strikes in the 1970s and of its success in curbing strikes. Industrial action is not a straightforward piece of evidence to use, however, to indicate either union strength or the 'quality' of industrial relations. Strong unions need not strike to achieve their objectives, weak ones may be pressed into action they would rather not risk taking. Edwards and Scullion (1982) have shown that strikes are only one form of industrial action or worker resistance. Indeed they suggested that more sophisticated union organisations relied less on strikes. The decision to strike, rather than to take other forms, will probably take into account factors like high unemployment. It is therefore quite possible to have fewer strikes, but an increase in other forms of action. Strike levels vary dramatically from one year to the next, so that figures for single years are unreliable as indicators of general trends. Table 6.5 compares the figures from 1975 to 1984. It shows that there has been little absolute change in days lost through strikes. In the more strike-prone industries the number increased because of the coal strike. Elsewhere in the OECD countries rising unemployment and depressed trading conditions reduced strike activity, so that Britain's 'league position' in terms of strike activity increased from seventh to fifth overall, and in strike-prone industries from sixth to third. Even this comparison flatters the government's record, however. The strike rate was three times its previous level in 1979 but the bulk of days lost were not during the 'Winter of Discontent' but during the national engineering dispute which occurred in September, after the general election.

Table 6.5   Industrial action 1975–9 and 1980–4.
Working days lost per 1,000 employees (WDL)
Place in league table of 21 OECD countries (Place)

	1975–9		1980–4	
	WDL	Place	WDL	Place
All industries and services	510	7	480	5
Manufacturing, mining and quarrying construction, transport and communications	980	6	1,070	3

Source: Department of Employment Gazette, July 1986, p. 267.

The pattern of industrial action does seem to have changed. The WIRS surveys found that the proportion of workplaces experiencing strikes increased by about half, from 13 per cent in 1980 to 19 per cent in 1984, but this was attributable to a fall of about half in manufacturing (and two-thirds in vehicles plants) and a rise in the public services sector. Strikes and other action by manual workers declined, but those by non-manuals increased. WIRS 1984 also investigated the reasons for industrial action. The most common reason for strikes continued to be pay disputes, but stoppages for other reasons, including disputes about privatisation, were important. These findings are significant when it is remembered that since the survey asked about industrial action in the previous twelve months the period 1983–84 is being compared with that of 1979–80, when there were several widespread stoppages in industry, including the national engineering dispute and the steel strike. Despite changes in the experience of particular sectors such as car plants, the overall figures for industrial action suggest that Thatcherism has not ushered in an era of industrial peace where there was previously strife. As with so much else, little has changed.

Substantive change at workplace level

Many of the claims made about changes in industrial relations over the period 1979–1986 centre on changed attitudes, increased cooperation, and the spirit of 'new realism' among workers. Batstone (1984, p.234) puts the case well:

> it does not follow that management have not tried to reduce the role which the unions in practice play within the workplace. If they were successful in such endeavours, then there would be little need to engage in a frontal assault on trade unions. Similarly if shop stewards and workers now demonstrated a new awareness of the importance of plant viability — whether due to their reduced job security, the shift in the balance of power or whatever — then it is possible that, far from being an obstruction, steward organisation might become a useful additional tool for management. That is the current economic situation might have in fact achieved what reform, according to many accounts, was meant to achieve in the 1970s.

Before considering the evidence for this, however, it is necessary to remember our discussion in Chapter 2 about the meaning of 'adversarial' industrial relations in Britain. This never meant that all shop stewards were at loggerheads with their managements all of the time. It is necessary to remember how managers in the 1960s and 1970s could both resent the impact of union organisation but also value the role which stewards played as leaders and mediators. They were as much a lubricant as an irritant in the industrial relations machinery. It is important, therefore, not to compare change and cooperation in the 1980's with an exaggerated picture of conflict and stagnation in earlier years.

Employers, particularly in manufacturing, felt that industrial relations did improve. In 1985 a CBI survey found that 59 per cent of employers in manufacturing thought that industrial relations in their industry were better than five years ago, compared with 35 per cent who thought they were the same and only 3 per cent who thought they were worse. Service sector employers, however, were as likely to think that relations has stayed the same (46 per cent) as had improved (47 per cent). It could be argued that a question about a whole industry, rather than particular workplaces, tends to elict responses which may not reflect actual rather than expected experience. The CBI survey went on to ask those employers who thought relations were better about different causes of better industrial relations. Table 6.6 shows the results. They confirm that employers have not seen the law as very important. Nor did they seem to think that the overall government's stance or moderation by their local union officials was decisive. Only one-third of the half of all employers who thought industrial relations were better saw fear of unemployment as 'very important'. The two factors which employers highlighted were improvement in their industrial relations skills and employee involvement initiatives. Edward's survey produced results which pointed to a similar conclusion. When he asked why the personnel function in companies had increased its role he found that half cited employee involvement.

Table 6.6 Employers' views of factors affecting industrial relations improvement (per cent)*

	Very important	*Not important*
Greater management skill and commitment to employee relations	53	3
Improved employee involvement	45	11
Fear of unemployment	35	16
More moderate union leadership locally	29	21
Stance of government	27	22
Trade Union Act 1984	16	45
Employment Acts 1980, 1982	9	48

Source: CBI (1985)
* Excluding responses of 'fairly important' and 'don't know'.

This seems to suggest that managers have adopted the sort of new approach to employees that the theorists of 'new industrial relations' discussed in Chapter 1 suggested. And it seems plausible that this is what many (but not all) employers *thought* they were doing. They could also point to high levels of cooperation with employees. Evidence of this is provided by the example of new technology. WIRS84, Edwards's survey and a Policy Studies Institute study (Northcott *et al.* 1985) showed that shop stewards and workers overwhelmingly accepted and cooperated with new technology and new working practices. Edwards's study of large manufacturing plants where one could expect unions to be strongest found that in 73 per cent of workplaces there was no workforce resistance, and in a further 18 per cent of cases there were negotiations followed by acceptance. Daniel (1987) reported strong resistance in only 2 per cent of cases where it affected manual employees.

However, such results do not necessarily point to a substantial change in industrial relations. Unions have always taken a positive view of technological innovation as such. Conflict has usually focused on the way changes are introduced, and what effects they would have on members' jobs and pay. In addition, the arguments about poor labour productivitity have focused not just on union and workforce opposition to change (for example, through demarcation rules) but on management's acquiescence in that opposition, its low expectations of the sort of change which could be attempted and its lack of interest in and poor record on the organisation and motivation of workers (see Nichols 1986). It is therefore conceivable that there was little union resistance because the sorts of changes employers introduced did not change all that much. The low level of capital investment in manufacturing cited in Chapter 5 suggests there has been no rush to substitute capital for labour. It seems pretty clear that most change has been in manufacturing where the impact of the slump was greatest, and the traditions of job control by unions strongest. Yet here there was evidence of areas of continued conflict. Daniel found that there was more opposition to organisational change as distinct from the introduction of new technology. Batstone (1984, p. 291) found that 62 per cent of managers in large manufacturing plants thought that working practices could be improved and three-quarters of them cited trade unions as a factor preventing such change. Batstone's finding is consistent with the other evidence when we remember that technical and organisational change at plant level, just like economic restructuring at the level of the economy, is an ongoing process. Much of it was achieved without conflict after 1979, just as most of it was achieved without conflict in the 1960s and 1970s. What was also true was that conflict remained when employers attempted what unions saw as 'unacceptable' changes, and that employers took the likely reaction of unions into account before proposing such change. It may be that the definition of what is 'acceptable' changed. Case studies in particular sectors like car plants bear this out. But it would be wrong to overestimate the degree of such change and how widespread it was.

Participation and involvement

Employers clearly believe that their new efforts in employee involvement are central to the achievement of better relations. Many others have seen a new 'participative' approach by British managers — in contrast to the ubiquitous *laissez-faire* plus bargaining approach described in Chapter 2 — as an important part of a move towards new industrial attitudes and the development by workers and their unions of 'enterprise consciousness'. But as we have already seen in the previous section, there is very little evidence of much procedural change. Less than one in ten stewards reporting more two-way communications does not add up to a changed system of workplace industrial relations. The Warwick survey of enterprise-level industrial relations found that 84 per cent of companies said they 'had an overall philosophy towards the management of employees'. Just under half had a written policy. But only one-sixth gave employees a copy (Marginson *et al.* 1986, pp. 8–9):

> Respondents were also invited to describe their overall policy in their own words. Many had great difficulty in doing so, which makes it difficult to summarise the results. But various 'keywords' cropped up regularly: 'fairness' and 'equity' were emphasised, as were 'caring' and 'looking after'. Many of the managers believed that their enterprises were 'progressive or 'forward looking' in their approach to the management of employees, reflected in the prominance of 'participation' or 'involvement' in their statements.

Case studies by Cressey *et al.* (1985) and MacInnes (1985) of participation in six companies found that such vague and general intentions about employee involvement often translated into little in practical management behaviour and less in terms of workforce response. Further evidence of the gap between managerial rhetoric or intention and its actual practice come from Daniel's (1987) study of the introduction of new technology. Using material from the WIRS 1984 survey (in which a third of managers had claimed to have taken initiatives to increase involvement) he found that consultation was infrequent except where managers were formally obliged to consult, or where their plans provoked unfavourable reactions. Daniel (1987, p. 295) concludes that managers' approach was 'quite simply opportunist. When managers wanted to make changes they simply set about introducing them and if they could get away with it without consulting anyone, they simply did so.' Employers claim that they have changed their approach to industrial relations and put it on a more sophisticated and participative footing. But the overall extent of any procedural or substantive change or demonstrable practical results seems to be small. Further evidence of the general absence of change in either behaviour or attitudes is provided by the British Social Attitudes Survey of 1985, reported in Table 6.7. Few manual workers decided their own tasks at work and many still had a little say in working changes. Most thought they needed strong unions to protect them and that they were on a different side from managers who would try to get the better of them. A MORI poll in 1986 (*Guardian*, 27 February

1987) 'suggested that three quarters of shopfloor workers believe there is urgent need to improve the quality of management, and shows that distrust of management is growing, not declining'.

Table 6.7 Views on decision making and industrial relations

| | Social class | | | | |
	All	1/11	111 White-collar	111 Manual	1V/V
Who decides specific tasks at work?					
Respondent	50	75	55	30	32
Someone else	46	21	41	67	65
Would respondent have any say in decisions that change the way of working?					
Yes	62	75	61	63	44
No	34	22	35	33	50
Percentage agreeing that:					
Workers and management are on opposite sides	51	41	46	56	59
Management always try to get the better of employees	52	35	45	63	61
Managers know best	35	34	30	36	41
Employees need strong unions to protect them	45	39	34	52	55

Source: Mann (1986)

There was evidence of an increase in the use of profit-sharing and employee share ownership schemes of various types. Millward and Stevens (1986, p. 20) estimate that the proportion of employees participating in share-ownership schemes rose from 5 to 7 per cent in industry and commerce. Cressey *et al.* (1985) expressed doubt about the impact of profit sharing and employee share ownership, and an IDS (1986, p.1) study noted that

> The growth in schemes (except for executive share option schemes) is not as dramatic as has sometimes been suggested ... While some major companies are enthusiastic, there is very little evidence from detailed analysis that these schemes do in fact change employee attitudes.

Research at Glasgow University (Baddon *et al.* 1987) found that neither managers nor employees saw share-ownership schemes as a means of promoting employee involvement, and that they exercised a negligible impact on collective bargaining. Profit-sharing schemes, especially cash-based ones, were more widespread but usually accounted for only a very small percentage of employees' wages.

The question of flexibility

Yet another area where the record of management change is controversial is flexibility. Flexibility has become a buzz word in the 1980s. Employers' leaders and government ministers have espoused it and ministers have claimed that developments in flexibility have been crucial to improvements in productivity: it has been held up as a prominent example of how markets have been made to work better and how changed market forces surrounding firms have produced changed working arrangements within firms. However, 'flexibility' is a concept like 'involvement' which is extremely difficult to define. No one is 'against' flexibility — it is as difficult to support rigidity and conservatism as it is to support autocracy. But flexibility is a contradictory and controversial concept which is limited in its potential application. Just as supporters of involvement can still see a role for managerial prerogative, so do advocates of 'flexibility' see the benefits of 'inflexible' rules and institutions. There are two main aspects to flexibility. The first is functional flexibility in a firm's internal labour market: how it organises its workforce. The second is numerical flexibility in the external labour market, and the associated division of the workforce into 'core' and 'peripheral' workers.

In a number of articles, Atkinson and his colleagues (Atkinson 1984, IMS 1985) have argued that employers are developing a new type of 'flexible firm'. It has an inner 'core' of stable, skilled employees with secure employment and good conditions. Here flexibility is qualitative. Traditional craft demarcations are relaxed and workers are trained to be multi-skilled. Around the core is an outer layer of workers with poorer conditions more directly determined by the market and with security of employment dependent on how busy the firm is. Here flexibility is quantitative. In addition, the firm may employ other still more peripheral groups: temporary workers on short-term contracts, part-time workers, trainees on special government schemes. Finally, the firm may depend less on direct employment. It can subcontract to specialised suppliers of services, to self-employed workers, rely more on outsourcing, and so on. The overall effect is to rely far more on the market to bring different aspects of production together than on management in a much larger production unit to organise everything with its own workforce.

In such a system it is clear that not everybody can find employment in the 'core' sector. This is where the government's emphasis on labour-market flexibility is relevant. The greater the proportion of the workforce in temporary, part-time or self-employment, the greater the scope for flexibility. For the system to work it is important that the terms and conditions of employment for such people are tied as closely as possible to labour-market forces rather than determined by comparison to the rewards 'core' workers receive. Hence the emphasis by the government that national wage bargaining, the use of job evaluation, the concept of the going rate or the annual pay round ought to be abandoned in favour of decentralised negotiations (preferably decentralised to the level of the individual employee) based on the worker's performance and the company's ability to pay. It argued that such increased flexibility in the labour market would increase the supply of the sorts of labour employers wanted at the rates they could afford.

These two dimensions of flexibility have had a considerable impact on industrial relations according to Brown (1986), both in individual workplaces, and on the entire system.

> For, at one extreme, it is becoming easier to play the labour market for some types of work, obtaining relatively cheap and easily disposable employees of the required competence, and allowing their anxiety about job loss to sustain acceptable effort levels. At the other extreme it is also becoming easier to build up a package of employment, training and payment practices that elicit high labour efficiency through the very different route of cultivating commitment.

The fortunes of the core group of employees are more dependent on their individual employer than on their particular craft skills or the industry in which they work. This encourages them to develop more solidarity with their employer than other workers in the trade and weakens their loyalty to the national union: 'the structure of trade unionism, originally developed for the needs of employee solidarity, is increasingly being shaped to the needs of employers' (Brown 1986, p. 163). Conversely, unions are faced with considerable problems in organising the peripheral workers because of their weaker bargaining position and the organisational problems of recruiting part-timers or temporary staff. They are faced nationally by a dual labour market. In the 'core' segment workers are relatively insulated from the market and have little need of the union in securing the sorts of employment conditions which employers feel are necessary to motivate them and secure their commitment. In the 'peripheral' segment workers might feel they needed the union, but the unions are relatively powerless to organise them effectively.

However, once we scrutinise the evidence on the actual existence of 'flexibility', as opposed to theories and intentions, it is extremely doubtful if there has been any extensive development of it in practice. Indeed the concept itself is contradictory. Doubtless flexibility is one of the goals employers pursue, but they have many other goals which often cut across it and limit its practical application. Many parts of the flexibility argument refer to long-established features of the way British employers have hired labour and unions have organised it. Employers have always sought ways of attracting and retaining skilled workers in relatively short supply. In turn these workers and their unions have in their dealings with employers tried to define themselves as core employees, distinct from the unorganised, and to maintain barriers between themselves and other workers to restrict the labour supply. By contrast the *laissez-faire* approach of employers towards labour has always encouraged a flexible 'hire and fire' attitude to less skilled workers. In this sense there has always been a dual labour market in Britain. So, too, have there been large employers which subcontract parts of their work to others — for example, car manufacturers mostly assemble components produced elsewhere. To sustain the flexibility thesis we need to show that these elements are being put together in a new and more purposeful way.

It does appear that employers are attracted to the idea of flexibility in principle. The CBI survey cited earlier found that a majority of employers wanted to 'reduce demarcation and increase multi-skills/job flexibility', a quarter wanted to use more temporary workers, a fifth wanted to employ more part-timers and a third wanted to subcontract more work. But data from the Census of Employment and the WIRS 1984 survey show that their actual employment *practices* have changed little. In manufacturing companies the incidence of part-time labour has been falling for both men and women. The number of part-time workers, most of whom are women, increased in the economy as a whole, but most of this expansion is explained by the growth of the services sector, both public and private: the proportion of part-time workers employed in different industries has hardly changed at all. As we saw in Chapter 5, the proportion of part-time workers in Britain grew from 21 per cent in 1981 to 23 per cent in 1986, representing an increase of 340,000 part-timers, while full-time employment fell by 1 million. Sproull (1987) calculated that in the service sector 'on average two-thirds of the increase in the total number of part-timers is accounted for simply by the growth of these industries'. He also found that employers' reasons for employing part-timers had not changed.

The WIRS 1984 survey provided estimates of the number of temps, contract, freelance and homeworkers used by different sectors of industry with 25 or more employees. The total of around half-a-million represented under 4 per cent of the labour force in these workplaces. It was estimated that while the use of short, fixed-term contracts had stayed the same, the use of freelances and outworkers had fallen. Millward and Stevens (1986, p. 210) found that 'there was a marked relationship between the use of non-core workers and capacity utilisation' because while 46 per cent of establishments working at full capacity used non-core workers only 36 per cent of those working 'considerably below capacity' did so. They contend that this 'adds some weight to the view that non core or "periphery" workers are, perhaps increasingly, being used by employers to make a closer connection between output and employment' and they cite Atkinson's study (IMS 1985). This is, to say the least, a surprising conclusion. If the incidence of the use of non-core workers rises by just over a quarter over the full range of output change that is hardly indicative of the sort of connection between output and employment change posed by the flexibility model. If the flexibility thesis were to be sustained it would surely also require that a far higher absolute proportion of non-core workers were found in the size of establishments the WIRS 1984 survey examined. It would also require some evidence of growth in non-core employment between 1980 and 1984 rather than evidence of decline. Nor does the pattern of non-core employment discovered by WIRS fit the thesis. It found only 122,000 non-core workers in manufacturing: about 2 per cent of the labour force, and most were temps: presumably agency secretarial staff and the like. Most workers on short-term contracts worked in education, where patterns of employment were quite different.

Most of the evidence used to generate the flexibility model in the first place is capable of sustaining different interpretations. First the number of companies used in the flexibility studies was very small. The two main studies by Atkinson used 72 and 31 firms respectively. Neither was a sample of firms statistically representative of the economy or of the four sectors (food and drink, engineering, retail distribution and financial services) which the larger study covered. In fact, the 31 firms in the later study were chosen 'because they were known to have introduced changes to work organisation specifically to promote greater flexibility, or because they represented clear examples of flexibility already achieved' (Atkinson and Meager 1986, p. 4). Second, the definition of flexibility used in Atkinson's study for the NEDC was very wide. It included virtually any initiative to change the working arrangements or pay of the workforce. Numerical flexibility focused on the use of part-time, temporary, short-term contract and casual workers, and on changes in working time such as new shift-working patterns or changes in overtime. Functional flexibiliy focused on changes in working practices and the range of tasks different types of employees were expected to do. But firms make these changes all the time in response to new methods of production and changing labour and product markets. What is important is not the fact of such initiatives but, firstly, the overall extent of these practices, secondly, whether any changes were part of an overall strategy consistent with Atkinson's flexibility model and, finally, whether the initiatives themselves were successful.

In terms of the extent of initiatives the CBI survey evidence and that from WIRS 1984 show that the actual level of management intentions are below those found by Atkinson and his colleagues, and that the extent of any actual change in numerical flexibility is, to say the least, very small indeed. Because of changes in the definitions it uses, the Labour Force Survey can only be used to examine trends in the use of temporary workers from 1983 onwards. It shows an increase of only about 70 thousand such workers to around 1.3 million in 1985. (It should be noted that the claim by Hakim (1987 p. 93) that the number of temporary workers doubled between 1981 and 1985 is wrong and based on a confusion of definitions (Department of Employment 1987, p. 218). Meager's (1985) study of temporary workers helps to explain this pattern. It showed that the main reasons for any increase in the use of temporary workers (an increase which WIRS 1984 suggests is unlikely) were the shift of employment towards services (where more temporary workers are employed) and the cyclical effect of temporary employment rising as the economy became more active. This was not a new trend but one visible in the 1970s, too. In fact Meager (1985, p. 4) suggests that 'the proportion of temporary workers in the workforce peaked in 1979, before declining rapidly in the recession and resuming an upward trend in 1982–1983, such that by 1985 it has regained the level of the mid 1970s'. However, Meager found that the main reasons most employers used temporary workers were 'traditional' ones of cover for holidays, seasonal workload fluctuations, special projects, and so on. 'Flexibility' was a rationale claimed by a minority of respondents, even counting those who also gave traditional reasons (Meager 1985, p. 42). And even where 'flexibility' was the claimed rationale it 'was not always part of a well-formulated manning strategy, but was often a process consisting of *ad hoc* and sometimes opportunistic adjustments to existing manpower policies' (Meager 1985, p. 7).

Self-employment has risen dramatically since 1979, from under 2 million to over 2.5 million. But it does not seem that this is connected with flexibility strategies in larger companies. Only one in six of the self-employed worked either in manufacturing or business services in 1985: about the same as in 1979. The Labour Force Survey produces some evidence on job switching. There is rapid turnover in self-employment: just over 200,000 of the self-employed in 1984 had been employees one year earlier; but only 18,000 were still in the same occupation, working for the same firm. Creigh *et al.*. (1986, p. 13) concluded that there was 'little evidence of direct switching of the nominal status of individuals between the employee and self employment categories'.

To the extent that numerical flexibility does exist (in the sense of the growth of part-time and temporary work associated with the growth of the service sector) it is fundamentally a question of gender (see Beechey 1984). Nearly two-thirds of the temporary workers in the IMS survey were female, and five out of six part-time workers are female. It also seems clear that the growth of part-time work is related to the trend rise in the employment of married women, and women's much quicker return to the labour market after childbirth. For example, in the bank studied by MacInnes (1988) part-time working was only possible because a pool of women existed who had left bank work in previous years, usually because of domestic obligations. It is perhaps in gender, rather than the concept of a flexible firm as such, that explanations of the trend towards dualism in the labour market ought to be sought. Craig *et al.* (1984), in their study of low pay in small firms, concluded that low-paid unskilled workers were rarely without skills of some sort. Most work situations required a stable, skilled, experienced and cooperative workforce. This implied that even employers of low-paid relatively unskilled workers could rarely afford high levels of labour turnover which poor conditions could cause (Craig *et al.* 1984, p. 93):

> The choice between risking high labour turnover or high wage levels can be avoided by changing recruitment policy and hiring labour from relatively disadvantaged labour groups that are generally more stable at low wages. Probably the most important group of this type is that of married women ...

Functional flexibility is by its nature more difficult to measure. We have already seen that changes in technology and working arrangements were widespread, accepted by employees and seldom resisted by unions. In this sense, functional flexibility is neither new nor necessarily part of a flexible firm strategy. But what is more significant is just how cautious Atkinson's conclusions were in the original study. He pointed out that functional flexibility arose mostly in the manufacturing sector. But while nine out of ten companies claimed to be trying to achieve it their actual achievements were modest. For example, one-third said they had achieved dual skilling in maintenance craftsmen. It is worth quoting Atkinson's discussion of the constraints on flexibility at some length (IMS 1985, pp. 153–4):

> Almost without exception, our management respondents cited union demarcation as the principal factor constraining [greater functional flexibility] ... such union attitudes are far from being absolute constraints; rather they condition the extent, the pace and above all the manner of implementation of such changes ... We found a very widespread readiness among employees and their representatives to acquire enhanced skills, subject to provisos on pay, training and safety issues, but the critical constraint was encountered when such acquisition would involve skills previously the sole preserve of a different bargaining group ... The 'catch 22' observed here was that many firms reported a high degree of informal flexibility; while it remained informal they were less able to provide training and reward the deployment of enhanced skills. This required formal agreement which would bring out the conflicting interest of the different unions; and this issue was not one which our management respondents wished to raise ... The most widespread constraints cited by respondents who had moved furthest were inadequacy of skills, the resulting costs of retraining and shortage of training resources.

It has to be asked just how far flexibility had in fact gone when training was still a major constraint, the boundary lines of bargaining groups were not crossed and its practical organisation remained informal. The real limitations and informality of functional flexibility in practice resemble an enthusiasm of government and employers from the 1960s and 1970s: productivity bargaining. This was supposed to be a means whereby workforces bargained away restrictive practices or inefficient or inflexible working in return for larger pay increases, and was therefore supposed to emphasise the common rather than conflicting interests of employer and worker, while benefiting the consumer, too, through higher productivity. In the event, it was fraught with problems. If it focused on specific, easily measurable changes in work and output by particular groups of workers it tended to reinforce low-trust adversarial bargaining attitudes, focused workers' attention on management shortcomings or on the productivity gains of other workers and even encouraged the development of new restrictive practices which could be 'sold' in the future. Conversely, if it focused on the organisation as a whole and emphasised the general importance of cooperation and efficiency, it faced the problem of becoming an irrelevant propaganda exercise or of provoking conflict about how far different work groups were contributing to the productivity bonus (see Cressey *et al.* 1985, ch. 5, and Batstone 1984, ch. 4). Whichever route was taken both measuring productivity and distinguishing between the influence of worker effort, technical change and management efficiency were notoriously difficult. The enthusiasm of senior management was liable to be frustrated by the heterogeneous interests and outlook of junior managers closer to production. For them, honouring the letter and spirit of the productivity agreement could be much lower in their list of priorities than getting the work out, or maintaining good relations with the local work-group.

The disillusion with productivity bargaining was presumably why the current government fixed on the new term 'flexibility'. Hence a recent publication from the Treasury (1986, p. 3) on flexibility argued.

> There were, of course, productivity deals in the 1970s and earlier. But recent flexibility agreements often differ from earlier agreements in a key respect. They involve a general commitment to flexibility in whatever form it may prove to be necessary, rather than a commitment to remove specific rigidities named in the agreement and no others. Examples of this very broad flexibility commitment are the British Shipbuilders National Enabling Agreement to Revised Working Practices, the agreement between Nissan and the Amalgamated Union of Engineering Workers for the new car plant at Washington, and agreements at Findus, Toshiba and Continental Can. Agreements of this sort signal a complete change in labour practices from the attempt to defend traditional positions against encroachment by market forces (which is likely ultimately to drive the firm out of business) to the attempt to develop the potential of the firm and its employees fully, thus giving the firm the maximum scope to reward its employees and safeguard their jobs.
> The evidence is that flexibility agreements are now quite widespread.

The study which the piece proceeds to cite is that by Atkinson which we have discussed above. It is possible that the examples cited by the Treasury do represent real moves towards flexibility, but this would not be proof of any general trend. Instead, echoing the Treasury's view that the commitments in flexibility agreements are 'general', it is clear that many agreements are simply 'enabling' agreements which set out the desire of both parties to pursue change in principle, but avoid the problems of the differences between managers and workers about what it ought to mean in practice. It seems that 'flexibility' agreements are rather like the 'general' type of productivity agreement, which failed to produce improvements precisely because what was promised was so amorphous. The contention that many workforces are offering a 'general commitment to flexibility in whatever form it may prove to be necessary' is utopian nonsense, and misses the point that there are other barriers to flexibility than workforce attitudes: training, pay and conditions relativities, management competence and so on.

There are many factors which restrict firms' ability to develop functional flexibility besides those outlined by Atkinson himself which we discussed above. There is growing evidence, even with high unemployment, of shortages of skilled craftspeople. A third of companies in the CBI survey claimed that the supply of skilled labour was hindering their improvement in competitiveness. It is thus reasonable to conclude that many skilled core workers did not feel constrained to agree to job flexibility which would undermine their established bargaining position. One effect of the slump was to cut the resources firms devoted to training, which, combined with the virtual collapse of the apprenticeship system, decreased the supply of skilled labour. Yet effective multi-skilling and flexibility would require much greater resources for retraining, not only for the skilled workers themselves, but for those who supervise and manage them.

There are also internal inconsistencies in 'flexibility' as an overall strategy. The first concerns the payment system. Atkinson reported two possible developments: one was the development of more rates of pay, 'multi-graded structures reflecting and encouraging skill acquisition'; the other was the reduction of different rates of pay, 'more simplified structures with fewer broad grades. The former was often seen as a transitional step to the latter.' This may have been the companies' genuine intent but it seems more like an attempt to reconcile two diametrically opposed principles in the implications of flexibility for pay. One is the principle of rewarding individual commitment, skill and effort. This is clearly what the government had in mind when it advocated the decentralisation of pay bargaining to plant level and below and that individual merit and performance should be rewarded. We have already quoted Kenneth Clarke's (1987) comment that 'It is only right to pay more to those who bring to their job enthusiasm, enterprise and initiative than those who are prepared merely to idle along'. Presumably such a principle is valuable in encouraging employees to become multi-skilled and responsible for new and more varied tasks. But the second is the principle of making the multi-skilled core workforce more homogeneous (instead of split into different skill and bargaining groups). It facilitates flexibility if workers expected to interchange tasks and skills are on the same grade of pay. These principles are often incompatible in practice. Thus flexibility could imply introducing a 'single-status' regime for all workers. But this would face most companies with a substantial drop in the weekly hours of their manual employees.

Another problem concerns the link between the numerical and functional flexibility. Meager (1985) points out that workforces faced with the former were often less convinced of the virtues of the latter because they believed they could be functionally facilitating their own numerically flexible redundancy. This raises the more general problem managers face in using the threat posed by adverse market forces to convince employees of the need for flexibility while maintaining credibility in their promises of job security for core workers if flexibility is adopted. Cressey *et al.* (1985, p. 166) showed that in the companies they studied workers' reactions to management appeal of this sort were complex. Very often the message would be interpreted in unanticipated ways.

> Discussions on company performance ... were all treated with cynicism by worker representatives, whereas managers hoped they would be useful. What managers saw as information on the types of challenge the company faced, representatives saw as 'rays of gloom', usually aimed at pay negotiations... Emphasising the importance and meritocratic nature of management focused representatives' attentions on an inefficient and inexpert management whenever it fell short... The argument that employees' commitment was vital became the argument that if employees' efforts and initiatives were so decisive they should be rewarded accordingly.

The obverse of this problem is the inflexibility of non-core workers. MacInnes (1988) reports how management in the bank he studied found that there were limits to how far part-timers could be used to cover peaks in demand because of their narrower range of skills compared to full-time trained staff.

A final question concerns who is to be in the core, and how it is to be protected. The prospect of job security for core workers could conflict with the drive to contract out work. One response of firms to recession and tight margins has been to use their own 'core' staff whom they wish to retain to do jobs previously done by contractors. This implies that subcontracting might *fall* in a recession. Yet it is during the slack market of a recession that the economic advantages of subcontracting are to be enjoyed. Conversely, in a boom subcontractors could enjoy a sellers' market just when the flexible firm would want its own core workers to concentrate on production! And just how large is the core? Flexibility includes such changes as production workers doing routine maintenance and interchange of tasks in semi-skilled and unskilled jobs. If it did not include this it could be of little contribution to overall increases in productivity. Yet if most of the workforce is in the 'core' (and the low figures for non-core workers suggest this is indeed the case) it is difficult to see what scope is left for numerical flexibility.

The high productivity growth in manufacturing in the 1980s which we described in Chapter 5 has often been cited as evidence of the achievements of flexibility. But the difficulties of equating productivity to worker effort and the importance of compositional effects which we discussed above along with the level of earnings rises that pushed labour costs per unit of output in Britain up faster than elsewhere suggests that many employers paid dearly for the rises in productivity they achieved.

Table 6.8 Employers' views of factors affecting competitiveness improvement (per cent)

	Hindering	*No effect*	*Assisting*
Other companies' pay settlements	36	59	4
Supply of skilled labour	32	49	17
Government policies	32	47	12
Trade union attitudes	27	58	12
Finance for investment	18	48	32
Employees' attitudes	15	18	65
Managerial skill	10	6	83

Source: CBI (1985)

A CBI survey (Table 6.8) showed that most employers thought that their own skills and employees' attitudes were the most important factors in the improvement of productivity. Trade union attitudes had on balance hindered it, but not by as much as government policies! This could be interpreted in different ways. It could be argued that the small role attributed to trade union attitudes suggested that few changes in industrial relations have occurred, while the positive evaluation of employee attitudes simply confirms that employees have continued to cooperate with technical and organisational change. Conversely, it could be inferred that managers felt they had established a closer and more direct relationship with their employees, such that the attitudes of their unions were more marginal in the process.

Indeed there is evidence that flexibility is actually decreasing both in the sense of labour-market change and in the sense of the force of the links between the external labour market and the internal organisation of labour in firms. Kenneth Clarke (1987, p.8) ruefully noted that analysis of WIRS 1984 'found that negotiated pay settlements were not influenced by a company's recent financial performance nor the trend in its output nor the sensitivity of the product's price to the level of demand'. His case was overstated, in that the links between pay bargaining and a company's market position are much less simple than Clarke's comments implied. Other researchers (Gregory *et al* 1987 for example) have found relationships, albeit less direct ones than we might expect.

But it does seem that unemployment actually decreased flexibility rather than promoting it. A study by Jones and McKay (1986) showed that as unemployment and redundancies increased, voluntary job changes — the essence of labour market flexibility — fell dramatically. In addition, measures to promote labour mobility were less effective when high unemployment made the rewards to mobility less certain.

> Measures designed to encourage flexibility do not exist in a vacuum. They cannot succeed against the background of declining opportunities in the UK as a whole ... Redundant middle aged steelworkers are unlikely to find employment writing computer software. Nor is it always possible for those without work to opt for a lower wage ... Interest in retraining and willingness to consider moving to other occupations and other areas critically depend on the demand for labour ... There is little point in encouraging transfer *until* there is something to transfer to (Jones and McKay 1986, pp. 1, 16, 25).

Further evidence of this process comes from the comparison between the unemployment total and the flows on to the unemployment register. In 1974, while unemployment was well under 1 million, over 3.5 million people became unemployed at some point each year. By 1984, with unemployment over 3 million, the annual flow on to the register had only increased by about 1 million. Eventually Lord Young, the Employment Secretary, found himself presenting a paper from his Department to a NEDC meeting in 1986 which admitted that the level of mobility in the labour market had fallen since the late 1970s and that 'there are probably relatively few vacancies in any part of the country which cannot be filled from within the local areas, possibly with some training' (*Financial Times*, 6 November 1986).

Training in the UK, has remained well behind its competitor countries at all levels (Nichols 1986, p. 106ff, pp. 225–8). There are fewer qualified scientists and engineers in the workforce, managers are less well qualified (only about 6% have degrees) as is the workforce they manage. Prais (1981) estimated that, in Germany 60 per cent of manufacturing workers had qualificatons such as apprenticeships compared with 30 per cent in Britain. But from 1979 onwards, as firms made savings in the face of the slump, training was cut back. Such a poor situation in training creates a poor environment for the development of flexibility. It also suggests again that British management has remained wedded to a short term, cost minimising attitude towards the labour it employs.

The level of overtime working in 1986 was back up to the levels prior to the slump, despite the fact that output was lower. The British Social Attitudes Survey in 1985 also found that three-quarters of manual workers thought the best way to improve their position was to stay with the same employer rather than move around. The only respondents who saw the external labour market as a better avenue of mobility were those with degrees, technical or professional qualifications (Mann 1986, p. 21). The 1985 Labour Force Survey provided evidence on the length of people's job tenure which shows that workers acted in line with their beliefs: 59 per cent of men and 44 per cent of women had been in their jobs for five years or more. Main (1982) estimated that nearly a half of adult male full-time workers were in jobs likely to last for 20 years or more. It seems that high unemployment, rather than forcing labour to be more flexible, can actually encourage the opposite. It leaves many employers and workers stuck with each other.

By 1985 the lack of training in British industry was reaching crisis proportions, and skill shortages were starting to reappear. A joint Manpower Services Commission and NEDO report in 1985 criticised industry's complacency on training, and advocated tax relief to companies as a way to encourage more training. In 1986 an Employment Select Committee report recommended a return to the system of levies to fund training which the government had abolished, as one way of tackling the growing training shortage.

There are no doubt some impressive individual examples, and the new Nissan plant at Sunderland, for example, may well be one. But even here there is other evidence to consider. The *Guardian* (8 May 1987) reported that several employees had left Nissan complaining that they were given 'no real responsibility', that consultation was a sham, and that the pace of work was so fast that targets were sometimes met by working on during breaks, 'a huge proportion of the workforce are said to be disillusioned with their much coveted jobs'. The history of British industrial relations is strewn with equally impressive individual examples which proved to be false dawns: such as the Fawley Productivity Agreements, and of individual companies with 'new' industrial relations policies which have nevertheless failed to catch on elsewhere, such as IBM. Batstone (1984, p. 149) noted

> The near-evangelical promulgation of 'success stories' of productivity agreements a decade ago shows a remarkable similarity to the more recent spate of 'success stories' about autonomous work groups: both frequently expatiate in detail over the intention and the process of introduction, but then become vague and confuse aspiration with reality when it comes to assessing results.

Since then 'success stories' have focused on quality circles, team briefing, 'just in time' management and flexibility. More remarkable, perhaps, than the short lifespan of some of these managerial fashions, is the credulity with which outside observers are prepared to take them. The internal logic of the concept of the flexible firm is flawed. There is little evidence for its achievement in practice. But what flexibility does do is fit with Thatcherite ideology and its belief that the solution to all of Britain's industrial problems lies in subjecting institutions to the most direct possible influence of market forces. The government believes that by doing this it promotes flexibility and efficiency. The government has therefore gone to great lengths to 'talk-up' the development of flexibility, arguing that many companies already practice it and that others should follow them. And that is why, in stark contrast to the real evidence, so much has been heard about it.

Wage inflation and earnings

The behaviour of earnings, like productivity changes or strike statistics, is not a straightforward guide to the state of management–worker relations, or to union bargaining power. It may be that employers 'reward' workforces who eschew radicalism and espouse cooperation with higher wage increases. However it would be difficult to argue that low wage increases did not reflect reduced union power, at least where bargaining is decentralised: we consider later on the question of whether the labour movement nationally could have an interest in containing wage rises. Earnings increases also reflect compositional factors: changes in the distribution of the workforce between high- and low-paying industries and between high- and low-paying occupations. But bearing in mind these reservations, changes in earnings can tell us a lot about what is happening at work. Moreover, since we have already seen that there has been relatively little change in *how* pay is decided since 1979, we can be fairly confident that the outcome of that process tells us quite a lot about relations between employers and workers. In this light the pattern of earnings growth which was demonstrated in Chapter 5 suggests that unions at workplace level maintained and perhaps even improved their bargaining power. There is no evidence that these earnings increases were *not* the result of normal collective bargaining processes. Metcalf and Nickell (1985) actually estimated that the 'union mark-up', that is to say the differential between earnings achieved by union members and those achieved by non-members, increased by half from 8 per cent to 12 per cent as free collective bargaining under the Conservatives replaced Labour's incomes policy. However, Blanchflower (1986) has suggested that the real 'mark-up' might be less so that this apparent move could be the result of other effects.

Far from reducing the level of wage settlements, there is every reason to suppose that decentralisation (which Thatcherism has espoused), when combined with workplace-based union organisation, is the system most likely to maximise earnings differentials, maximise earnings for the best organised, and maximise unemployment and insecurity for the rest. In a decentralised system each employer and bargaining group can only influence the level of their own agreements. They have no institutional influence on other bargainers. They influence them only through the market effect of their own bargains. Despite high unemployment it is still possible for the smaller, surviving sectors of manufacturing to trade profitability. Indeed profits have recovered strongly since 1981. Therefore employers have the resources to reward their stable labour forces with relatively large increases. Even if these increases were such as to threaten future employment levels, or were dependent on productivity increases which would do so, it is still in the interests of the workforce to maximise their wage gains, since any redundancies will probably be voluntary and in any event affect only a minority. This is because the high level of unemployment has reduced voluntary turnover so much (as we saw above) that plenty of people who might wish to move have hitherto not done so. Redundancy payments, however, compensate for the adverse state of the labour market. The firm's labour market therefore becomes progressively more and more separate from the external labour market as its workforce becomes smaller and progressively more specialised and skilled in that firm's particular work. It is therefore quite possible for the firm's profits to keep rising and for the level of earnings to keep rising. Even if this process starts to put other firms out of business (as they fail to match the level of wages afforded by others) it need not affect the profits or wage levels of those who are able to survive. The workers in these firms might wish to lower the level of wages overall, in order to increase the general level of employment for fellow workers, but they have no certain means of doing so. If they forgo a wage rise it could simply result in higher profits for their employer, or higher real wages for other workers who benefit from lower prices but do not themselves forgo high wage increases. On the contrary, it will always be in the interests of any one group to secure as large a wage increase as possible, in the hope that it will be marginally above the general rate of settlements, and therefore above the rate of price inflation. Far from increasing employment, linking pay to performance, or companies' ability to pay, could actually progressively decrease it. Sir Pat Lowry (1985), chair of ACAS, argued that unions had

> the responsibility, therefore of persuading their members that the traditional role of maintaining and improving living standards is sometimes better served by not pressing a wage claim too far or by not opposing as a matter of principle any measures designed to improve efficiency.

But such appeals and similar ones from ministers were bound to be ignored given the structure of bargaining arrangements unionists faced.

While this is the process for workers in the primary labour market, conditions in the secondary labour market could get progressively worse. Where jobs are sufficiently poorly specialised or unskilled that the advantages of retaining the current workers are low, then so will the costs of labour turnover be low and the attraction of bidding down wages fairly great. Because of high unemployment there will be a ready supply of alternative labour and union organisation will be difficult.

But it is not clear whether lower wages in this sector could create much employment. Abolishing Wages Councils, restricting their remit to adult workers and repealing the Fair Wages Resolution may lower wages for workers in the secondary sector and make life more miserable and insecure both for them and many of their employers who will be faced by wage-cutting competitors. But it will not affect the level of wages in the primary sector, especially if the criterion to be followed (as urged by the govenment) is ability to pay.

The increase in earnings differentials across high- and low-paid workers and between manual and white-collar workers and between part-time and full-time women workers might be taken as evidence of the development of the 'flexible' firm. But it is unclear whether the growth of the latter should produce such a pattern of differentials. If it were leading to greater harmonisation of working conditions one could expect the differential between white-collar and manual workers to reduce. The increase in the differential between full- and part-time workers might be seen as a consequence of the *fall* in demand for part-time workers in manufacturing caused by the absence of the development of flexibility.

But the pattern of increase in differentials does suggest that the dualism of the labour market is increasing. This also helps to explain why unemployment has not checked wages growth, because it suggests that 'internal labour markets' have become relatively more important for employers, and a major way of retaining the cooperation and motivation of their labour force is high earnings. Hence the industrial relations director of Ford (Roots 1986) has argued that

> Many politicians and economists are surprised that, despite high unemployment and falling inflation, wage settlements have continued to run at a high level. That is because they do not understand that employers are interested not in wage rates but in labour costs. Firms are willing to grant wage increases if the labour costs do not go up. When the CBI and the Government say we have to reduce the level of wage settlements they are missing the point.

Sacking an experienced workforce because cheaper labour from the dole is potentially available is simply not an option. It is also risky for managers to emphasise the insecurity of the workforce's jobs or prospects of a plant's closure, while at the same time securing their commitment and ensuring that valuable skilled workers do not seek more secure jobs elsewhere. Once profits recovered strongly after 1981, it was even more difficult to maintain that companies could not 'afford' higher wages. Because it is the relatively more productive areas of industry which have survived the recession and because redundancies have left smaller workforces, companies have been prepared to buy cooperation in changes in working practices through larger pay increases. Hence a *Financial Times* Marplan survey in October 1985 found that 73 per cent of directors thought wage settlements in their company 'just about right' compared to only 9 per cent who thought them 'excessive' (Rutherford 1985).

The government's policies have encouraged this inflationary process, not just by the emphasis on decentralising bargaining but also by its determination to 'depoliticise' trade unionism. As Gamble (1974, p.144) notes, this has long been an aim of Conservatism. But under Thatcherism this process has taken a different turn. Not just political unionism but almost any form of leadership by unions has been defined as illegitimate. This runs contrary to an earlier strand in Conservative thinking that 'responsible' leadership should be nurtured and left with enough power to channel the aspirations of members in constructive directions. 'Giving unions to their members' might well reduce their influence when that membership is divided, or in a poor bargaining position, or has expectations less ambitious than its officials. But the situation can just as easily be reversed. For example 189 of the 246 pre-strike ballots known to ACAS in 1986 had resulted in a majority for action. And one reason for this, according to Roots, is that the members have little to lose by voting yes and watching management's reaction. In such a situation appeals by government ministers or the CBI to bring down wage settlements is not likely to have much effect. There is also the problem of practising what is preached. One of the reasons for the much bigger increase in white-collar pay is the extremely strong performance of managerial pay since 1979. The top decile of male white-collar pay in the private sector rose 28.5 per cent by 1986. At the 1985 CBI conference which condemned excessive pay settlements one of the speakers was Ralph Halpern. In 1984 he had earned £348,000, a 75 per cent increase on the previous year. But by 1986 he was Britain's highest paid executive, at slightly more than £1 million per annum.

Almost from the start of the Thatcherite experiment ministers have been concerned about wage growth. From 1983 onwards their public pronouncements have increased in urgency, but to little effect. True to the government's faith in the ability of markets to produce 'flexibility' (and therefore to bring the supply of and demand for labour into equilibrium by lowering its price) it concluded that labour-market institutions must still be a barrier to flexibility. In order to overcome this it argued that all the methods traditionally used to bargain about pay such as comparability, job evaluation, considerations of fairness, and so on, ought to be abandoned, and instead pay should be related simply to the company's performance and ability to pay, on the one hand, and the employee's performance, on the other. In effect it has wanted to leave everything to the market. However, even its own behaviour demonstrated the impracticality of such an idea. In the public sector, both within the nationalised industries and public services, virtually all pay continued to be decided by collective bargaining at national level. The government came in committed to ending the use of comparability in public sector pay, and enforcing cash limits or ability to pay instead. This was supposed to replicate the effect of market forces within the public sector. In practice the situation was a good deal more complex. In the course of the 1979 election the Conservatives promised to honour the awards to public sector workers awarded by the Standing Commission on Pay Comparability chaired by Professor Hugh Clegg. Its solution to the public sector's 1979 'Winter of Discontent' was therefore to award it the appropriate 'catch-up' wage increases. In August 1980 it wound up the Commission and in November it suspended the Pay Research Unit for civil servants' pay.

In practice, however, cash limits worked rather like a public sector incomes policy. Most public services, like the National Health Service for example, had only extremely limited scope to increase wages either by increasing labour productivity or by finding savings in relatively small non-wage budgets. Cash limits effectively meant direct control of employment numbers and wage increases. As with incomes policies the limits did not prove to be inviolate. After extensive industrial action nurses, civil servants and others succeeded in breaching the limits. In turn such industrial action produced pressure to find better procedures for determining public sector pay which in turn led to the rediscovery of the benefits of comparability. A new pay-review body for nurses and midwives was established which promptly ignored cash limits in its first set of recommendations. Strikes in the civil service led to the setting up of the Megaw inquiry, which in turn led to protracted negotiations with the civil service unions. In March 1987 the Institute of Professional Civil Servants concluded a long-term agreement with the Treasury on the determination of pay for scientific and technical civil servants. The agreement provided for an annual pay review, for negotiations to be influenced by the 'going rate', for regular 'comparability' studies, job evaluation and a single national pay scale. All these practices had been attacked a matter of days earlier by the Paymaster General, Kenneth Clarke. This drew the astonishing on-the-record comment from a Treasury official that Mr Clarke's agenda was 'not totally realistic ... Pay negotiations have to stay in touch with what is happening in the big wide world' (*Financial Times*, 4 March 1987).

Comparability was the essence of the government's problems in education, too. However much it might want to determine wages by 'ability to pay' it faced the problem that once salaries fell sufficiently behind the private sector, recruitment of skilled and committed teachers became difficult and plummeting morale turned the teaching profession into a workforce which sustained one of the longest, most imaginative and (in terms of immediate wage gains) successful programmes of industrial action the labour movement had seen. Again cash limits were breached. This time the government sought revenge by abolishing the teachers' collective bargaining machinery in England and Wales but it was not clear that this unparalleled measure was not simply storing up further trouble: both teaching unions immediately secured large majorities in secret ballots for protest strike action. As the main procedural change pursued in the public sector, the attempt to move away from comparability in collective bargaining was a dismal failure. Brown (1986, p.167) noted how:

> For all their carefully chosen phrases, the current pay review bodies for nurses, civil servants, soldiers, judges and the like .... argue for the use of effective comparability and they warn of the danger of disrupting the loyalty and commitment of employees.

Hence the government's proposals on labour-market flexibility were ignored, not only by employers but by the Treasury itself. Employers valued collective bargaining because it controlled the possibility of endless individual or group 'leapfrogging' comparability claims produced by permanently deciding everybody's claims on their continually changing merits. Geographical staff mobility would be difficult if they faced changing bargaining groups every time they moved rather than a nationally agreed rate. Abolishing the institutional determination of pay might fit with the dogma that market forces always work best, but it would bring chaos to the real world of labour market operation in practice.

Conclusion

This chapter began by describing British employers' fears about the limits to their autonomy to make their own decisions which further moves towards corporatism might imply. These worries, combined with their own internal divisions of interest and outlook made the Thatcherite programme of dramatic deflation an acceptable alternative. As the process continued it gathered some momentum of its own. By definition those employers who were able to survive were more likely to look favourably on the policy, and it chimed in with the fundamental *laissez-faire* beliefs in the virtues of the market characteristic of British employers that we reviewed in Chapter 2. We then looked at how far the new economic and legal environment was used by employers to change their relationship with labour: how far it altered the balance of power in the workplace and what new managerial strategies towards labour were adopted. It seemed that there was much less change than might have been expected. A major reason for this was the importance of 'internal labour markets' for employers which meant that, except in special market conditions, there was little reason for employers to want to use the law or unemployment to alter their approach to their unions or undermine their bargaining position. As Batstone and Gourlay (1986, p.266) conclude: 'Employers .... have been prepared to accept less than 'optimal' changes in the wage effort bargain from their point of view in order to preserve the cooperation of the workforce and the union.' Where internal labour markets are less important, workers have fared less well, resulting in the very rapid growth of earnings differentials. But the development of dualism in the British labour market is not a new feature of management strategy or industrial relations in Britain, nor is it necessarily taking new forms, as the discussion of 'flexibility' pointed out. And fundamentally, regardless of how low conditions are driven in the secondary sector, they would still exert little influence over terms in the primary one.

But there is a more striking argument to consider. If we look at the nature of British employers, the history of British management's strategy towards labour and the traditions of the British industrial relations system outlined in Chapter 2, then we should not expect Thatcherism to have led to widespread change because its main effect was to encourage unions and employers to revert to some of these older traditions. The nature of the management of labour is a complex process to analyse or describe. The best starting point is the labour contract between employer and worker. This usually sets out the rates and method of payment, and makes some description, explicit or implicit, of the sort of work and effort the worker is to deliver in return. But as Baldamus (1961, pp. 90–1) stressed, the second part of the contract is inevitably vague:

> who can define ability, restricted output, capacity ('fullest' or otherwise)? If the intensity of effort expected from the worker is left undefined, then, surely, everything else that is stated about wages, hours, and method of payment is equally indeterminate ... the formal contract between employer and employee is incomplete in a very fundamental sense.

One result of this 'incompleteness' is the actual need for the everyday management of labour. It has to be put to work effectively and this is inevitably a joint process involving both manager and worker. Management, no matter how expert, cannot set out in advance exactly what must be done under all circumstances and how, but must rely to some extent on the workers' cooperation, initiative and experience. Just how it does so both arises from and gives rise to, different systems of workplace industrial relations. But a second result of this 'incompleteness' in the labour market (and of comparable incompleteness in product markets) is that it inevitably renders the process of economic calculation approximate and relative.

This second result is of fundamental importance because it takes us back to the concept of organisational pluralism we examined in Chapter 3. It implies that neither entrepreneurs in a market nor planners in a socialised economy can really calculate the effects of their actions either in advance or after the event. They will be able to tell the general result but not the detail of how it was arrived at, which elements of the collective labour were most effective or the precise relationship at any point in time between effort and result. The entrepreneur cannot read off from market forces what must be done, nor is it possible to arrive at a fully comprehensive plan which lays down to a workforce precisely what they must do to maximise efficiency. There will always be room for, and indeed a decisive reliance upon, creativity, imagination and autonomy at all levels of an enterprise. And, because the precise result and potential alternative outcomes of different forms of creativity, imagination and autonomy can never be measured precisely or unambiguously, there will always be room for argument within the enterprise that different courses of action ought to be followed, different work groups within the enterprise given a different role or rewarded differently. Within the external logic of market forces or a central plan there will always be a degree of space for groups and individuals within the enterprise to argue about how its ends ought to be achieved (and indeed what, precisely, its ends are) and how well or badly these ends have been achieved in the past and what contribution was made by different parts of the enterprise to that performance.

In the management of labour this difficulty of linking cause and effect is made more acute because managers have mutually exclusive and contradictory aims which they must try to reconcile. On the one hand, there is a need to enforce order, create stability and predictability, make rules and enforce them: to create a formal division of labour and police its operation. On the other hand, there is the need to foster innovation and change, ensure creativity, encourage informality, autonomy, self-responsibility and flexibility. It is frequently difficult to reconcile these mutually contradictory goals in practice, and impossible to lay down a general policy which spells out in advance how they are to be reconciled in every particularity. Thus there is always a difference between what has been called the 'espoused' and 'operational' policies of managers towards labour. The first refers to their formal rules, the second to the informal processes of compromise and trade-off by which they are applied. Brewster *et al.* (1981, p. 6) found that 'The espoused policies are themselves inconsistent ... may be no more than pious aims or statements, breached with impunity and unrewarded where followed.' This will tend to be true in any system of management. And this casts doubt on the extent to which procedural reform in industrial relations, which inevitably concentrates on formal policies and rules, can be used to change the ways in which managers and workers behave. This helps explain the limits to the reform of industrial relations achieved by the approach of the Donovan Commission. The essential point for our consideration of British management strategy, however, is that its *laissez-faire* ideology and the structure of its organisation are likely to produce a particular combination of espoused and operational policy that is both resistant to change and fits well with Thatcherism.

First of all the 'espoused' policy of management towards labour in Britain has been particularly vague and general because according to *laissez-faire* ideology the management of labour is virtually a problem that by definition should not exist. The relationship between employer and worker is governed by a labour contract that ought in principle to be complete; the entrepreneur ought to know what is to be done with the labour that has been bought, and have the right to direct it accordingly. In practice, as we showed in Chapter 2, this softened into the doctrine that employers and workers had legitimate differences of interest over the price of labour but not over the control of labour, the organisation of work or the process of management. Employers combined a pluralist approach to wages with a unitarist approach to management. One result was that British management did not develop any distinct strategy for dealing with or managing labour. It did not see any distinct need to plan in detail the social relations of production: how labour was to be trained, motivated, deployed and developed. These matters were often left to local management to work out informally. Within such a unitarist approach the only 'espoused' policy towards labour that was necessary was to ensure discipline, proclaim managerial prerogative and keep down labour costs. This might be accompanied by recognition of the need for 'leadership' or the importance of good communications to stress the harmony of interest between manager and worker. However, unions often depended on their ability to control the organisation of work in order to bargain more effectively over wages. This was true not just for craft workers where such traditions were strongest, but for any group of workers in an internal labour market. Collective bargaining depended less on the state of the external labour market and more on the organisation of the internal one. Within the internal labour market management's commitment in principle to absolute prerogative threatened the roots of the workers' bargaining power. In practice, therefore, unions ceded the principle of managerial prerogative while reserving the right to oppose it in practice when it has adverse implications for their members' bargaining position. Indeed the potential to bargain formally over the management of labour was viewed with suspicion because it could incorporate the unions into management decision-making. That is why many unionists as well as managers were hostile to the development of industrial democracy as envisaged in the Bullock Report, in case it should undermine the independent and oppositional stance of free collective bargaining.

Thus beyond the espoused managerial strategy of total prerogative over work organisation has lain the operational policy of admitting limits to it in practice, and in effect submitting the organisation of work to a process of low trust bargaining, mostly local and informal, about what will be acceptable to both sides. In addition, the reality of bargaining over work organisation is reciprocal in its effects. Management become aware of the dangers of premature disclosure or discussion of its plans, lest this facilitate opposition to them. There will be little management expectation of a genuine workforce commitment to cooperation with management over work organisation, and an emphasis on money as a motivator in securing such cooperation as does exist. In turn 'accounting' concepts of labour come to dominate managerial thinking. It is a cost to be reduced, not a resource to be developed.

The material organisation of British management adds a further dimension to the process. As we have seen, most bargaining is done at plant level, particularly in the private sector and particularly in manufacturing. In keeping with *laissez-faire* ideology the main method of monitoring plant performance is profitability. Yet capital investment and longer-term production strategy are typically decided at enterprise level. Management and workers at plant level are therefore left with responsibility for developing an effective and profitable relationship without gaining the corresponding power to ensure its continued existence. Such a structure also works against the ability to implement any strategy for labour relations from the centre. Local management may prefer to circumvent it to follow other priorities (for example, the need to minimise throughput times in the face of a slack product market), knowing that what matters most is not the formal policy, but 'results' and 'the bottom line'.

This model fits well with the evidence we have reviewed in this chapter about management under Thatcherism. In the face of exhortations from the CBI and government about the need to 'involve' employees and secure their commitment to production senior management has mounted 'communications' initiatives and espoused participative ideals. There have been flurries of interest in a succession of techniques which held out the elusive promise of greater worker cooperation and commitment: quality circles, team briefing, 'just in time' management, autonomous work groups, videos, and so on. Nor has this usually been a cynical or opportunist exercise. In the face of severe product market pressures managers have sought ways to reorganise work, shake out unnecessary labour and encourage flexibility. Hence the production of agreements which recognise the 'need' for greater flexibility. But in practice, as the policies have been operationalised, bargaining, informality and local deals have been the rule. Hence there have been few institutional changes in participation, and little evidence of real worker involvement or less adversarial or suspicious attitudes. Consultation on new technology has been minimal and flexibility in practice has come to an abrupt halt at the boundary of the bargaining group, regardless of the fine words the formal agreement or annual company report may contain.

It seems that exhortation and communications have after all remained the main way managers have sought increases in productivity when even the advocates of productivity bargaining themselves were sceptical of the value of such results. It is worth considering the caution urged by Flanders (1964, pp. 237–8) about

> our delusion that productivity can be raised by propaganda ... In this sort of activity cooperation between trade unions and employers has been easily obtained ... its actual impact on management and union behaviour in the workplace has not been impressive. The fatal flaw of productivity propaganda is also the source of its attraction: it involves no commitment to act. Propaganda is mainly concerned with persuading other people to do something ... The manifest lack of response can be explained as an unfortunate consequence of prejudice or ignorance; the failure of propaganda then serves simply to demonstrate the need for more.

Finally, money has remained the main motivator. One explanation for the record rise in the level of real earnings is that management is content to buy flexibility and feels that in the context of restored levels of profitability it can afford to do so. Financial participation too has been one of managers' preferred strategies, despite the paucity of evidence on its real effects. But employers have been much less keen on 'profit-related pay' schemes proposed by the government. They argue that workers would be very reluctant to share losses, that it could constrain their ability to change employment levels and that it could provoke *too much* union interest in the whole process of management and new demands for information disclosure. By contrast profit-sharing schemes are usually sufficiently low key and general to preclude too much argument about whose efforts were responsible for greater profits, or what ought to be done to increase them further. In other words, management values financial participation because any 'participation' effect is indirect and general. Employees will identify more with the company, but not so much that they start demanding a greater say in how it is to be managed.

What Thatcherism appears to have produced is neither new realism nor flexibility but a system of workplace industrial relations with much the same features as were previously seen as responsible for Britain's economic decline. It was argued that in the past managers have given too little attention to motivating labour and organising work efficiently and in practice colluded with unions at local level to allow restrictive practices to continue to permit inflationary wage deals despite the fine words contained in their productivity agreements or in statements emerging from their consultation committees. Yet this is a fairly accurate description of the current situation. Local collusion has become a good thing if it is known as 'decentralisation'. Thus we find one employer arguing that:

> The move to a unit-based organisation means that those who work in such units have close links and can identify directly with the aim of the enterprise; above all it offers them the prospect of more control over their working lives, which is why it will prevail (Cadbury 1985).

Record levels of real wage inflation have led to a situation where Britain's international labour competitiveness is worsening, despite large productivity gains, and has been offset only by a steady and large devaluation of sterling. Britain's manufacturing balance of trade continues to decline. But so long as 'ability to pay' is to be the main principle in negotiations, and profit levels are high, then high wage increases fit with Thatcherism's emphasis on markets. The decisive problem here, as it was identified by Fox and Flanders after the Donovan Report 20 years ago, is firstly, that there is no reason why the sectional interests (both of employer and employee) in play in any bargaining unit should be congruent with a wider industrial or national economic interest, or the interest of those not present at the bargaining table such as the unemployed. Worse, as we pointed out above, it is simply not rational for bargainers to try to take such interests into account, because there is no reward for doing so, no guarantee that others will follow suit and every possibility that the bargainers themselves lose out without any benefit accruing to those they hoped to help. This problem does not arise for those who believe in the infallibility of markets. If they worked perfectly, with perfect knowledge and total flexibility, there would indeed be no problem. Such a world, as we have seen, is perfectly impossible. Rather than enjoy the utopia of labour-market flexibilities we face the real problem of dealing with the negative externalities which sectional decentralised bargaining produces through its actual inability to take wider interests into account. Rutherford (1985) summarises the current situation incisively:

> companies are settling for a small, highly paid workforce and will not willingly increase permanent employment even if output is expanding ... The arrival of unions more interested in industrial agreements than in pursuing national politics ... may accelerate the trend.

In the light of this discussion we might summarise the predicament of British workplace social relations as follows. In the nineteenth century employers' *laissez-faire* outlook led them to neglect how labour was to be organised and deployed, and also turned this into an area of low-trust bargaining with unions which emphasised a short term outlook towards labour of minimising costs. This neglect extended to the organisation of management and capital itself. Other countries in their attempt to compete with Britain developed more conscious structures for organising industry and training, deploying and rewarding labour. The Post-War Settlement did little to alter management's approach to labour, and found increasing problems in the

1970s of reconciling full employment and free collective bargaining partly because of the continued poor productivity growth in industry. But the return to *laissez-faire* plus legal restrictions on unions under Thatcherism has emphasised leaving the deployment of labour to market forces once again. Employee involvement has become a matter of 'communications' (which is probably a euphemism for 'leadership') and financial participation. Productivity has been bought by higher wage increases. A short term outlook has been encouraged by currency fluctuations, high interest rates and a takeover boom, all of which emphasise the importance of quick profits at the expense of long term planning. Individual performance and reward has been emphasised at the expense of collective and collaborative result. Training and research and development remain underfunded. These problems are likely to become more serious as product sophistication and the division of labour needed in production becomes more elaborate. Unfettered market forces might produce higher labour productivity in a sweatshop using simple technology. They are less likely to produce the working relationships needed to motivate and coordinate labour in the era of microelectronic technology.

This raises the problem of producing institutions which can represent the interests which market forces cannot and command legitimacy from both managers and workers who would have to obey not only the letter of any procedures proposed, but their spirit, too. We are back to the problem raised by Kalecki of the need for 'new institutions'.

CHAPTER 7

The Trade Unions and Labourism

Mrs Thatcher might proclaim and Norman Willis complain that Thatcherism has eviscerated the trade unions, but then both have a vested interest in that belief. For the right it is evidence of the success of their policies, for the left it proves their class nature. It would be foolish to claim that unions have not been hit since 1979. But it is remarkable how little evidence there is that unions have been clobbered. The last chapter discussed how at workplace level, especially in the primary sector of the labour market, Thatcherism often meant 'business as usual' for the unions. The institutions of workplace union organisation remain largely intact, and there is surprisingly little evidence of a dramatic shift of bargaining power away from the unions. Brown (1986, p. 163) has argued that there has been a move towards enterprise-based unionism, that technological changes and the switch from manual to white-collar labour has exacerbated inter union disputes, and that 'unions have to cope with more individualistic criteria and more enterprise oriented members'. Changes in training have been eroding the unions' ability to use skill definitions to maintain their bargaining power.

> Nor are there fresh organisational opportunities for unions among those workers more exposed to the vagaries of the labour market ... it is hard to avoid the conclusion that the structure of trade unionism, originally developed for the strategies of employee solidarity, is increasingly being shaped to the needs of the employers (Brown 1986, pp. 163, 165).

It might appear that the sorts of fear voiced by Lane (1982) and others which were discussed in Chapter 1 have in fact materialised. Yet again the evidence presented in Chapter 6 casts great doubt on this. There was less structural change in industrial relations than could well have been expected. The effects of economic restructuring were long established and not clearly linked to union decline. Unions coped with economic restructuring in the 1960s and 1970s. They appeared to have continued to do so in the face of considerable obstacles in the 1980s.

There is another grave problem with such 'new industrial relations' analyses. Few of the features Brown identifies are new, nor are many of the practices criticised by

Hobsbawm (1981) or others. British unionism has always had a strong tradition of craft- and workplace-based sectional, decentralised collective bargaining as Chapter 2 showed. Technological change threatening the demarcation lines between areas of union organisation is not new. Nor are leapfrogging wage claims, disunity or allegations that unions pay too much attention to money or too little attention to rights at work. It is far from clear that such aspects are becoming more important in the labour movement. We have already pointed out that 'no-strike'-type union agreements cover only a tiny proportion of workers. There is also the problem that such agreements are by definition ambiguous. In arbitration the arbitrator is still likely to weigh up the power of the two sides as well as the quality of their case. Harper (1986) reported on the progress of one EETPU 'no-strike' deal:

> The workers struck for two weeks after the sacking of three workers, one of whom had been elected as EETPU shop steward the night before. After the strike, pendulum arbitration was used to resolve a dispute about pay for double day-shift work and came down in favour of the union. It cannot have been a coincidence that the only decision by pendulum arbitration to find in favour of a work force came after the only strike under a no-strike deal. Whatever deals are made between unions and management, workers are still going to find that collectively withdrawing their labour will from time to time be a necessity.

Today it may be the EETPU which is taking the initiative in supposedly 'soft' greenfield deals. But it is not so long ago that the GMBATU enjoyed a similar reputation. It was not clear then, nor is it now, that the fine print of procedure counts for much against the actual organising ability of the union and its substantive aims. Many of the features of 'new' industrial relations are thus rather old. This chapter looks at the actual effects of Thatcherism on the labour movement between 1979 and 1987, and examines the ways in which it responded to the government's new (and historically virtually unprecedented) approach to them, the new economic conditions it produced and to the problem of how to pose an alternative to Thatcherism. For although unions maintained their formal position in the workplace, as Chapter 6 showed, this does not mean that other aspects of their role were unaffected. On the contrary Thatcherism precipitated a crisis in the unions, and their relationship to the Labour Party. The unions responded in a variety of ways.

Trade unions and the dual labour market

The unions did not maintain the gains in membership which they achieved in the face of restructuring in the 1970s. But as Bain (1986) points out, the latter was in many ways 'an exceptional decade' for union membership growth. Increasing dualism in the labour market was an important problem for unions but not a new one. Unions have always found it difficult to organise the low paid, those in sweatshops, homeworkers, workers in industries with poor working conditions and high labour turnover. The rationale for the Wages Council system itself was that there would be industries where union organisation and stable collective bargaining would be difficult to achieve. The main factor here appears to be the 'substitutability' of the labour involved. So long as employers are less dependent on the acquired skills and experience of their labour force, then maintaining their morale and commitment becomes less important, while the ability to bring in new labour to replace those prepared to organise or resist becomes easier. It was thus in this secondary labour market that the rise in unemployment affected workers' bargaining position the most. The vast increase in pay differentials since 1979, shown in Tables 5.11 and 5.12, was clear evidence of this. It is also the case that anti-union legislation probably undermined the ability of unions to organise in this weaker labour market far more than it affected their relations with employers in the primary sector. While 'good' employers may be reluctant to reach for injunctions, the potential cost of lost employee goodwill is much less for others. Longer qualifying periods for unfair dismissal and the emphasis on removing 'barriers' from small employers reduced the protection most for workers in the private services sector where small businesses and shorter lengths of employment are more common. Len Murray, then General Secretary of the TUC, was correct in claiming in 1979 that the government's proposed employment legislation was 'a charter for backward employers which would restore to them the right to treat workers unfairly without infringing the law'. (Gennard 1979, p. 122) In 1986 the Northern Region Secretary of the TGWU complained that employer scare tactics had hit a membership drive by his union: 'One company paraded their employees in front of a dustbin and instructed them to discard their union application forms' (*Guardian*, 17 January 1986). Union organisation in some parts of the private services sector has always been weak because high labour turnover and small employment numbers made the cost of organising high, while the low profit margins, high competition, low entry costs and the importance of labour costs made many employers resist collective bargaining, or made it difficult for unions to negotiate real improvements. Here neither unions nor markets have served workers well, but again this was not a new phenomenon. Nor were the restructuring trends all working in the same direction. For example, mergers and the trend towards both bigger retailing companies, bigger shops and larger hotel chains probably made the conditions for union organisation slightly better.

While the 'substitutability' of labour in the secondary sector makes it more difficult for workers there to organise by their own efforts, union and employment legislation made it more difficult for more powerfully organised groups, or political agencies like local councils, to use their position to encourage or enforce union recognition elsewhere. Thus Rodney Bickerstaffe of the National Union of Public Employers argued at the Wembley Special Conference of the TUC in 1982 that

> In limiting trade disputes to matters solely between an employer and his own employees, the Bill effectively rules out sympathetic action. It clearly isolates those who have no industrial muscle and those who have muscle but who feel

constrained not to use it because of its effect on fellow workers. Women, part-time workers and low paid workers will suffer the hardest.

Education and social welfare services — where will support come from [for] those? People have already said they must be supported. I look forward to it in the future. Hospitals — where you cannot stand with us shoulder to shoulder in our problems, but where every two bit do-gooder with a one day conscience can break through our picket lines to look after their dear patients for a few hours if there is a blaze of publicity. They will not do what our workers do: care for them in silence year after year, decade after decade (TUC 1982, p. 389).

So that even though Conservative ministers publicly regretted that trade unions had, over the years, come to represent the strong rather than the weak (Young 1986) their own employment legislation probably made it more difficult for unions to organise in the secondary sector rather than the primary sector of the labour market.

The structure of the two faces of unionism

In Chapter 3 we noted the distinction made by Flanders (1961a) between the two faces of unionism: those of 'sword of justice' and 'vested interest'. The evidence from Chapter 6 suggests that despite high unemployment the unions have been able to continue to play their role of 'vested interest', but Thatcherism has had a much bigger and more destructive impact on their role as 'sword of justice'. These two roles tend to be pursued by unions as distinct activities in separate places. Collective bargaining of wages is done mostly at plant and company level, often by shop stewards who know more about the details of their own company than full-time officials. Conversely, the pursuit of social justice is more a matter for national action (much of it is focused on government and Westminster) organised by full-time officials. It comprises exerting pressure on government about its economic, social and industrial policies, pursuing appropriate legal action on behalf of members, mounting campaigns to influence public opinion and putting a labour movement view across to the media. It also, of course, embraces the special relationship between the trade unions and the Labour Party.

The separateness of these two spheres of action is a distinctive feature of British industrial relations. But it is not total. Bargaining in the public sector tends to be more centralised, as we have seen. There are also national negotiations in the private sector, as well as Wages Councils, but these national negotiations are often nearer to the 'social justice' purposes of unions in so far as they tend to be concerned with setting floors for minimum earnings or dealing with the wages of low-paid workers. 'Sword of justice' issues can arise at workplace level, too — over rights at work, for example.

Three factors have undermined union influence at national level. The first is the overall loss of membership caused by the fall in employment and by the way it has been concentrated where unions previously had members. Table 7.1 shows the fall in national union membership since 1979, the year in which post-war membership

Table 7.1 Trade union membership and density 1979–85, UK.

	1979	1980	1981	1982	1983	1984	1985
Union membership (millions)	13.3	12.9	12.1	11.6	11.2	11.0	10.7
Number of unions	453	438	414	408	394	375	373
Employees in employment (millions)*	23.1	22.9	21.8	21.4	21.1	21.2	21.5
Density (per cent)	57.4	56.4	55.4	54.2	53.3	51.9	50.0

* Seasonally adjusted June figure
Source: Department of Employment Gazette, February 1987

reached its peak after an uninterrupted rise. Despite maintaining membership levels and density in the workplaces where they are represented, trade unions have lost some 2.5 million members since 1979. This loss of membership has meant sharply declining income for most unions at a time when the demands on their resources have increased, and came after a decade when unions had been used to steadily rising membership levels. One result of this has been the merging of several smaller unions with larger general unions over the period, and a weakening of the contrast in identity between 'craft' and 'general' unions. For example, the Boilermakers' Union, faced with a plummeting membership, eventually merged with the General and Municipal Workers Union. Thus some eighty unions disappeared between 1979 and 1985.

The second source of union weakness has, of course, been government policy itself. The Prime Minister spoke scornfully of the irrelevance to the nation's economic problems of 'beer and sandwiches at No. 10' (as she called talks with trade union leaders). Tripartism was abandoned. Union leaders and the TUC were simply not consulted about relevant government policy, or their views and advice were ignored. This broke up a relationship which had endured for over a century. It became an even firmer policy once James Prior was moved from the Department of Employment. In 1982 the Cabinet Office was (secretly) instructed to 'freeze out' unions from the membership of public bodies at national level. Relations between the TUC and the government reached their nadir when the government banned trade union membership at GCHQ, the intelligence-gathering unit in Cheltenham. The government claimed that threats of industrial action in the past during pay disputes in the civil service made the union presence there a 'threat to national security'. Despite offers from the TUC which were remarkably conciliatory, amounting effectively to a no-strike agreement, the government stuck to its original intention. As a result the TUC withdrew from the NEDC. The government took little notice of this, and employers voiced fears that if the unions boycotted this essentially tripartite body for too long it might be abolished by the government.

Thirdly, the unions could not be confident of the committed support of their own membership. As we saw in Chapter 3, many union members shared the view that while their own local union organisation might be fine, unions as a whole had too much power. Thus in contrast to the demonstrations the TUC had been able to mount against Heath's Industrial Relations Bill, the unions' early promises of mass opposition and even civil disobedience in response to the Government's programme of union legislation failed to materialise. A lobby against the Employment Bill in March 1980 attracted 140,000 people according to the TUC, but only 30,000 according to the police. A Day of Action two months later brought uneven support mostly from the public sector where the effects of the government's attitude to trade unions were potentially more direct. Many large workforces in the private sector refused to back calls to participate. It was the last attempt by the TUC to use its industrial strength against the government's employment policies.

The trade union response to legislation

This loss of influence and the more hostile environment for unionism caused by the government's legislation and the slump opened up many fissures in the national face of trade unionism. This was not simply a question of different political outlooks of union executives, or the different interests of unions organising different types of worker. There was a more general confusion and uncertainty about how to respond to the twin problems of a radical challenge from above by the state combined with the apparent ambivalence of the membership below.

At first, as we have seen, the TUC sought simply to resist the government's legislation outright. In February 1980 the General Council of the TUC decided that all unions should refuse to accept public money for ballots. In 1982, at the special TUC conference held to discuss how to organise against the Employment Bill of that year, Terry Duffy of the AUEW recalled how the refusal of his union to comply with the Industrial Relations Act had helped its demise. That action had cost the union sequestration of its funds and he hoped that a future Labour government would reimburse unions retrospectively for the financial consequences they might endure under the Conservative's legislation. He added:

> no union should break with the Congress policy concerning the use of public funds for elections. We say that, even though every one of our 201 officials is elected by postal ballot, not by my decision but by a decision of the membership. If you want democracy, then you take your orders from the bottom. Our union will always insist that all our officials periodically face the electorate, but in spite of that tremendous expense, we have decided not to accept one penny from this Government for postal ballots.
>
> Further we must agree to give full support, where necessary, to a union that requires assistance when facing legal action by an employer. This support must come from the solidarity of the Movement (TUC 1982, p. 396).

But not only was such outright opposition potentially cripplingly expensive in terms both of public money refused, assets sequestrated or fines paid for contempt of court: it raised the problem of how to challenge the law and on what basis it could be challenged. The TUC drew back from blanket endorsement of any resistance by an individual union to the law, since that threatened to commit it in advance to action whose consequences were quite unpredictable. The watchword was to be unity in the face of the government's challenge, with the basis of that unity determined by the TUC General Council. Thus the GMWU at its conference that May wanted to grant it 'authority to instruct normally autonomous unions' but this simply flew in the face of the reality of the decentralisation of power and decision-making in British trade unions. Terry Duffy's remark (TUC 1982, p. 384) was to prove nearer the mark: 'may I give a word of caution and remind you it will remain the prerogative of individual unions to do what they like'. The first major test of the TUC's strategy came with the dispute between the NGA and the *Stockport Messenger* at Warrington. In December 1983 it refused to back the NGA's attempts to ignore the law and in effect withdrew its support.

Len Murray had argued of the government's legislation:

> This is not the use of the law, the proper and legitimate purpose of the law, to generalise good practice or to correct occasional errors. On the contrary, this is an abuse of the law. This is the Government bringing politics into industrial relations — and that must be our answer if they accuse us of playing politics (TUC 1982, p. 407).

The difficulty in sustaining this position was that what constituted 'good practice' had become a political question. To accuse the government of 'bringing politics into industrial relations' would have been a severe criticism during the era of voluntarism, the separation of politics and economics and the state 'holding the ring'. But after the developments of the 1970s it seemed rather thin. Moreover it was unclear to the outside observer (even if it was obvious to veterans of the union movement) how far the demand to take the law out of industrial relations went, and what its full implications were, because such a demand could be linked to quite different sorts of challenge to the government. Arthur Scargill of the NUM, for example, argued that the issue was the survival of the trade union movement and that implied challenging the state outright. It was not a matter of seeking to resist and repeal bad law, but of destroying any law that threatened unionism:

> [Conference] has recognised the fundamental principle that it is no longer sufficient to defend the interests of our members — it is imperative that we begin to take the offensive against the Tory Government, who are designing a Bill to destroy the British trade union Movement ... We can go through this legislation line by line ... but if we begin to tackle the problem in that way we will be making a fundamental mistake. It is not the responsibility of the British trade union Movement to try and argue the pros and cons of legislation that seeks to destroy us. Our responsibility is to fight and destroy the Bill and all that goes with it ... We have to make up our minds today on what we are going to do in the face of this declaration of war — because that is what it is. It is a declaration of class war against the trade union and labour Movement ... I have constantly advocated defiance of the law (TUC 1982, pp. 383–4).

Therefore beyond the trade unions' common recognition of a need for 'unity' to resist the government's legislation there was neither agreement about how to resist it, why to resist it or the material means to commit unions to a common strategy to oppose it, even if one could be fully agreed. Beyond this was the fundamental problem that aspects of the legislation were popular with the public and the membership. Eric Hammond of the EETPU argued:

> Does anyone here really believe that the Tories have produced this Bill to improve industrial relations? No! They calculate that if they are seen to be union-bashing they will then gain electoral advantage. And are they wrong? Does not every measurement of public — indeed, trade union members' — opinion show that we only have minority support? Why? Why? Why? That is the question that we should ask ourselves ... Why are we so unpopular that this disastrous Government can gain support by anti-union legislation? When we get the answer and act upon it, when we are properly representative of our members, then no legislation and no government can hold fear for us (TUC 1982, pp. 393–4).

In the event the TUC edged away from supporting action that was unlawful because of the potentially disastrous financial consequences. Unlike the Industrial Relations Act of 1971 the new employment legislation stuck. In part this was because it had been designed to emphasise penalising financially trade unions rather than individuals. In its early years of operation it successfully avoided creating 'martyrs' while effectively facing unions with crippling penalties if they lent official support to action which was unlawful. In part it was because the alternative of 'keeping the law out of industrial relations' was no longer credible and finally the greater unpopularity of unions and their alleged abuse of their power played a part too.

After the Conservative landslide in 1983 the TUC re-examined its stance. Congress supported a motion on the 'lessons of the 1983 election' which re-examined the unions' outright opposition to government policy. In September the TUC held talks with Norman Tebbit, the Employment Secretary. An internal strategy document argued that the TUC should recognise its previous dependence on government cooperation, and seek instead to revitalise unions' branch networks at the grassroots. In practice this policy of 'new realism' came to little. The government's banning of trade unions at GCHQ made it clear that it would offer few concessions to moderates in the TUC which would allow them to argue that 'new realism' worked. By 1984 the tremendous conflict of the miners dispute froze relations between the unions and the government once more. The interlude did have one important effect, however. Norman Tebbit's successor, Tom King, was persuaded by the TUC to drop the original intention of replacing the ability of union members to 'contract out' of paying contributions to political funds with the requirement for them to 'contract in'. A similar move in 1927 had cut the number of unionists paying such contributions (much of which went to support for the Labour Party) dramatically. Instead unions were required to hold secret ballots of their members to approve having a political fund at all, but members would have to 'contract out' of it once it was approved.

But the TUC's move towards new realism, even if it proved unsuccessful, cast doubts over the credibility of the previously established policy of 'no compliance'. In November 1984 the EETPU, closely followed by the AUEW, voted to break ranks and apply for public money to pay for secret ballots. This was in clear breach of the TUC's policy and reversed their own previous stance. This provoked a severe crisis in the TUC. The General Council voted to discipline both unions in January 1985 and matters came to a head at the Congress in September that year. On one side the TUC faced the fact that both unions had deliberately flouted clear Congress policy, and undermined the unity of resistance to the government's proposals. Both unions were fulfilling Tery Duffy's warning three years earlier that the TUC's authority need count for little if powerful unions decided to ignore it. Aside from the issues of policy involved it would be humiliating for the TUC to let this happen. For their part the two unions were convinced that the refusal to accept ballot money was anachronistic. The amounts of money involved were large, and the point of principle now obscure since most unions were moving towards acceptance of ballots as the best means of internal democracy. At the eleventh hour a face-saving formula was produced, a classic British industrial relations fudge, which essentially allowed the unions to take the money without censure. The alternative for the TUC could have been yet worse: the secession of the two unions and the emergence of a rival trade union confederation.

By March 1986, when the TUC held a special conference on labour-law reform, there was a further shift in approach. It was accepted that secret ballots were an established and popular fact which trade unions ought to accept. The demand for complete autonomy in deciding how to organise their internal affairs was seen to be untenable. Whilst some proposed measures sought to continue the trend of the 1970s to greater legal support for collective bargaining and union organisation, there was also a new emphasis on individual rights. This represented the realisation by unions that increasing dualism in the labour market made it unrealistic to expect unions to be able to defend all individual workers through collective action. There would need to be a wider framework of rights, which unions might help police but would not be dependent on them. This was a substantial change of emphasis. In the past unions had embraced voluntarism and been wary of blanket legal remedies lest these made unions less important for employees. But now they were coming to see the law as a potential ally rather than a competitor in regulating the labour market.

The industrial response

It was not just over union legislation that the union movement found itself divided. In some major disputes union leaderships found themselves at loggerheads where the immediate interests of their own memberships clashed. The ability of individual unions or of the TUC to take the initiative and exercise leadership in the struggles they entered foundered on their inability to command the loyalty of their members or support from the general public. In January 1981, in the wake of the steel strike of the previous year, a 'Triple Alliance' between the Iron and Steel Trades Confederation (ISTC), National Union of Railwaymen (NUR) and NUM was formed, reminiscent of that of 60 years before. Its purpose was to stand together against government attempts to push through closures and redundancies in the three industries which were intimately linked (steel production depended on supplies of coking coal delivered by rail). The alliance was not as comprehensive as it really needed to be. The power workers, for example, were not party to it. In the event, during the coal dispute it fell apart. While the NUM demanded that steel production should stop, and promised to blockade imports of steel from rival producers, the ISTC insisted that they be allowed sufficient coking coal to avoid closures. Once the NUR followed the NUM's demands the ISTC cooperated with management to organise ore and coke deliveries by road. At its June 1984 conference the ISTC pledged support for the NUM but asked that it 'recognise the precarious state of the British steel industry and in particular the effect on the mining communities should any works suffer irreparable harm either of a mechanical or a commercial nature resulting from inadequate fuel supplies' (Marsden 1984, p. 412).

Just as the steel workers' support for the miners fell short of practical support, so too was the Transport and General Workers Union (TGWU) unable to halt the movement of coal by road. Nor was it likely that, had they asked their members, the electricians or the power workers could have commanded their support. The TUC did not even feel able to order a levy of union members to support the miners and while the 1984 Congress offered fine words of support it could offer little practical help. The circumstances surrounding the coal strike, the strategy adopted by the NUM and the response of the state, including the police, have been widely debated elsewhere. It would be superfluous to repeat them here, but some of the implications of the course of the dispute for unionism in general can be noted. The dispute emphasised the real conflicts of outlook and objective held by unions behind the rhetoric of Congress unity. All might agree in principle on the justice of the miners case, but that did not mean that there was agreement, even within the NUM itself, about how best to advance it. There was no central authority powerful enough to weld these divergent objectives into a common strategy, nor would the NUM itself have been happy to hand over the conduct of its own dispute to the TUC. On the contrary the NUM avoided involving the TUC as far as possible. The tensions between the interests of the miners and the movement as a whole were never clearly articulated or resolved. The dispute also showed the real problems the union movement faced in commanding popular support for its actions. This problem became focused on the twin issues of ballots and mass picketing. The NUM's case was unequivocal. A ballot was unnecessary: it was immoral to vote 'other people out of a job', while mass picketing was seen as a key symbol of the union's unity and determination not to be intimidated by anti-union legislation.

Richard Hyman (1986) makes some trenchant observations about both these issues: 'Both sides endorsed the simple equation: to oppose the strike is to support the ballot; to support the strike is to oppose the ballot'. But ballots were a long-established feature of the NUM's traditions.

> A successful ballot campaign could have been a potent symbol of legitimacy, not only in presenting the unions' case to the world outside, but also in its internal relations. To refuse a national ballot on the grounds that it might be lost was to concede, in effect, that many of those actually on strike participated unwillingly (Hyman 1986, p. 335).

Hyman also casts grave doubts on whether mass picketing achieved its objective, rather than being counterproductive both in terms of public support and relations within the NUM. At some point the purpose of a mass picket turns from peaceful persuasion to intimidation:

> many participants in a mass picket may take it for granted that if reasoned argument fails, the veto of force is the logical alternative ... the early picket line confrontation turned the divisions between Yorkshire and Nottinghamshire into an unbridgeable chasm ... To present the issue starkly: what happens if persuasion fails? Admit defeat or employ more forceful methods? ... Unless fellow workers are regarded as by some means open to reasoning and conviction, the very notion of class politics is futile (Hyman 1986, pp. 336, 343, 349).

The objection to voting on other people's jobs was essentially that a majority could override the legitimate interests of a minority in the union. But such an objection implied either that there was a better procedure available to reconcile these differences (such as collective discussion) or that the rights of minorities were always sacrosanct. This was not a position the NUM leadership itself would sustain in the future. When in 1987 British Coal proposed to sanction a new pit at Margam in South Wales only on condition that a six-day working week was introduced, the NUM nationally sought to overturn the local lodge's acceptance of the proposal. On this occasion it was indeed demanding the right for others to vote people out of a job. In both instances it was a question of balancing the sectional and general interests, albeit in different circumstances and on different issues.

The miners' strike highlighted the potential for division within the trade union movement, but it would be wrong to conclude from this that the whole movement was hopelessly weak. Least of all should the outcome of the miners' strike be taken as some symbol of the overrall balance of power between government and the unions because the miners were in a very poor bargaining position. The government had spent almost a decade preparing for the dispute. It was prepared to 'invest', to use Chancellor Lawson's term, billions to win it. Coal stocks were at very high levels. The local productivity-payments scheme imposed by the NCB had fostered disunity. There were ample alternative sources of energy. Other unions were poorly placed to offer assistance. And even then, in June and September 1984, the NCB offered agreements which would have been a long way short of victory for the Board. Other prominent disputes told a rather different story of the unions' ability to campaign and win popular support. In particular the two long-running disputes by teachers in Scotland and in England and Wales stretching from January 1985 to 1987 effectively left the government's public sector pay policy in tatters. The teachers' unions learnt from the miners' failure: they made sure of their members' support, and that of parents and the general public. Avoiding 'set piece' confrontations, they engaged in a variety of tactics which allowed them to develop and escalate the campaign over a long period without losing popular support or sapping members' morale. They broke cash limits and put 'comparability' firmly back on the agenda. In doing so the major rival unions representing teachers in England and Wales overcame years of mutual suspicion and hostility to work together.

The crisis of Labourism

So far we have considered the tensions and strains caused to the unions by the changed attitude of the state. Equally significant, especially for their attempts to develop a 'sword of justice' role, was the profound crisis of Labourism which erupted after the 1979 election. In Chapter 3 we considered the development of Labourism and how it had coped with growing pressures and changes in the 1970s. In the 1980s these pressures became too great, exploding into schisms in the Labour Party and alarm in the trade unions. In the aftermath of its defeat in 1979 there was the usual post-election post-mortem within the party. But in the context of disillusionment with the Social Contract and the disintegration of the unions' Praetorian Guard role, the usual demands of Conference for more radical policies were now tied to the demand for constitutional change which would stop what was seen as the 'betrayal' by the Parliamentary Party of the socialist aspirations of the membership. Tony Benn became the parliamentary spokesperson and exponent of this analysis but it was not just the left who thought the Party's poor record in office was because the leadership had escaped the control of the rank and file. At the 1979 Conference the Party's General Secretary, Ron Hayward, argued that its recent defeat had happened because 'For good or ill, the Cabinet supported by MPs ignored Congress and Conference decisions. It was as simple as that' (quoted in Butler and Kavanagh 1984, p. 46). Crucially, enough of the trade unions lent their support to such moves to enable them to succeed. This was not just because of their frustration with the Social Contract, but because of the internal democratisation of trade unions we outlined in Chapter 3. While the 1978 conference rejected mandatory reselection of MPs because AUEW leader Hugh Scanlon 'forgot' to cast his union's block vote in favour of the move (Butler and Kavanagh 1984, p. 48) the 1979 Conference passed this and also supported moving control of the manifesto from the PLP to the NEC. In June 1980 the unions supported the move for an electoral college rather than the PLP to choose the Party leader. This was finally sanctioned by a Special Conference at Wembley in January 1981. This system was used to elect the deputy leader in that year. Denis Healey, the clear favourite of the PLP, only just beat Tony Benn and over one-third of the union votes went in support of the latter.

These moves propelled more than 20 MPs to leave the Party and form the SDP. They not only objected to the leftward drift of the Party's policies — that was something the PLP had lived with for some time. They were also alarmed by the prospect of the trade unions dropping their automatic support for the PLP and joining forces with its left-wing critics on some issues. As we have seen this was a virtually inevitable development of the closer relationship between politics and economics in the 1970s. It would have been almost unthinkable for the trade unions to bargain with the Labour leadership over the terms of the Social Contract yet simply rubber stamp the leadership's position at Party Conference. Even if union leaders had desired such a relationship, their delegations might well have baulked at it. The unions were certainly conscious of their predicament and anxious not to over-exert their influence. For those who joined the SDP however, the loss of the Praetorian Guard turned the 'democratisation' of the Party into the prospect that the PLP would no longer be free to develop its own policies and could be forced leftward. Thus in the name of democracy itself they abandoned the 'democraticised' Labour Party. Lord Houghton of Sowerby (1981, p. 157) describes the essence of their thinking:

> The role of the trade unions in the Labour Party is becoming crucial, disturbing and even dangerous. The unions have traditionally been a steadying and stabilising influence. They are now in the fray [between left and right] and as we saw at the Wembley Conference they may behave very strangely indeed ... The Labour Party is too dependent on union money and is too easily swayed on policies by volatile block votes.

Butler and Kavanagh (1984, pp. 70–1) argue that the schism was not inevitable. The constitutional decisions which prompted the exodus were won by narrow margins. 'And if Mr Healey had been elected Leader in 1980 and had fought, as Michael Foot would never fight, against the constitutional changes and left wing tendencies, many who deserted would have remained.' While this is a significant point, we also have to consider the forces making for the constitutional changes and left-wing policies, which had grown dramatically in the 1970s. Chapter 3 also analysed how these tensions had been contained in the past. The difficulty of containing them in the future would surely have been ever greater. As we shall see, the formation of the SDP did not remove them. As Miller (1984) makes clear, Labour's internal ructions were disastrous for its popular support. Long before the Falklands campaign, Labour's support in the opinion polls fell from nearly 50 per cent in December 1980 — some 15 per cent ahead of the Conservative Party — to under 30 per cent one year later. Union concern at Labour's electoral fortunes prompted a meeting at which the unions agreed not to support the left in the Party so long as the right agreed to abide by the new constitution. In 1982 Tony Benn was voted off the TUC–Labour Party Coordinating Committee. But what the unions could not deliver was a credible assurance on their role in the future economic policy pursued by a potential Labour government. Its proposed National Economic Assessment embraced the concept of 'planned incomes' but its precise implications were vague: it was emphasised there would be no return to government-imposed wage restraint.

In the 1983 election fewer trade unionists than ever before supported the Labour Party. As Table 7.2 shows, this was a long-term trend, but what was decisive was the haemorrhage of unionist support to the Social Democratic/Liberal Alliance. Using pollsters' traditional market-research-based definitions, 35 per cent of skilled manual workers voted Labour, as against 39 per cent who supported the Conservatives. Again this continued a long-term trend. As well as being an electoral disaster for Labour, these results suggested that 'class dealignment' which had worked for Labour, as we pointed out in Chapter 3, was now working against it.

Table 7.2 Trade unionists voting for political parties (per cent)

	1964	1970	1974	1974	1979	1983
Labour	73	66	55	55	50	39
Conservative	22	28	30	23	35	31
Others	5	6	15	22	15	30

Source: Butler and Kavanagh 1975; 1979; 1983; Taylor 1982

However, analysis of class and voting by Heath, Jowell and Curtice (1985) suggested a very different picture. They redefined social class from the normal pollster's definitions so that workers were allocated between the categories of 'salariat', 'routine white-collar' foremen/technicians (manual workers who exercised supervision or enjoyed considerable autonomy whether or not they were formally skilled) and all other manual workers (skilled or unskilled). They also defined married women's class by that of their own occupation, not that of their spouse. Their analysis of the 1983 election on this basis produced the results shown in Table 7.3. On the basis of similar reanalysis of earlier elections, they concluded that apparent class dealignment in voting was due to the growing divergence between pollsters' definitions of class and its workplace reality. Manual workers' support for Labour remained strong, but their numbers had shrunk dramatically because of economic change: from nearly half of the electorate in 1964 to around one-third in 1983. Meanwhile the 'salariat' increased from 19 to 27 per cent. What this also meant was that the 'new' unionists among the white-collar workers and salariat were not supporting Labour: the electoral basis of Labourism was crumbling away at the same time as its organisational expression was in crisis.

It was in this context that the post-1983 election period brought a loosening of the ties between the Labour leadership and the trade unions. In part this expressed a return to the older arrangement whereby the unions provided vital finance for the Party, but left the leadership free to get on with its business. However, there were

Table 7.3 1983 General election voting by social class (Heath *et al* definitions)

	Conservative	Labour	Liberal/SDP
Petty bourgeouisie	71	12	17
Salariat	54	14	31
Foremen/technicians	48	26	25
Routine white-collar	46	25	27
Manual	30	49	20

Source: Heath *et al* (1985, p. 33)

other factors, too. Even after 1983 the TUC found itself unable to wean itself from its commitment to free collective bargaining and reach agreement with the party on wage restraint. Meanwhile, The Labour leadership and a substantial majority in the TUC had become convinced of the case for the retention of ballots in internal union government and industrial relations. In a decisive speech to the Congress in 1986, Neil Kinnock distanced himself from the unions and emphasised that they needed him more than he needed them. After outlining his proposals for economic regeneration he added pointedly: 'If cooperation and agreement are not given in any quarter it might slow the pace, it might retard progress, but it will not change the direction of these policies for jobs and for growth in our country (*Financial Times* 3 September 1986).

Labourism did, however, survive its severest test of the second Conservative government: the ballots on political funds. As we saw earlier, one of the fruits of the attempts by unions to talk to the Thatcherites, even if the latter saw little point in talking to them, was the political funds ballotting arrangements of the 1984 Trade Union Act. It seems that the government expected that several unions would fail to win the vote to operate political funds, thus forcing them to end all financial support for the Labour Party. Its expectations were based on the basis of the low level of unionists' support for Labour in the general election. However, they would have done well to recall Churchill's more perceptive analysis which we cited in Chapter 2. In the event unionists drew an important distinction between voting for Labour, allowing their union to support Labour financially and be linked to it politically and having political funds to campaign on a broad range of issues. As a result, every single ballot produced high turnouts and substantial majorities for the retention of political funds. Steele *et al.* (1986, p. 456) recorded that just under 3 million unionists in 37 unions voted to keep the funds, 83 per cent of those voting. Four unions, two just before and two just after the Act became operative, voted to establish political funds for the first time. Campaigns around the Act also increased numbers paying the levy in some unions. It also inspired the creation of the organisation Trade Unionists for Labour, whose object was to make available the industrial machinery of the unions to the Labour Party to assist in its campaigning. Far from throwing the link between unions and the party into crisis, the Trade Union Act breathed new life into it. Tom King, who as Employment Secretary had overseen the Act, found himself following the path of one of his equally unpopular predecesors, James Prior, to the Northern Ireland Office. The campaign for retention of political funds had another major benefit for the unions. 'The political fund retention campaign made trade unions return to their members and rediscover the skills of communicating with, campaigning amongst and winning the arguments. The members, in turn, responded by giving their overwhelming support' (Steele *et al.* 1986, p. 461).

The unevenness of 'New Unionism'

The threatened schism between the TUC and the AEU and EETPU appeared to symbolise for many the gulf between a new realism approach, on one hand, and the old style collectivism of the TGWU or NUM on the other. It was not just over ballot money that the two unions confronted the TUC. In the News International dispute at Wapping the EETPU was accused of collaboration with the employers in recruiting and training a workforce which would take the jobs of the Fleet Street workforce who were members of the NGA and SOGAT. The eventual prize the EETPU hoped to secure was a single-union agreement in an industry which technological change made it keen to expand into. Elsewhere, especially amongst Japanese electronic companies in Wales, it had pioneered various forms of 'no-strike' greenfield site agreements. In a similar fashion, the AEU concluded a single-status no-strike deal at the Nissan car plant in Sunderland.

These trends have to be placed in perspective, however. As we have discussed above, both the extent of such agreements, their novelty and their divergence from existing practice have tended to be greatly exaggerated. The idea that Britain is starting to experience an 'Americanisation' of industrial relations leading to growing non-unionism or business-style unionism just does not stand up to the evidence. As we saw in Chapter 2, there are many features of traditional unionism in Britain which are 'business-like' in the sense of basing their rationale on controlling the labour market. Indeed the approach of the AEU and EETPU is in important ways more closely wedded to the old voluntarist system than that of many other unions. The most forceful speaker against TUC support for minimum wage legislation at the Congress debate in 1986 was Eric Hammond, leader of the Electricians. Supported by the AEU, he spoke up for differentials and against ill-judged interference with market-based collective bargaining. The AEU, along with other unions in the Confederation of Shipbuilding and Engineering Unions had been discussing flexibility and moves towards single-union agreements with the EEF for over two years when in February 1987 its executive voted to continue the discussions by only a single vote. By contrast many of the 'traditional' unions have been turning away from their reliance on voluntarism and collective bargaining in response to the new environment of a hostile government and increasing labour-market dualism. The TUC voted to support minimum wage legislation for the first time at its 1986 Congress, revising its established stance that such legal protection might interfere with collective bargaining. The TGWU with its 'Link Up' campaign and GMBATU with the 'FLARE' (Fair Laws And Rights in Employment) initiative sought to try new methods of recruitment and new types of trade union activity and organisation to appeal to the particular position of workers in the 'secondary' sector of the labour market, particularly part-timers and temporary workers.

While single-union no-strike deals might be a new trend for the craft unions there were different new trends emerging elsewhere, particularly in public sector white-collar unions, such as the rolling strikes and lightning industrial action orchestrated by the teacher's unions or the token strike action taken by the Association of University Teachers: a body which a decade earlier would have denied that it constituted a 'union' rather than a professional association with the ear of the Department of Education and Science. Its growing radicalism was a function of its members' frustration at the impact of public expenditure cuts. Similarly the Royal College of Nursing, another 'moderate' union, discussed dropping its commitment to avoid all strike action in the face of the problems faced by the National Health Service.

The growing tension between policy and practice

In their 'sword of justice' role British unions have stood publicly for greater equality in various forms: more equality between classes through greater rights for employees, or more industrial democracy and better public services which reduce the relative advantages of private education or health care. They have stood for greater equality between men and women, and for the rights of ethnic minorities. They have stood for the rights of unemployed workers, calling for economic policies which would reduce unemployment and for better provision for the unemployed. However, this 'sword of justice' role has been weakened not only by the Conservative onslaught on the unions' national role, but by the crisis of their traditional political arm: Labourism. Their pursuit of a 'sword of justice' role has been hampered by their structure, and even by the very success and relative strength of their locally-based 'vested interest' role. This has underlined the tendency for the policy and fine words of Congress and national conferences to come into conflict with the everyday practice of what happens in the workplace or union branch. In turn this reflects the fact that there are often deep conflicts of interest between the different sectors of the unions' membership, and an absence of structures where these conflicts can be openly debated and resolved.

One source of division is gender. The vast rise in women's membership of unions has seldom been paralleled by a corresponding increase in their representation on local, regional or national governing or policy-making bodies (see, for example, Ellis 1981). Behind the policy commitments to gender equality lies the real problem for the unions in practice that greater opportunities for women could mean relatively fewer opportunities for their male members. While some of the public sector unions have made considerable advances, others, particularly in the private sector, have found it difficult to alter their branch structures or methods of organisation to respond to the different needs or interests of women. They have neither altered the assumption that union activists will have their domestic labour done for them, nor challenged the culture of masculinity that pervades the movement's organisation. Their structures make it very difficult for them to tackle one of the major sources of gender inequality: occupational segregation. Unions as much as employers have tended to accept the asumption that women's real orientation is to the household rather than to work, and that their link with work is less strong. Yet most of the evidence shows that both women's rationale for working and their attachment to it are very similar to men's, despite their responsibility for the bulk of domestic labour and child care (see, for example, Dex 1986; Martin and Roberts 1984; and Coyle 1981). Unions have been able, albeit imperfectly, to take up issues of equal pay and discrimination, but they have not been able to raise the gender stereotyping of work, or the masculinity of technology (Cockburn 1983b) partly because the roots of union organisation are firmly embedded in masculinity itself (Cockburn 1983a). This has also been relevant to the unions' approach to working hours.

Table 7.4 Time use, Spring 1985 (hours per week)

| | Employees | | | | Housewives |
| | Full-time | | Part-time | | |
	Male	Female	Male	Female	
Work and travel	45.0	40.8	24.3	22.2	—
Domestic and personal labour*	33.1	45.1	48.8	61.3	76.6
Free time:					
total	33.5	24.6	38.3	27.5	32.2
weekday	2.6	2.1	4.5	3.1	4.2
weekend day	10.2	7.2	7.8	5.9	5.6

* Cooking, shopping, children, eating, washing, getting up and going to bed.
Source: Social Trends vol. 17, p. 163, Table 10.1

Individual unions and the TUC have campaigned officially for shorter working hours, both as part of general social and economic advance, and as a strategy for reducing unemployment by sharing participation in work more easily. Nor has this campaign been without its successes. The standard working week of many employees has been reducing gradually, for example the EEF conceded a cut in hours in 1981, and there has been a substantial increase in workers' holiday entitlements. However, the issue of hours of work is very relevant to gender inequality, too. Women have argued that their responsibility for the mass of domestic labour prevents their equal participation in the labour market. Table 7.4 certainly confirms this. Women workers do between one-quarter and one-third more domestic labour than their male equivalents, whether they work full- or part-time, and housewives do even more: about two-and-one-third times what the average full-time male worker does. And average figures understate the inequalities because a basic amount of domestic labour is of a sort that cannot usually be shared or done for others: eating, washing, getting up and going to bed. If we allowed 15 hours a week for these activities (surely a conservative estimate) then we would have to conclude that housewives did about three-and-a-half times as much domestic labour as full-time male workers. These inequalities show up more starkly when we compare the amount of 'free' time left to women. Full-time male workers, even though they spend an average of 45 hours a week on their work, nevertheless enjoy more free time than housewives or women who work part-time because they do so much less domestic labour, especially at weekends.

One factor here is the length of the male working week. Shorter hours would be a first step enabling many men to take part in domestic labour. But this means discussing what is done with shorter hours and how they are distributed. In practice formally shorter hours tend to produce greater overtime at premium rates. Thus, average hours worked by operatives in manufacturing rose by 3 per cent between 1980 and 1986. Nor have unions faced up to the relative merits of large blocks of time off at once (usually favoured by men) or shorter working days (favoured by women). The policy aspirations of unions at a national level have cut across the sectional interests of their members at local level, where the real power has been exercised.

A parallel problem faced the unions on industrial democracy. The presence of EEC legislation and absence of British employer initiatives gave the unions an attractive opportunity. It was an issue which was popular and which the unions were alert to. It was a clear example to them of their lack of 'positive' power and the reality of managerial prerogative in contrast to the image of union power and weak employers; thus Len Murray argued (TUC 1982, p. 379)

> The truth is that unions have not too much, but too little, power. Even where unions are well organised, employers set themselves to restrict and limit union influence to a narrow range of issues. In no other organisation in this country are the commitment to, and the practice of, democracy more deeply embedded than in the trade union Movement. Far from limiting freedoms, it is unions which provide workers with their only means of enlarging their freedoms against powerful employers.

This was also an issue to which many observers sympathetic to the unions had urged they turn their attention. Just as Flanders in the 1960s urged that unions take up the issue of status and rights at work, many who doubted the progressive nature of sectional wage bargaining in the 1970s advocated that they should focus instead on industrial democracy. Kitching (1983, p. 125) articulates this stance well:

> the British working class ... must sell itself in a planned, thought-out and expensive fashion; ... the class should sell its cooperation in making capitalism in Britain more competitive and efficient not simply in return for material

benefits, but in return for increasing rights to control and decision-making — in return for power, in short.

But once again the structure and practice of union organisation made such a perspective seem utopian. The TUC formulated such documents as *Economic Planning and Industrial Democracy* along with the Labour Party at national level which advocated the widespread development of union-based participation in management decision-making. But at local level precisely the attitudes and relations with management that ensured that there was little development of new realism or enterprise consciousness, meant that little attention was paid in practice to these ideas by the rank-and-file membership. Lane (1986) shows how the structures and resources of British unions and their staffs remained ill-suited to developing such an approach to industrial democracy. Thus unions might wish to exercise 'positive power' but the real structures and traditions of bargaining made such developments unlikely. There was no widespread discussion by unionists of alternative plans or alternative ways of organising work, nor of the conflicts of interest between work-groups or bargaining groups which these might create and how they would be resolved. If, as we argued in Chapter 3, the immediate economic militancy and political or strategic weakness of British labour were two sides of the same coin, this relationship was reinforced by Thatcherism. For while industrial democracy became neglected, wages bargaining continued its central importance.

Wages

The contrast between the 'vested interest' and 'sword of justice' roles of trade unions, and the way in which their structure worked in favour of the first at the expense of the second was demonstrated most clearly in the issue of wage bargaining. Chapter 6 examined why unions and employers managed to produce very high real wage settlements after 1982 under a free collective bargaining regime. It became clear that any substantial fall in unemployment would require a much slower rate of wage growth unless other factors in the economy changed significantly, such as the rate of capital investment, the balance of retained to distributed profits, interest rates, and so on. This was recognised by the TUC in its discussions with the Labour Party over its economic strategy and over its plans to reduce unemployment. The TUC itself put forward various versions of an alternative economic strategy endorsed by successive congresses. Its *Economic Review*s in 1980 and 1981 called for a return to expansionary economic policies, with higher public expenditure. This was also the basis of the document 'Partners in Rebuilding Britain' launched for the 1983 election and the 1987 statement 'Work to Win'. But what neither the TUC collectively nor unions individually have been able to deliver is more than a fudge or worse on specific proposals to restrain wages or have any national planning of incomes. Some in the Labour Party have argued that this simply recognises the realities of what incomes policies, statutory or voluntary, were really like. The spirit and letter of the policy were frequently evaded by companies and unions who had little individual incentive to follow it. Policies created anomalies which built up resentment and leapfrogging 'catch-up' claims once the policy finished which nullified the original objective. But it is doubtful whether this is the basic motive for such disillusionment with incomes policies, or that vague voluntary restraint as opposed to a formal policy would overcome such difficulties. Launching 'Work to Win', TUC General Secretary, Norman Willis, argued, 'The issue of pay, productivity, exports, costs and jobs are certainly linked together now much more closely in people's minds', and Labour leader, Neil Kinnock, argued that union conference resolutions showed that union members were willing to put job creation before rises in the standard of living and that this would be achieved by voluntary restraint:

> in the private sector, the discipline is competitiveness and costs. Everyone is acutely aware that unless their wage demands and other costs conform to the requirement of final costs and the ability to sell in the market, they are not being realistic or securing the future of their company (*Guardian*, 31 March 1987).

The problem with such an analysis, as we saw in Chapter 6, is that there is no reason why the wages and employment objectives of individual companies or their workforces should coincide with the interests of the economy as a whole or of the unemployed.

The real dilemma for the trade unions and the Labour Party is that the unions' continued vitality at workplace level and their ability to bargain high wage increases for those in employment who are well organised, particularly in the private sector, has meant that 'free collective bargaining' is popular with their membership. As we discussed in Chapter 3, it is doubtful if union leaders have the power, even if they wanted to, to deliver the members behind an incomes policy which threatened to reduce the trend of real wage increases substantially. Crouch (1982, p. 184) argues: 'Union activists will not exchange the real strength they have won on the shop floor for the often shadowy talking shops that comprise national tripartite activity.' If it is accepted that the level of wages settlements are significant in determining the level of employment then the structure of bargaining we described in the last chapter acts to boost wages while accentuating unemployment. This does not mean that unions are to blame for creating unemployment by accepting such wage increases: under decentralised bargaining they have no way of ensuring that refusing them would create employment. Nor does it mean that cutting wage increases in the secondary sector of the labour market (something which has been achieved by the current government) or making low pay still lower will do much to create employment in either sector (see Craig *et al.* 1982). What it does mean is that an alternative economic policy to Thatcherism which accepted that market forces did not automatically produce either economic recovery or full employment would find it difficult to show that such market forces nevertheless proved the most effective form of wage determination. The evidence to the contrary is substantial and does not depend solely on econometric arguments about the Phillips curve or automatic trade-off between employment and wages.

Cameron (1984) has provided compelling evidence about the ability of social democratic parties with 'corporatist' policies and structures to hold down unemployment while forgoing higher money wage increases. Batstone and Gourlay (1986) make a similar point when they compare the average rise in unemployment and rise in wages in OECD countries according to the centralisation or decentralisation of their trade union and bargaining structures. Centralised systems have been able to hold down the rise in employment through moderating wage demands since, unlike the individual bargaining group at plant level, they can ensure that the wage restraint is shared and also influence macroeconomic policy to direct the benefits of such restraint towards employment creation. Batstone and Gourlay looked at the average unemployment rate and rise in real earnings in manufacturing between 1978 and 1984 for 13 OECD countries, divided into three groups according to the degree of centralisation of their union movements. Those with 'centralised' movements had an average unemployment rate of around 4 per cent, while real earnings had not increased over the period. The decentralised systems had delivered annual earnings increases of around 2 per cent but at the cost of an average unemployment rate of 8 per cent. Britain had the highest rate of earnings increases and the fourth highest level of unemployment behind Belgium, Eire and the Netherlands (Batstone and Gourlay 1986, p. 286). As we discussed in Chapter 3, union leaders in Britain cannot simply demand that their members renounce the struggle for higher living standards particularly when that has been an especially important focus of British industrial relations, for the reasons we examined in Chapters 2 and 3.

Perhaps Labourism's greatest problem, given the collision of economics and politics, is the inability of the industrial arm of the movement to find a new role to replace that of the Praetorian Guard. It is surely utopian to expect that the unions could ever return to such a role in the future. It would be very hard, to say the least, for the unions to offer support in the Party Conference or NEC for policies which they as unions sought to resist in the country. This implies that the special relationship between the unions and the Labour Party becomes either a closer corporatist one, or something looser and more vague. The first would entail the exercise of 'positive' union influence on economic policy of the sort they have urged in the past: expansionist policies, better social services, and so on. But it would also entail 'positive' government influence over the unions in the form of sufficient control of wages to facilitate further expansion without excessive inflation. Even after eight years of market forces, free collective bargaining and massive unemployment the party and the unions have not been able to construct such a relationship. Here perhaps lies the key to the stagnation which Crick (1983, p. 349) identified in the Labour Party after its 1983 defeat, and its image as 'A party of government and high taxation, of state and local council interference, preservationists of run-down industries, defenders of obsolescent working practices, a self-preservation society of professional dispensers of welfare'. Neither the trade

unions nor the Party seemed able to tap into public opposition to government
economic policies, despite widespread evidence of the failure of Thatcherism to
create a sea change in values. The Post-War Settlement was and is tremendously
popular and powerful. For example, the BSA survey in 1983 found that more than
twice as many people thought unemployment ought to be a higher government
priority than inflation as thought the reverse. Even a majority of Conservative
supporters thought so. Public views of the causes of economic problems was also
widely at variance with those of the government, as Table 7.5 shows. Most thought
the gap between high and low incomes too large, a tiny majority thought it too
small. The subsequent surveys produced similar results. Mann (1986, p. 28),
reporting on the 1985 survey, describes how a substantial majority of respondents
opted for Keynesian solutions to the country's economic situation: 'The consistency
of viewpoint is striking: there is too much unemployment and inequality;
something should be done about it; the government is the appropriate agency to
tackle these problems.'

Table 7.5 Views on causes of economic problems (1983)

	Not true (%)	*True and important (%)*
Decline in world trade	10	82
Energy costs are too high for industry	11	80
British workers reluctant to accept new ways of working	22	69
The government has not done enough to create jobs	26	67
British industry is badly managed	26	64
Employers are not investing enough	27	63
People are not working hard enough	37	60
Manufacturing industry is not attractive to the best school and college leavers	34	45
Government spending has been too high	45	45
Wages are too high	64	30

Source: Jowell and Airey, 1984.

The paradox of British trade unions today, in so far as they aspire to be part of a
wider labour movement, is that the means available to them to play their economic
role increasingly frustrate their ability to play a political one: this is the nub of the
crisis of identity and strategy. In its 'sword of justice' aspect the labour movement
would like to see an expanding economy with higher investment complemented by
more flexibility, more training, shorter hours, less occupational segregation and
more industrial democracy in the sense of greater union involvement in planning
changes. Such a sector would need to be more competitive and productive.
Industrial democracy would have to mean active cooperation between unions and

management and in some instances the scrapping not just of traditional defences and boundaries but the abandoning of many keenly felt sectional rivalries. Wages would have to be restrained and priority given to investment and training. Most of these measures are anathema to the trade unions in their economic defender role. Bargaining power for individual work-groups often depends on maintaining just those sectional boundaries and rivalries which they would now be invited to dismantle for a longer-term return which would by its nature be uncertain. Moreover, real equal opportunities, shorter hours, a pay policy which really helped the low-paid would all mean measures which promoted the interests of some union members and often non-union members *at the cost* of other members. More promotion opportunities for women means less than in the past for men. Less sexist job evaluations means less benefits for men. Greater labour-market equality for women means more domestic labour for men. Less low pay means lower differentials. More state intervention to promote fairness in wages and work means less relative power for those who have a strong market position. Under free collective bargaining market forces arbitrate between these competing claims but, as we have seen, in a way which does not necessarily produce a structure that is either rational, fair or efficient. The alternative to free collective bargaining implies some discussion of the priorities and principles that ought to inform the determination of incomes. It implies the development of what Fox and Flanders (1969) termed a 'normative order'. Without the development of such a policy there is (to borrow a phrase) no alternative to free collective bargaining.

The unions are aware of this dilemma, while the changing structure and balance of power in the union movement — the shift in emphasis towards public sector and white-collar unions, the erosion of craft identity and changes in the structure of the TUC General Council — has given the union movement some of the institutional means to pursue its resolution. The commitment of the TGWU to minimum-wage legislation, for example, represented a decisive change in policy which was bound to exert pressure for change elsewhere in the movement. What must be realised however, in the light of our discussion in Chapter 2,3 and 6 is just how powerful the historical forces are which impede the labour movement developing any such new strategy, and how from 1979 onwards Thatcherism has reinforced them.

CHAPTER 8

Conclusions

> I am more than ever impressed with the extraordinary gap that exists between the perceptiveness, intellectual grasp, and technical competence of the people who work in industrial concerns, and the cumbrous, primitive and belittling nature of the administrative structures by which they direct their efforts, and of the constraints they see fit to impose on their thinking and liberty of action.
>
> Burns 1961, p.xxii

The system in 1987

In the light of the arguments and evidence presented in this book, it is worth asking what the prospects for industrial relations and economic change are in 1987, after two terms of Thatcherite government. Full employment has been abandoned, and employment lies perhaps a million jobs below its potential level. Industrial output, boosted by North Sea oil, has passed its 1979 level, but manufacturing output has not. Productivity increases have not been sufficient to reverse the relative decline of manufacturing's market share and exports, so that deindustrialisation has continued at a faster pace than elsewhere. For example, since 1980 exports of consumer goods have increased 4 per cent while imports have increased 44 per cent. Balance of payments problems have been avoided through oil exports and income from abroad earned on the capital exported in the wake of exchange controls (yet another reminder of the era before the Second World War). Price inflation has been reduced but not all the domestic sources of inflation. Thus only the devaluation of sterling has prevented a faster decline in the competitiveness of British industry (which even so was some 15 per cent below its 1979 level in 1986) and only falling prices for imports such as raw materials have prevented such devaluation fuelling higher domestic price inflation. Earnings inflation (the main domestic source of inflation) continues to be high. Since 1979 unit labour costs in Britain (taking account of productivity improvements) have risen 60 per cent, compared to rises of 15–29 per cent in West Germany and Japan. However, the rise in earnings has been distributed unequally for those in work while those made unemployed have suffered a substantial drop in income. As a result, as we saw in Chapter 5, real incomes for many households have hardly improved at all but for a substantial (employed) minority there has been rapid progress. Other elements of the macroeconomic environment do not look very healthy. Manufacturing investment is still below the level of the late 1970s, research and development is still far below the levels of competitor countries, and training is inadequate. The 'supply side' of the economy seems to face much the same set of problems, with much the same sort of institutions and organisation of both management and labour as in the 1970s.

In effect, inflation has not been 'squeezed' out of the system. Price inflation has been low now for four years, but unemployment has stayed very high and growth remained relatively poor. Fundamentally, inflation is low because unemployment is high and growth poor, because only by maintaining high interests rates, relatively high exchange rates and a low PSBR is price inflation kept at its current level. Its more immediate causes, such as wage inflation, have not been removed. We do not have a qualitatively new domestic economy, but much the same structure run at a different setting. Instead of high inflation we have high unemployment. In contrast to the government's claims about eschewing short-term gains for long-term recovery, almost the reverse could be said. Despite high unemployment, a collapse in manufacturing output and employment, a government-engineered-fall in international competitiveness that has bequeathed an unprecedented deficit in non-oil trade and despite zero net growth in GDP from 1979 to 1983, the basic features of workplace industrial relations remain unchanged. Meanwhile, the social costs of these economic policies have been made possible only by oil revenues which have paid for unemployment benefit, and wage rises and cheap imports which have kept those with a job in rising real living standards. Rather than solving the problems outlined by critics like Jay and Brittan in the 1970s, the government has taken the pressure off the system by letting unemployment rise. The pressure of rising expectations and sectional conflict has been released by creating a growing pool of unemployed who have no means to participate in the increased living standards of those in work. But this army of unemployed has neither made the employed work more efficiently nor curbed their power to pursue rising expectations. What we have, in a sense, is therefore Thatcherism not at work.

The resurgence of older traditions

The strength of the *laissez-faire*, the limited role of the state in the genesis of Britain's industrial order, the strength of individualism (perhaps expressed most strongly in the common law), the conviction that the pursuit of self-interest (by individuals, employers or unions) was ultimately for the best while the actions of government tended naturally towards the worst; all these traditions which we discussed in Chapter 2 help to explain why it was in Britain that the monetarist ideas of tight money, balanced budgets and liberation from state regulation took firmest root. Thatcherism above all identified collectivism and public enterprise as its main object of attack, while it applauded individual initiative, market forces and enterprise as the means towards recovery. At an ideological level, then, Thatcherism blended well with many long-established features of the British social order. It was not an alien doctrine, but one central to much British economic and political thought before the changes wrought by the Second World War and the Post-War Settlement. It is surely no coincidence that so many of the 'driest' of Mrs Thatcher's economic ministers and the Prime Minister herself, have had a background in the legal profession, where the concept and definition of individual rights takes its strongest form.

As well as these ideological factors, there are material ones too. If we recall Ingham's (1984) analysis cited in Chapter 2, then it seems that Thatcherism's policies have been consistent with defining the needs of the City as paramount in Britain's economic order. It is far beyond the scope of this book to examine in detail the development of government policy towards the City since 1979, and compare the effect of its macroeconomic policies on the City and on domestic industrial capital. But it does appear that a set of macroeconomic policies which have only worsened conditions for domestic production, combined with the determination to abandon industrial strategy and proclaim a new lease of life for *laissez-faire* make little sense from the point of view of domestic industry itself, but are made possible by, and sustain the City's role and the overseas activities of Britains multinationals.

The identity between Thatcherism and earlier British traditions also points towards why it has been so unsuccessful in changing the industrial social order. For if Britain's economic and industrial relations problems started long before 1945 then it is far from clear that a return to the policies of the 1920s or 1870s should solve them. This is why the claim that Thatcherism has generated an enterprise culture is suspect. For in the sense of absence of state regulation and hostility to state control, combined with economic liberalism and freedom for the pursuit of individual self-interest in economic matters, Britain perhaps more than any other country, has always had a culture of enterprise. In this sense Mrs Thatcher's espousal of Victorian values is quite consistent, although they might also be termed Puritan, Cromwellian or even Whig. Therefore that part of Britain's economic malaise which is rooted in its structure of industrial relations — in the sense of shopfloor conflict, barriers to innovation and faster productivity growth, anarchic systems of pay regulation and the absence of high trust, cooperative workplace relations — is a *result* of the very enterprise culture which Thatcherism espouses. In a sense this *is* that enterprise culture, not an opposed social force. Because employers chose extreme economic liberalism, trade unions organised and responded with their own economic strategies. The state could not outlaw these strategies (in large measure because the capitalist classes feared a strong state); to preserve the social order they had to be permitted, incorporated and legitimated. In the absence of regulation of the economy to preserve social order the economic parties themselves had to contrive such regulation themselves *voluntarily*. At different times then and since the employers or the state might wish to escape from this regulation, to kick over the traces and wish for enterprise without its social or cultural fetters, but that has always been more a rhetorical flourish rather than a realistic project. Just as in the nineteenth century employers and the Home Office each bemoaned the other's lack of spirit in repressing combinations, so today some more hawkish employers call for more legal restrictions on trade unions, while the government has waited in vain for an employers' offensive in the private sector.

Lord Young's protests about 'anti-enterprise culture' in Britain miss the point that the set of attitudes and dispositions which are held to comprise this culture are an intimate part of 'enterprise' itself, and that indeed their pervasive hold in British industrial life can be found precisely in the enterprise culture in which the British industrial revolution was forged. For example, Lord Young regrets that most people would advise youngsters to take up a career in the professions, while jobs in the service sector (where Lord Young sees the future of the country's prosperity) are seen as the least popular (Financial Times, 5 December 1985). Such results, however, simply confirm people's commitment to the sort of 'enterprise' Lord Young espouses of following market forces. One need only compare the wage rates and employment conditions in private services with those enjoyed by the 'professions' to see why.

The obsession with markets

There is a certain inscrutable, self-fulfilling determinism about Thatcherite economic philosophy's faith in market forces. If market forces are perfect and government 'interference' can only distort them then what they give rise to is, by definition, what people actually want and the economy needs. But what people want or the economy needs is sometimes far from clear. For example two of the major market forces relevant to the rate of wage growth are the rate of company profits and the state of the labour market: unemployment. Through its emphasis on companies' ability to pay and such measures as profit-related pay the government has made it clear that high profits ought to lead to higher wages, ensuring that successful companies which produce goods or services which people value can attract the best labour. Through its emphasis on 'pricing people into jobs' and refusal to try to maintain employment levels in the face of earnings rises, the government has made it clear that higher unemployment ought to lead to lower wage rises. But from about 1982 onwards the economy has experienced *both* very strong increases in company profits *and* a very high level of unemployment. How ought this constellation of market forces to determine the behaviour of workers and employers when striking wage bargains? If market forces are perfect it is far from clear how anything has ever gone wrong with any economy in the first place, or how a simple policy of 'hands off' by government should not quickly set things right. The government has sometimes tended towards the latter view. Addressing the Scottish CBI in 1986, Chancellor Nigel Lawson castigated British industry for taking too short-term a view over pay (paying too much), training and research and development (spending

far too little). The CBI itself concurred in seeing British export industries'
performance as precarious.

Despite the devaluation of sterling after 1981 exports were growing at only half
the rate of world trade and market share was being lost. As an editorial in the
Financial Times (5 September 1986) put it: 'Industry has not made the transition
from rationalisation to expansion'. But the basis of the Chancellor's criticism was
unclear. For if market forces (and the business decision-makers who effectively
create them) know best, how could the Chancellor — a *state* official after all —
apparently know better? The 'short-termism' complained of by the Chancellor in
fact appeared to be pretty much a consequence of the rule of market forces. In a
period of high interest rates and a lot of takeover activity it was important for
companies to maintain the value of their share price (and so avoid being taken over)
by paying substantial dividends to share holders. This made provision for long-term
R and D or training more difficult, while high profits and high dividends
encouraged companies to accede to high wage rises, which in turn (in the absence of
an incomes policy) encouraged similar wage increases elsewhere. The Chancellor
was in any event not averse to enjoying a few short-term gains himself. The boosts
to the government's tax receipts caused by high profits, earnings increases and the
consumer boom allowed him to cut income tax in his 1987 budget, despite the
adverse implications for the balance of trade, with a (short-term) view to improving
the electoral fortunes of the Conservative Party.

What this suggests is that, from the viewpoint of the economy as a whole, as
opposed to the individuals directly engaged in a market transaction, markets are far
from perfect. They are imperfect for two main reasons. First, individual bargainers
do not have perfect information on which to base their behaviour. The state of
market forces now implies little about the state of market forces in five or ten years
time when investment or training might come to fruition. It is far from clear, for
example, how market forces can instruct British export industry to take over from
declining oil exports when the investment necessary to undertake this or the winning
of new markets or extra market share can take years to execute. It is also true that
planners and state officials do not have perfect information either, but it can surely
be agreed that different types of information are more suited to one or the other
form of decision-making: markets do not enjoy a monopoly of virtue. Second,
individual market transactions at the micro level can and do have unanticipated
consequences at the macro level. There is no automatic harmony of interest between
individuals, interest groups or society as a whole. A level of profits, prices or wages
which is best suited to an individual company's needs may nevertheless have
undesirable consequences for other parts of the economy. Our discussion of wage
bargaining in Chapters 6 and 7 focused on this point. Indeed, an underlying theme
of this whole book has been that the labour market bears little resemblance to an
abstract model of markets, especially at the level of the individual firm, where it
virtually ceases to function as a market at all. The blanket appeal to the virtue of
market forces therefore suffers from two fundamental errors. The first is the
assumption that encouraging unfettered market forces at the micro level will

improve how institutions work. We have suggested that this is not the case. The second assumption is that such reform of the micro level does not have costs or negative implications at the 'macro' level of the economy as a whole. Clearly the 'macro' costs of the government's strategy have been very large indeed, in lost output, lower growth and high unemployment. In so far as micro-level reform has aggravated wage inflation pressure it will have further 'macro' costs in the future.

Thatcherism's faith in the virtue of market forces also underpins two other important features of its policies. First, it explains the assumption that rising price inflation was caused by the frustration or blockage of the market mechanism — for example, by trade unions or by government economic activity. This led to the conclusion that freeing up markets, curbing union monopolies and government intervention would remove market imbalances and reduce inflation. But precisely the opposite conclusion could just as well be drawn. It could be argued that it was the continued over-dependence on market forces in an advanced industrial society, and the inability during the Post-War Settlement to develop a greater consensus on the means to regulate wages, focus investment or direct macroeconomic policy which was responsible for inflationary pressure.

A second feature of advocating the superiority of market forces is that it allows people to escape from the vexed question of how to match up effort and result, how to evaluate the worth of individual or group contributions to a collective or social effort or how to recognise the handicaps of social disadvantage or real inequalities of opportunity that face people. In a world of perfect market forces, perfect information and no externalities everybody's economic fortune is their own responsibility. No one is 'exploited'; the market simply matches up the demand and supply of people's needs and abilities. It is a world where individual effort and initiative are the only determinants of rewards and benefits. Poverty or unemployment is just as much one person's fault as wealth and prosperity is another's just reward. At times it appears that some Thatcherites espouse the belief that the world is indeed like that. Thus unemployment is caused by people choosing not to work or equip themselves with sufficient skills, regional inequalities are caused by negative attitudes towards industry. Inequality of wealth and income is positively desirable because it comes from personal effort. Such an outlook fits well, both with the traditions of individualism in Britain, and with many people's personal experience: for many white-collar workers, for example, promotion is a question of personal endeavour, of studying for qualifications, of working hard.

There are two problems here. First, given the imperfections of markets, there is no necessary connection between individual effort and rewards. Some enjoy windfall gains for little effort, others work earnestly only to find that their efforts turn out not to prove valuable in the market. Second, given the inevitably social and collective nature of production, how can markets distinguish the relative worth of different contributions? This was the question we examined in discussing 'organisational pluralism' in Chapter 6. Both these problems point to the importance of developing directly social criteria for evaluating individual effort and its contribution to collective result which complement the verdict given by market forces, and which command widespread legitimacy. The meagreness of vision and clumsiness of organisation of which Burns despaired in the passage cited at the start of this chapter are surely rooted in the history we outlined in Chapter 2. It bequeathed to the modern age a tradition of individualism strong enough to sustain the idea that economic success was mostly achieved by dint of personal effort. And in turn this tradition was nourished by Britain's experience of a process of industrialisation and a century of world dominance both of which proceeded within a *laissez faire* framework, requiring little in the way of new forms of economic organisation within firms or of direct partnerships between industry and the state, the city or the labour movement. Thus the preoccupation with *laissez-faire* at a micro level has been compounded by its parallel effects at a macro level.

The Post-War Settlement in perspective

As we suggested in Chapters 2 and 3, the British Post-War Settlement was far from perfect, but what surely stands out from the vantage point of eight years of a Thatcherite project committed to abandoning that Settlement is just how powerful an achievement it was. Keynesian policies got to grips with the problems caused by the free rein of market forces and established an international economic order that lifted economic growth from its century-old trend rate of 2.25 per cent per annum to around 4 per cent till the mid-1970s. Cairncross (1985) puts the establishment of the Post-War Settlement in perspective:

> commitment to full employment meant commitment to prosperity. But if production had to be enlarged, so had the infrastructure of capacity on which it rested. All over the world, investment had to be expanded to keep pace ... Fortunately governments were in an expansionist mood and were, if anything, too ready to sustain demand while the public and financial markets had not yet learnt those self-fulfilling truths that made them treat increases in the money-supply as the inevitable harbinger of inflation ... Those years appear in retrospect, and rightly so, as years when the government knew where it wanted to go and led the country with an understanding of what was at stake.

Unlike the aftermath of the First World War, when wartime cooperation and rosy government promises about the future turned into industrial strife and mass unemployment, the sentiments expressed in the *Times* editorial we cited in Chapter 2, sentiments which went against the grain of the individualistic traditions of the British social order, were actually put into practice. Anderson (1987) and others have argued that the central cause of Britain's current economic decline was the weakness of the modernisation produced by the Post-War Settlement and its failure to develop new institutions, produce a new industrial social order or prioritise the development of its national economy over the interests of the City or imperial pretensions. The ease with which the government was able to let unemployment rise after 1979 without eroding its popular support is evidence perhaps of the strength of the forces which the Settlement worked against. Conversely, the continued commitment of the electorate to the basic institutions of the Welfare State, such as the National Health Service, is evidence of the strength of some of the newer traditions the Settlement fostered: that gross inequalities of wealth and income were unjust, that the problems of regional unemployment or poverty imposed an obligation on society as a whole to address them rather than pretend that self-help was the only issue. It is ironic, given the Prime Minister's professed admiration for Churchill, that the Thatcherite programme in effect constituted the real end of the Second World War in the sense that it has attempted to roll back the social reforms to which that conflict gave rise.

The lessons of the post-war period in Britain, in the market economies of the West, and in the centrally planned economies of the East are that neither markets nor plans have a monopoly of virtue or efficiency (Nove 1983). Some economic decisions are best left to market forces — those relating to consumer goods, for example. There are others which markets clearly cannot handle — natural monopolies, long-term decision-making or training, for example. Economic decisions concerned with people's jobs are particularly problematic. The work they perform, the effort and responsibilities expected of them, what they are paid, what their future prospects are and alternative opportunities: all these are issues where the relative advantages and disadvantages of markets and plans seem especially acute. A market in labour implies the possibility of unemployment. But abolishing unemployment by replacing markets with a plan implies introducing industrial conscription. Planning of wages and incomes appears an impossibly difficult task given the fluidity of the demands for labour in a dynamic economy, yet leaving wages to market forces can also produce undesirable results when there is no automatic mechanism to align the interests of individual firms and the entire economy. Finally, within the production units themselves there is the need to balance the stability, order and planned relationships needed actually to perform work and organise production, with the change and innovation implied by market demands for new products, or the changing abilities, interests and composition of the workforce.

If these lessons are correct, then it is likely that what the British economic and industrial order needs is not a further dose of market-based decentralisation but the nurturing of attitudes and institutions which can emphasise communal and public interests over and above the individual and the sectional, which can give a material foundation to this process (rather than relying on propaganda and exhortation) and which can bring together the desirable aspects of markets and plans, institutions which can develop 'the will, in an increasingly interdependent world, to be as concerned with what one must do jointly with others, to have as much pride in this achievement, as one has in what one does for oneself' (Galbraith 1987).

But such developments are an anathema to Thatcherism. Through its emphasis on market forces it has emphasised the priority of individual and sectional interests over public and collective ones. It has been successful in attracting many workers, especially white-collar ones, to its political programme, while they have also continued to benefit from the achievements of workplace trade unionism. This has meant that the prospects for the return to an economic and industrial order based on priorities arrived at through recognising the national interest of the economy might be much more difficult. Posner (1986, p. 313) has described one of the possible scenarios for the future development of the British economy as follows: 'that the size of the UK traded goods and services sector becomes steadily smaller (compared with the path that it could follow), while real wages *within* that shrinking sector continue to grow at the rate determined by "aspirations" '.

In this sense, then, it may have been the signal achievement of Thatcherism to give a further powerful twist to the process of the decline of the British economy and society in the name of doing precisely the opposite. Such a policy could also be continued for quite some time, with appropriate changes of emphasis perhaps, to deal with the increasing problems for social order caused by escalating inequality and poverty. For the essence of the economic order bequeathed by Thatcherism is that, whatever the long-term consequences for the economy as a whole, there will be large sections of the population, in the right areas, in the right industries, with the right jobs, who in the short term will enjoy (and certainly have enjoyed since 1982) substantial rises in their personal standard of living. In proportion as the general problem of decline becomes more acute, so will the gap grow between the living standards of those who still have a stake in the system and those who have not, and so will the task of securing their assent to a genuine programme of national economic reconstruction become more difficult. It is perhaps in this process that can be glimpsed the real mechanism by which democracy could 'eat itself up by the tail': the fear expressed in the mid-1970s by the monetarists. Rutherford (1983, p. 43) has shrewdly observed that the process of economic and social decline is rarely cataclysmic: 'Countries don't fall over cliffs. Decline can continue indefinitely. Look at other countries and other centuries.' The evidence presented in this book suggests that the Post-War Settlement represented an imperfect but powerful reversal of such a process of decline and that its overthrow by Thatcherism has only served to return Britain to its former downward trajectory.

Glossary of Abbreviations

ACAS	Advisory Conciliation and Arbitration Service
AEU/(AUEW)	Amalgamated Engineering Union (formerly Amalgamated Union of Engineering Workers)
CBI	Confederation of British Industry
CIR	Commission on Industrial Relations
CSEU	Confederation of Shipbuilding and Engineering Unions
DE	Department of Employment
DTI	Department of Trade and Industry
EAS	Enterprise Allowance Scheme
EEC	European Economic Community
EEF	Engineering Employers' Federation
EETPU	Electric Electronics Telecommunications and Plumbing Union
GCHQ	Government Communications Headquarters
GDP	Gross Domestic Product
GLC	Greater London Council
GMBATU	General Municipal Boilermakers and Allied Trades Union
IDS	Incomes Data Services
IMF	International Monetary Fund
IMS	Institute of Manpower Studies
IPCS	Institute of Professional Civil Servants
ISTC	Iron and Steel Trades Confederation
LFS	Labour Force Survey
LRD	Labour Research Department
NALGO	National and Local Government Officers' Association
NCB	National Coal Board
NEC	(Labour Party) National Executive Committee
NEDC	National Economic Development Council
NEDO	National Economic Development Organisation
NGA	National Graphical Association
NHS	National Health Service
NUM	National Union of Mineworkers
NUR	National Union of Railwaymen

NUPE	National Union of Public Employees
OECD	Organisation for Economic Cooperation and Development
PLP	Parliamentary Labour Party
PRP	Profit Related Pay
PSBR	Public Sector Borrowing Requirement
SCOMER	Scottish Manufacturing Establishments Record
SDP	Social Democratic Party
SOGAT	Society of Graphical and Allied Trades
TGWU	Transport and General Workers' Union
TUC	Trades Union Congress
UDM	Union of Democratic Mineworkers
VAT	Value Added Tax
WIRS80	Workplace Industrial Relations Survey 1980
WIRS84	Workplace Industrial Relations Survey 1984
YTS	Youth Training Scheme

Bibliography

Abrams, M., Rose, R. and Hinden, M. 1960. *Must Labour Lose?* Harmondsworth, Penguin.

Aldington, Lord 1985. *Report from the House of Lords Select Committee on Overseas Trade on the causes and implications of the deficit in the UK balance of trade in manufactures.* HL 238/1.HMSO.

Aldington, Lord. 1986. Britain's Manufacturing Industry. *Royal Bank of Scotland Review*, 151, 3-13.

Anderson, P. 1965. Origins of the Present Crisis. *New Left Review*, 23.

Anderson, P. 1986. The Figures of Descent. *New Left Review*, 161, 20-77.

Armstrong, P. 1982. 'If it's only women it doesn't matter so much'. In West (ed) 1982.

Atkinson, J. 1984. Manpower strategies for flexible organisations. *Personnel Management*, August, 28-31.

Atkinson, J. and Meager N. 1986. New Forms of Work Organisation, *IMS Report No 121*, Brighton, IMS.

Bacon, R. and Eltis W. 1976. *Britain's Economic Problem: Too Few Producers.* Macmillan.

Baddon, L., Hunter L.C., Hyman J., Leopold J., and Ramsay H., 1987. *Profit Sharing and Employee Share Ownership: Research Report.* University of Glasgow. Centre for Research in Industrial Democracy and Participation.

Bain, G. 1983. (ed) *Industrial Relations in Britain.* Oxford, Blackwell.

Bain, G. 1986. Introduction to a Symposium on The Role and Influence of Trade Unions in a Recession. *British Journal of Industrial Relations*, 24, 157-9.

Bain, G. and F. Elsheikh 1976. *Union Growth and the Business Cycle.* Oxford, Blackwell.

Baldamus, G. 1961. *Efficiency and Effort.* Tavistock.

Barnett, A. 1984. 'The Failed Consensus'. In Curran (ed) 1984.

Barnett, C. 1986. *The Audit of War: the illusion and reality of Britain as a great nation.* Macmillan.

Bassett, P. 1986. *Strike Free.* Macmillan.

Batstone, E. 1984. *Working Order.* Oxford, Blackwell.

Batstone, E. and Gourlay S. 1986. *Unions Unemployment and Innovation.* Oxford, Blackwell.

Beaumont, P. B. 1985. High Technology Firms and Industries: A Consideration of Some Industrial Relations Features. *Department of Management Studies Working Paper No. 3.* University of Glasgow.

Beaumont, P.B. 1987. *The Decline of Trade Union Organisation.* Croom Helm.

Beechey, V. 1984. Women's Employment in Contemporary Britain. Mimeo. The Open University, February.

Beechey, V. 1985. The Shape of the Workforce to Come. *Marxism Today*, August, 11-16.

Bendix, R. 1956. *Work and Authority in Industry.* Berkeley and Los Angeles, University of California Press.

Beynon, H. 1983. What about the Workers? *Guardian*, 23 June.

Blackaby, F. (ed) 1978. *Deindustrialisation*. National Institute of Economic And Social Research Economic Policy Papers 2. Heineman.

Blanchflower, D. 1986. What Effect Do Unions Have on Relative Wages in Great Britain? *British Journal of Industrial Relations*, 24, 195–204.

Brewster, C. J., Gill, C. and Richbell, S. 1981. Developing an analytical approach to industrial relations policy. *Personnel Review*, 10, 2, 3–10.

Brittan, S. 1975. The Economic Contradictions of Democracy. *British Journal of Political Science*, 5, 129–159.

Brown, R.K. 1978. From Donovan to where? Interpretations of industrial relations in Britain since 1968. *British Journal of Sociology*, 29, 439–461.

Brown, W. 1981. *The Changing Contours of British Industrial Relations*. Oxford, Blackwell.

Brown, W. 1986. The Changing Role of Trade Unions in the Management of Labour. *British Journal of Industrial Relations*, 24, 161–8.

Burns, T. 1981. Rediscovering Organisation: Aspects of Collaboration and Managerialism in Hospital Organisation. Mimeo. Department of Sociology, University of Edinburgh.

Burns, T. and Stalker, G. 1961. *The Management of Innovation*. Tavistock.

Butler, D. and Kavanagh, D. 1974. *The British General Election of February 1974*. Macmillan.

Butler, D. and Kavanagh, D. 1984. *The British General Election of 1983*. Macmillan.

Cadbury, Sir A. 1985. *Hitachi Lecture*. Institute of Manpower Studies, November.

Cairncross, A. 1985. *Years of Recovery*. Methuen.

Cairns, L. 1985. New Towns Unionisation Survey – Glenrothes and Irvine. *M. Phil Dissertation*, University of Glasgow.

Calder, A. 1971. *The People's War*. Panther.

Cameron, D.R. 1984. Social Democracy, Corporatism, Labour Quiescence and The Representation of Economic Interest in Advanced Capitalist Society in Goldthorpe (ed) 1984. pp. 143–78.

Carlton, D. 1986. Paying a high price for the new Jerusalem. *Times Higher Educational Supplement*, 18 April.

Carr, S. 1984. Changing Patterns of Work. *WEA Studies for Trade Unionists*, vol. 10 No. 40, December.

Cavendish, R. 1982. *On the Line*. Routledge and Kegan Paul.

Clarke, K. 1987. Changing the Labour Market: More Flexibility. Lecture at City University and Business School, February.

Coates, K. and Topham, T. 1986. *Trade Unions and Politics*. Oxford, Blackwell.

Cockburn, C. 1983a. *Brothers: Male Dominance and Technological Change*. Pluto Press.

Cockburn, C. 1983b. Caught In the Wheels. *Marxism Today*, November, 16–20.

Commission on Industrial Relations 1971. The Hotel and Catering Industry, Part 1. *Report. No. 23* Cmnd 4789. HMSO.

Commission on Industrial Relations 1974 Retail Distribution. *Report No. 89*. HMSO.

Confederation of British Industry 1985. *Attitudes Towards Employment. A Survey of Employers, Employees and The Unemployed Conducted by Gallup for the Confederation of British Industry*. CBI.

Coyle, A. 1981. *Redundant Women*. The Women's Press.

Craig, C., Rubery, J., Tarling, R. and Wilkinson, F. 1982. *Labour Market Structure. Industrial Organisation and Low Pay*. Cambridge, Cambridge University Press.

Craig, C., Garnsey, E. and Rubery, J. 1984. Payment structures and smaller firms: women's employment in segmented labour markets. *Department of Employment Research Paper no. 48.* Department of Employment.

Creigh, S., Roberts, C., Gorman, A. and Sawyer, P. 1986. Self Employment in Britain Results from the Labour Force Surveys 1981-1984. *Department of Employment Gazette.* June, pp. 183-194.

Cressey, P., Eldridge, J.E.T., MacInnes, J. and Norris, G. 1981. Industrial Democracy and Participation: a Scottish Survey. *Department of Employment Research Paper no 28.* Department of Employment.

Cressey, P., Eldridge, J.E.T., and MacInnes, J. 1985. *Just Managing.* Milton Keynes, Open University Press.

Crick, B. 1983. The Future of The Labour Party. *Political Quarterly,* 54, 346-353.

Crouch, C. 1982. The Peculiar Relationship: The Party and The Unions. In D. Kavanagh (Ed) 1982. pp. 171-190.

Curran, J. (ed.) 1984. *The Future of the Left.* Polity Press.

Daniel, W.W. 1987. *Workplace Industrial Relations and Technical Change.* Frances Pinter/PSI.

Daniel, W.W. and Millward, N. 1983. *Workplace Industrial Relations in Britain The DE/PSI/SSRC Survey.* Heinemann.

Department of Employment 1984. *Employment – the challenge for the nation.* Cmnd 9474.

Department of Employment 1987. Homeworking in Britain. *Department of Employment Gazette,* April, p.218.

Dex, S. 1986. *The Sexual Division of Work.* Brighton, Wheatsheaf.

Disney, R. 1979. Recurrent Spells and the Concentration of Unemployment in Great Britain, *Economic Journal,* 89, 109-19.

Donovan, Lord 1968. *Royal Commission on Trade Unions and Employers' Associations: Report,* Cmnd. 3623. HMSO.

Dorfman, G. A. 1983. *British Trade Unionism against the Trades Union Congress.* Macmillan.

Edwards, P. 1985a. *Managing Labour Relations through the Recession.* Mimeo, University of Warwick, Industrial Relations Research Unit.

Edwards, P. 1985b. Myth of the Macho Manager. *Personnel Management,* April, pp. 32-35.

Edwards, P. 1986. Industrial Relations: Challenges and Prospects. A Report on the Warwick Conference of March 1986. *Warwick Papers in Industrial Relations No. 6,* Coventry. IRRU.

Edwards, P. and Scullion, H. 1982 *The Social Organisation of Industrial Conflict.* Oxford, Blackwell.

Elliott, J. 1978. *Conflict or Cooperation. The Growth of Industrial Democracy.* Kogan Page.

Ellis, V. 1981. *The Role of Trade Unions in the Promotion of Equal Opportunities Policies.* Manchester. Equal Opportunities Commission.

Ellman, M., Rowthorn, R., Smith, R. and Wilkinson, F. 1974. Britain's Economic Crisis, *Spokesman Pamphlet,* No. 44

Evans, S. 1985. Research Note: The Use of Injunctions in Industrial Disputes, *British Journal of Industrial Relations,* 23, 131-137.

Feinstein, C. (ed) 1983. *The Managed Economy.* Oxford, Oxford University Press.

Fidler, J. 1981. *The British Business Elite.* Routledge and Kegan Paul.

Fine, B. and Harris, L. 1985. *The Peculiarities of the British Economy.* Lawrence and Wishart.

Flanders, A 1961a. Trade Unions in the Sixties. In Flanders, 1968.

Flanders, A. 1961b. Trade Unions and Politics. In Flanders, 1968.

Flanders, A. 1964. *The Fawley Productivity Agreements*. Faber.

Flanders, A. 1968. *Management and Trade Unions*. Hutchinson.

Fothergill, S. and G. Gudgin 1982. *Unequal Growth*. Heinemann.

Fox, A. 1985. *History and Heritage*. Allen and Unwin.

Fox, A. and Flanders, A. 1969. The Reform of Collective Bargaining: From Donovan to Durkheim. *British Journal of Industrial Relations*, 7.

Galbraith, J.K. 1987 *A View From the Stands*. Hamish Hamilton.

Gamble, A. 1974. *The Conservative Nation*. Routledge and Kegan Paul.

Gardiner, J. 1984. Caught in the Gender Trap. *Marxism Today*.

Gennard, J. 1979. Chronicle. *British Journal of Industrial Relations*, 17.

Gershuny, J. and Miles, I. 1985. *The New Service Economy*, Frances Pinter.

Goldthorpe, J.H. (1980) *Social Mobility and Class Structure in Modern Britain*. Oxford. Clarendon Press.

Goldthorpe, J.H. (ed) 1984. *Order and Conflict in Contemporary Capitalism*. Oxford. Clarendon Press.

Gregory, D. 1987. *A Million New Jobs Since 1983?* Oxford. Ruskin Colledge Trade Union Research Unit.

Gregory, M., Lobban, P. and Thomson, A. 1987. Pay Settlements in Manufacturing Industry, 1979–84: a Micro-data Study of the Impact of Product and Labour Market Pressures. *Oxford Bulletin of Economics and Statistics*, 49, 129–150.

Hadjimatheou, G. 1987. Is Public Expenditure Growth a Problem? *The Royal Bank of Scotland Review*, 153, 17–24.

Hakim, C. 1987. Homeworking in Britain. *Department of Employment Gazette*, February, pp. 92–104.

Harper, K. 1986. Unions ponder strike-free deals as industry sets the pace of change. *Guardian*, 28 September.

Harrison, A. 1984. Economic Policy and Expectations. In Jowell and Airey 1984, pp. 47–64.

Hay, D., Linebaugh, P., Rule, J.G., Thompson, E.P. and Winslow, C. 1975. *Albion's Fatal Tree*. Harmondsworth, Allen Lane.

Hayek, F.A. 1944. *The Road to Serfdom*. Routledge.

Heath, A., Jowell, R. and Curtice, J. 1985. *How Britain Votes*. Oxford, Pergamon.

Henderson, R. A. 1980. An Analysis of Closures Amongst Scottish Manufacturing Plants Between 1966 and 1975. *Scottish Journal of Political Economy*, 27.

Hirst, P.Q. 1981. On Struggle in the Enterprise. In Prior (ed) 1981, pp. 45–75.

Hobsbawm, E.J. 1968. *Labouring Men*. Weidenfeld and Nicholson.

Hobsbawm, E.J. 1981. *The Forward March of Labour Halted?* Verso.

Hobsbawm, E.J. 1984. Labour: Rump or Rebirth. *Marxism Today*, March, 8–13.

Holmes, M. 1985. *The First Thatcher Government 1979–1983*. Brighton. Wheatsheaf.

Houghton, D., Lord of Sowerby 1981. The Party We Love. *Political Quarterly*, 52, 149–159.

Huhne, C. 1985. Thatcherism may work in the house, but not in Britain. *Guardian*, 14 February.

Huhne, C. 1986. Renaissance Plan at No. 10 Downing Street. *Guardian*, 27 March.

Hyman, R. 1986. Reflections on the Mining Strike. *Socialist Register*, pp. 330–354.

Hyman, R. and Streeck, W. (ed) 1988. *New Technology and Industrial Relations: International Experience*. Oxford, Blackwell.

Incomes Data Services 1986. Profit Sharing and Share Options, *Study No. 357*, IDS Publications.

Ingham, G. 1984. *Capitalism Divided? The City and Industry in British Social Development.* London, Macmillan.

Institute of Manpower Studies 1985. Flexibility, Working Practices and the Labour Market. *IMS Manpower Commentary No. 32.* Brighton, IMS.

Jay, P. 1977. Englanditis. In Tyrell (ed) 1977.

Jones, D.R. and MacKay, R.R. 1986. Labour Adjustment and the limits to Voluntary Choice. Mimeo. Institute of Economic Research, University of North Wales, Bangor.

Joseph, K. 1975. *Reversing the Trend.* Rose Books.

Jowell, R. and Airey, C. 1984. *British Social Attitudes, the 1984 Report.* Aldershot, Gower.

Jowell, R. and Witherspoon, S. 1985. *British Social Attitudes, the 1985 report.* Aldershot, Gower.

Jowell, R., Witherspoon, S. and Brook, L. 1986. *British Social Attitudes, the 1986 Report.* Aldershot, Gower.

Kalecki, M. 1943. Political Aspects of Full Employment. *Political Quarterly,* 14, 322-331.

Kavanagh, D. 1982. *The Politics of The Labour Party.* Allen and Unwin.

Keegan, W. 1984. *Mrs Thatcher's Economic Experiment.* Harmondsworth, Penguin.

Kellner, P. 1985. The CBI in conference: an exercise in futility. *New Statesman.* 22 November p. 9.

Kilpatrick, A. and Lawson, T. 1980. On the nature of industrial decline in the UK. *Cambridge Journal of Economics,* 4, 1, 85-102.

Kitching, G. 1983. *Rethinking Socialism.* Methuen.

Labour Research Department 1986. *The Widening Gap.* LRD Publications.

Labour Research Department 1987. *A State of Collapse.* LRD Publications.

Lane, T. 1982. The Unions: Caught on the Ebb Tide. *Marxism Today,* September.

Lane, T. 1986. Economic Democracy: are the trade unions equipped? *Industrial Relations Journal,* 17, 321-328.

Layard, R. and Clark, C. 1987. No change on the job scene. *Guardian,* 1 May.

Lever, W. 1984. Industrial Change and Urban Size. A Risk Theory Approach. Mimeo, University of Glasgow, Department of Social and Economic Research.

Leys, C. 1983. *Politics in Britain.* Heineman.

Leys, C. 1985. Thatcherism and British Manufacturing: a Question of Hegemony. *New Left Review.* 151, 5-25.

Llewellyn, J., Potter, S. and Samuelson, L. 1985. *Economic Forecasting and Policy - the International Dimension.* Routledge and Kegan Paul.

Loney, M. 1986. *The Politics of Greed.* Pluto Press.

Lowry, Sir P. 1985. Trade Unions and Positive Rights. *Jim Conway Foundation Annual Memorial Lecture.*

McCarthy, W.E.J. and Ellis; N. 1973. *Management By Agreement.* Hutchinson.

MacInnes, J. 1985. Conjuring Up Consultation. *British Journal of Industrial Relations,* 23, 93-113.

MacInnes, J. 1987. Economic Restructuring Relevant to Industrial Relations in Scotland. *Centre for Urban and Regional Research Discussion Paper no. 26,* Glasgow, CURR.

MacInnes, J. 1988. New Technology in Scotbank; Gender, Class and Work in Services. in Hyman and Streeck (ed) 1988.

MacInnes, J. and Sproull, A. 1986. Union Recognition in The Electronics Industry in Scotland. *Centre for Research in Industrial Democracy and Participation Research Report No 4.* Glasgow, CRIDP.

McKenzie, R. 1982. Power in the Labour Party: the Issue of Intra-Party Democracy. In

Kavanagh (ed) 1982, pp. 191–201.

McLoughlin, J. 1986. Secret Ballots do more harm than silver bullets. *Guardian* 27 February.

Main, B.G.M. 1982. The Length of a Job in Britain. *Economica.* 49, 325–33.

Mann, M. 1986, Work and the Work Ethic. In Jowell *et al.* 1986.

Marchington, M. and Armstrong, R. 1985. Involving Employees Through The Recession. *Employee Relations,* 7, 5, 17–21.

Marginson, P., Edwards, P., Sisson, K., Purcell, J. and Martin, R. 1986. The Management of Industrial Relations in Large Enterprises. A Summary Report of the WIRS Company Level Survey. *Warwick Papers in Industrial Relations.* No. 11. IRRU, University of Warwick.

Marsden, D. 1984. Chronicle. *British Journal of Industrial Relations,* 22.

Martin, J. and Roberts, C. 1984. *Women and Employment: a lifetime perspective.* HMSO.

Meager, N. 1985. Temporary Work in Britain: Its Growth and Changing Rationales, *Institute of Manpower Studies Report No 106.* Brighton, Institute of Manpower Studies.

Metcalf, D. and Nickell, S. J. 1985. Jobs and Pay. *Midland Bank Review.* Spring.

Middlemas, K. 1983, *Industry, Unions and Government: Twenty-One Years of the NEDC.* Macmillan.

Midland Bank. 1986. UK Manufacturing: Output and Trade Performance. *Midland Bank Review.* Autumn, 8–16.

Miliband, R. 1978. A state of de-subordination. *British Journal of Sociology,* 29, 399–409.

Miller, W. L. 1984. There Was No Alternative: The British General Election of 1983. *Parliamentary Affairs,* 37, 364–84.

Millward, N. and Stevens, M. 1986. *British Workplace Industrial Relations 1980–1984 The DE/ESRC/PSI/ACAS Surveys.* Aldershot, Gower.

Morgan, K.O. 1985. *Labour in Power 1945–51.* Oxford, Oxford University Press.

Mulhearn, C. 1984. Urban Employment Decline and Labour Movement Response. mimeo. Department of Town Planning, Polytechnic of the South Bank.

Nichols, T. 1986. *The British Worker Question.* Routledge and Kegan Paul.

Nickell, S. J. 1987. Why is Wage Inflation in Britain so High? *Oxford Bulletin of Economics and Statistics,* 49, 109–127.

Northcott, J., Fogarty, M. and Trevor, M. 1985. *Chips and Jobs.* PSI.

Nove, A. 1983. *The Economics of Feasible Socialism.* Hutchinson.

Orwell, G. 1982. *The Lion and The Unicorn.* Harmondsworth. Penguin.

Panitch, L. 1986. The Impasse of Social Democratic Politics. *Socialist Register,* pp. 50–98.

Phelps Brown, H. 1983. What is The British Predicament? in Feinstein (ed) 1983 pp. 207–225.

Pimlott, B 1985. The road from 1945. *Guardian* 27 July.

Pimlott, B. and Cook, C. 1982. *Trade Unions in British Politics.* Longman.

Pollert, A. 1981. *Girls, Wives, Factory Lives.* Macmillan.

Posner, M. 1986. The state of the economy. *Scottish Journal of Political Economy,* 33, 305–316.

Prior, J. 1986. *A Balance of Power.* Hamish Hamilton.

Prior, M. (ed) 1981. *The Popular and the Political.* Routledge and Kegan Paul.

Riddell, P. 1983. *The Thatcher Government.* Oxford, Martin Robertson.

Roots, P. 1986. Collective Bargaining: Opportunities for a New Approach. *Warwick Papers in Industrial Relations No. 5.* IRRU. University of Warwick.

Rutherford, M. 1985. Unemployment Could Breed Unemployment Even at Three Per Cent

Inflation. *Financial Times*, 25 October.

Shonfield, A. *Modern Capitalism*. Oxford, Oxford University Press.

Singh, A. 1981. 'Full Employment Capitalism' And The Labour Party. *Socialist Register*.

Smith, T. 1985. Review of Middlemas 1983. *British Journal of Industrial Relations*, 23, 168–170.

Sproull, A. 1987. Part-time Employment and The Flexible Firm. mimeo. University of Glasgow Department of Social and Economic Research.

Steele, M., Gennard, J. and Miller, K. 1986. The Trade Union Act 1984: Political Fund Ballots. *British Journal of Industrial Relations*, 24, 443–468.

Stewart, H. 1986. No Good at Creating Jobs. *Guardian* 21 February.

Stewart, S. 1985. Letter in *Financial Times*. 19 December.

Storey, D. and Johnson, S. 1987. Are small firms the answer to unemployment? *Employment Institute*.

Taylor, R. 1982. The Trade Union 'Problem' Since 1960. In Pimlott and Cook (ed) 1982, pp 188–214.

Terry, M. 1977. The Inevitable Growth of Informality. *British Journal of Industrial Relations*, 15, 75–90.

Thompson, E.P. 1965. The Peculiarities of the English. *Socialist Register*.

Thompson, E. P. 1977. *Whips and Hunters*. Hammondsworth, Penguin.

Tomlinson, J. 1986. *Monetarism: Is There an Alternative?* Oxford, Blackwell.

Trades Union Congress 1982. *Annual Report*.

Taylor, R. 1982. The Trade Union 'Problem' Since 1960, in Pimlott and Cook (ed) 1982, pp 188–214.

Terry, M. 1977. The Inevitable Growth of Informality. *British Journal of Industrial Relations*, 15, 75–90.

Treasury 1986. Economic Progress Report No. 182. The Treasury.

Turner, G. 1981 *Daily Telegraph*. 13 February.

Tyrrell, J. 1977. *The Future That Doesn't Work*. Doubleday.

Unemployment Unit 1986. *Bulletin* No. 20, Summer.

Wedderburn, Lord W. 1986. *The Worker and The Law*. Harmondsworth, Penguin.

West, J. 1982. *Work, Women and The Labour Market*. Routledge and Kegan Paul.

Wintour, P. 1987. Manufacturers shift spending to overseas jobs. *Guardian*, 5 May.

Young, Lord of 'Graffham 1986. *Stockton Lecture*. London Business School, April.

Index